THE CHURCH OF THE BRETHREN
PAST AND PRESENT

CONTRIBUTORS

DESMOND W. BITTINGER
Head, Department of Sociology and Anthropology, Chapman College, Orange, California

DALE W. BROWN
Professor of Christian Theology, Bethany Theological Seminary, Oak Brook, Illinois

B. MERLE CROUSE
Church Development Consultant, World Ministries Commission, Church of the Brethren, Elgin, Illinois

DONALD F. DURNBAUGH
Professor of Church History, Bethany Theological Seminary, Oak Brook, Illinois

VERNARD ELLER
Professor of Religion, La Verne College, La Verne, California

WARREN F. GROFF
Professor of Christian Theology and Dean, Bethany Theological Seminary, Oak Brook, Illinois

ROGER E. SAPPINGTON
Professor of History and Political Science, Bridgewater College, Bridgewater, Virginia

EDWARD K. ZIEGLER
Former Chairman, Committee on Interchurch Relations, Church of the Brethren, and Pastor, Bakersfield, California

Woodcuts by I. J. Sanger

THE CHURCH OF THE BRETHREN
PAST AND PRESENT

EDITED BY

Donald F. Durnbaugh

THE BRETHREN PRESS

Elgin, Illinois

PREFACE

This volume was originally prepared at the invitation of the editors of the ecumenical series, Churches of the World (*Die Kirchen der Welt*). The stated purpose of the series is to provide for modern readers self-portrayals of contemporary churches. Publisher of the comprehensively planned series is the *Evangelisches Verlagswerk* in Stuttgart. Bishop Hans Heinrich Harms of Oldenburg initiated the request to the Church of the Brethren which resulted in this book. The undersigned enlisted the aid of contributors who, in his judgment, were able to write authoritatively on the respective topics.

These contributors prepared their chapters in English for later translation into German for continental publication. Through the kindness of the European editors and the publisher, the completed manuscript was made available to the Church of the Brethren for publication in the United States. There has been no alteration in the contents of the book for the American edition, except for the provision of this preface.

Appreciation is extended to the following, for making possible the publication in this form: the General Services Commission of the General Board, Church of the Brethren, and its executive secretary, Galen B. Ogden; Howard E. Royer, director of communication; and Elizabeth Weigle, copy editor. Several persons gave the manuscript critical readings, including Larry Fourman, Herbert Hogan, and Howard A. Miller, and their comments were helpful. Special gratitude is expressed to the members of the class on the History of the Church of the Brethren, Bethany Theological Seminary (Winter Quarter, 1970) for their searching and encouraging critiques.

It is understood that this book is not to be considered as an official or authorized denominational statement. Views here expressed rest on personal opinion. However, all of the contributors are informed and active members of the Church of the Brethren, and to that extent, their views may represent a certain consensus.

Each writer was given freedom to develop his topic as he thought best, within the general framework adopted for the book. For this reason, a careful reader will notice some duplication. In the judgment of the editor, occasional repetition is outweighed by the coherence and integrity of each contribution.

Those connected with writing and editing this book believe that it can be a useful resource for members and potential members of the Church of the Brethren. It can provide information about past and current beliefs and practices. It is also hoped that the book will be of some interest to the broader Christian community in describing the pilgrimage of a company of followers of Jesus Christ. Both the success and the failures here recorded may be instructive to those of all traditions who attempt to be faithful witnesses to Christian truth.

1970   DONALD F. DURNBAUGH

CONTENTS

1

EARLY HISTORY

Donald F. Durnbaugh

The historical sketch presented in these first two chapters has two purposes. The first is to provide a general framework of information for the more
detailed discussions of specific topics which follow. For this reason matters
which should receive more extensive development will be mentioned but
briefly. A second purpose is to relate in narrative form the origin and expansion of the movement known as the Church of the Brethren.

Some problems attend this attempt. For one thing, large portions of the
story have been inadequately charted. Early generations did not encourage
record keeping and history writing, for these tended toward vanity and self-
serving. For the same reason they refused to keep statistics, so that with
the important exception of 1770 there are no accurate records of membership
or numbers of congregations until 1882. Unlike the Quakers, the Brethren
did not develop a tradition of writing diaries and travel accounts, which reveal
so much about the inner life of that important movement. Although remarkably active in publication of devotional material for a people of their limited
educational background, the Brethren typically issued their hymnals and
books of poetry without attribution of poet or composer. So far was this
penchant for humility carried that early Brethren would allow only initials to
be placed on their gravestones made from common fieldstones.

Another problem deals with terminology. The movement was most
reluctant to give itself a name, and therefore has been called by a variety
of terms by outsiders. Members were content to call themselves "brethren,"
much like the unrelated nineteenth-century group known as the Plymouth
Brethren or Darbyites. In Europe the Brethren (as we shall refer to them)
were designated New Baptists (*Neue Täufer*) or Schwarzenau Baptists to
distinguish them from the Mennonites (*Alte Täufer*) with whom they had so
much in common. The use of the name *Brethren* has been confusing, for
many other denominations have appropriated this biblical term. Though the
Brethren have had contacts with the Moravian Brethren, the Brethren in
Christ (River Brethren), and the United Brethren, they should not be
identified with any of them. They are all distinct entities.

In 1836 the Brethren decided that they should officially be known as
the Fraternity of German Baptists, changed in 1871 to German Baptist Breth-

ren. This in turn caused them to be related to the Baptist movement. There is logic here, for the most striking of the Brethren practices was the baptism of adult believers by immersion (although this was by a threefold, forward motion, not a single, backward motion as practiced by the Baptists). This form of baptism gave rise to the most common nickname for the Brethren — Dunkers (derived from the German *tunken* — to immerse). The nickname is often corrupted to Dunkards, and it is by this that Brethren are still known in parts of the United States. Since 1908 the official title has been the Church of the Brethren.

European Beginnings

Pietism as a reform movement within German Protestantism is a well-known phenomenon and has been duly recorded in the annals of church history. Many studies have analyzed the Pietist attempts to renew the church, to recover the essence of the Reformation, to break through a hardened and disputatious Protestant scholasticism. Less studied is a concurrent development of the late seventeenth and early eighteenth centuries, best designated Radical Pietism. This had many of the same features as did Pietism, but was further marked by its dependence upon the mystical theology of Jacob Boehme (1575-1624) and its separatist stance toward the state churches. The historical understanding of the Radical Pietists was shaped by the erudite Gottfried Arnold (1666-1714), who convinced them of the necessity of looking to the early Christian church as their norm and also of the decadence of the institutionalized churches of their day.

By its very self-understanding, Radical Pietism tended to be antagonistic to church structures, but several movements did crystallize from it. One which has interested scholars was the Community of True Inspiration, founded in 1714. Stemming originally from the Camisard movement among suppressed Huguenots in late seventeenth-century France, the Inspired caused a wordy war of books and pamphlets to break forth from the ranks of the theologians. This was because of their astonishing claim that their leaders (J. F. Rock and E. L. Gruber) had the gift of speaking under direct, divine inspiration. Such important figures as A. H. Francke and Count Zinzendorf were impressed by the claims of these New Prophets who traveled as far afield as the Netherlands and Switzerland. In the nineteenth century their remaining members migrated to America where they formed communitarian colonies, first in Buffalo, New York, and then at Amana, Iowa.

Emerging from Radical Pietism at the very same time, but of quite a different temper, was the Brethren movement. Although numerically larger than the Inspired, the Brethren passed virtually without notice by the scholarly world. Scattered condemnations in synodical protocols, some documents in administrative archives, a few critical comments in the writings of the Radical Pietists — these are about all that research has discovered to date. Yet, unlike the Amana movement which is something of a religious fossil, the Brethren are currently an active, if small, Free Church with worldwide commitments and contacts. Counting all branches of the Brethren family, there are some 270,000 adult members today, primarily in North America, but also in Asia, Africa, and Latin America.

There are certain explanations for the paucity of notice at the time of the Brethren inception. First of all, the Brethren were of the genus of the "Quiet Ones in the Land" *(Die Stillen im Lande)* who lived to themselves and bothered no one. They ordinarily came only to the attention of the authorities through their immersion baptisms which sometimes caused public excitement (much like the early history of the Baptist converts in nineteenth-century Germany), or through their refusal to accept military service. The Brethren were indeed zealous in spreading their faith, by all that can be learned, both in America and in Europe, but over the years they have been a retiring, inoffensive, and unobstructive people. A historian in colonial America said of them: "They are meek and pious Christians; and have justly acquired the character of the *Harmless Tunkers.*"[1]

Another important reason is that within twenty-five years of their start they had left the continent for America. How they might have developed had they stayed in Europe is impossible to say. The fact is that they left, and their history has been primarily centered in the United States.

Perhaps the most important reason for their European obscurity is that as the Brethren formed themselves into a brotherhood or *Gemeinde,* they discarded many of the ideas and positions of the Radical Pietists. These included Böhmism, communitarianism, celibacy, refusal to work, antisacramentalism, and vocal criticism of authority. The best way to understand the early Brethren is to see them as a Radical Pietist group which appropriated an Anabaptist view of the church. They stressed a gathered church of believers, the discipline of church members, a nonresistant approach to the state, and a theology of obedience. To be sure, they retained some characteristics of their Pietist background, but they were almost indistinguishable by the outsider from the Mennonites. These descendants of the sixteenth-century Anabaptists had won for themselves a tenuous tolerance in the Palatinate as sturdy farmers and in other areas of Germany as skilled craftsmen. Therefore, in most places where the Brethren came they were considered to be identical with the Mennonites and therefore enjoyed similar tolerance.

Since many of the Brethren came from the Palatinate, it is necessary to portray briefly the situation obtaining there at the beginning of the eighteenth century. The area had hardly recovered from the devastation of the Thirty Years' War when repeated French invasions during the War of the League of Augsburg wreaked renewed havoc. Add to this the burdens of an unfeeling ruler, a profligate court, an oppressive bureaucracy, and several years of crop failures, and it is easy to understand why much unrest was present. So many subjects left for other lands that the term *Palatine* became the generic term for all German immigrants in America.

In the religious sphere there was much turmoil. Under the *Simultaneum* (1698) those Palatines who had become Roman Catholics during the French occupation were guaranteed protection. As there were also some Lutherans in the Electorate (which had repeatedly changed its official religion under the principle of *cuius regio, eius religio* — as the prince so the religion — there was continual strife among these confessions. The consistory repeatedly called its clergy to task for unbecoming behavior such as drunkenness at funerals.

By all accounts, church life was at a low ebb. Many of the devout were hungering for nourishing spiritual food.

This some of them found in the teachings of Ernst Christoph Hochmann von Hochenau (1670-1721), a Radical Pietist leader. Of noble birth, Hochmann studied at several universities and seemed destined to a promising career in law. But, after his conversion under Francke at Halle, he refused attractive positions in order to spend the rest of his life as an itinerant evangelist of radical persuasion. Jung-Stilling ranked him with Dippel as the two "mainsprings of enthusiasm, pietism, separatism, and along with it, of true Christianity in Germany." According to Goebel, Hochmann devoted his life to his own conversion and to the "thorough awakening and conversion of his brethren in Christ." In doing so, he came into conflict with the authorities, especially when he taught that separation from "Babylon" — the state churches — was essential for true salvation. All accounts agree that he was a personable and winsome individual, who quickly found friends and supporters among noblemen and the humble alike.[2]

In 1706 Hochmann was invited to come to Schriesheim, north of Heidelberg. Here he held meetings at the mill owned by Alexander Mack (1679-1735), a member of a substantial family of Reformed faith. Mack became one of Hochmann's closest associates and accompanied him on his travels. The Pietists at Schriesheim preached to laborers coming home from the fields, and soon word of their activity reached the local government. The soldiers sent to seize them reported that the group had left the area, but Hochmann and some companions were captured in nearby Mannheim and placed at hard labor. Rather than cease participating in the illegal conventicles, Mack himself sold his property and left his home with wife and children.

Similar incidents occurred in Strassburg, in the Basel area, and in Württemberg, with much the same result. Those unwilling to follow the state church line had to leave their homes, often suffering the confiscation of their personal and real property.

Hochmann had earlier lived in Wittgenstein and doubtless indicated to his sympathizers that relative religious freedom was available there. The isolated and modestly sized county in the region between the Eder and Lahn rivers soon became notorious as the place of refuge for religious dissenters. They centered at Schwarzenau/Eder, the site of a manor house belonging to the Sayn-Wittgenstein family. Count Henrich Albrecht (1658-1723) and his sisters shocked their peers by associating with these commoners on a familiar basis.

As might be expected, among the several hundred refugees who gathered in Schwarzenau and the surrounding hills there were intense discussions about the true faith. Some became discouraged and returned to their homes and their former faiths. Others became dissatisfied with the extreme individualism of many of the Radical Pietists. The issue which brought matters to a head was baptism. As the Wittgenstein radicals studied the New Testament and the lives of the early Christians they were impressed by the biblical injunction to be baptized upon their faith as "an appeal to God for a clear conscience, through the resurrection of Jesus Christ" (1 Peter 3:21). Some became convinced that a form of brotherhood or *Gemeinde* was necessary if they were to be completely obedient to the New Testament. A visit by two "foreign brethren" who may have been Dutch Collegiants brought these growing concerns into the open.

It was decided that an open letter should be sent to those of their acquaintance, announcing the intention to proceed with baptism. (They had earlier asked Hochmann for his opinion; he concurred that water baptism was commanded biblically, but cautioned that they not become sectarian by demanding it of everyone.) The open letter stated, in part:

> Our inner joy increased and we were strengthened in the Lord not to be negligent, and to come together in the fear of the Lord. . . . As we found that we all agreed with one spirit in this high calling, we have decided to announce this to our beloved brethren and friends through an open letter. This is to see whether they also find themselves convinced in their hearts to help confirm this high calling to the pride and glory of our Savior Jesus Christ, and to follow the Creator and Fulfiller of Faith. . . . So then, if some more brethren wish to begin this high act of baptism with us out of brotherly unity according to the teachings of Christ and the apostles, we announce in humbleness that we are interceding together in prayer and fasting with God.[3]

In late summer 1708 five men and three women participated in baptism in the Eder river, and thus began the Brethren movement. An unnamed brother baptized Mack, their leader, who proceeded to baptize his baptizer, and then the other men and the women.

News of the event spread rapidly, although it had been performed privately. Criticism came from two sides — from the rulers of the surrounding territories who saw in the group a revival of the kingdom of Anabaptists at Münster (1535), and from the Radical Pietists, including Hochmann, who looked upon the development as an unfortunate fall back into the institutionalization of error which they had known in the established churches. Henrich Albrecht was able to ward off the outside attacks, and Mack wrote several treatises to answer the religious critics. Thus there was time for the small number to develop and to expand.

They immediately began to witness to the newfound faith, and gained converts among the inhabitants of Wittgenstein. Meetings in Schwarzenau grew so large that no house there would hold them; so they met outside. They sent several of their spokesmen on journeys into Switzerland, the Palatinate, Hamburg-Altona, and elsewhere to establish new congregations. The most important of the daughter groups came into being in the Marienborn area near Büdingen, where there was also considerable religious toleration. This branch, however, was forced to leave in 1715, and made its way to Krefeld where members continued their activity, much to the dismay of the Reformed clergy. One of the annoyed officials satirized the religious pluralism there which he found so distasteful in this quatrain:

> Lutheran and Mennonite,
> Catholic and Israelite,
> Calvinist and New Baptist
> All in Krefeld now exist.[4]

Records of the early years are spotty, but it is known that often missioners and their converts were imprisoned, fined, and otherwise punished. The most notable incident involved six men of Solingen of Reformed faith, who were baptized in the Wupper river. They were seized and imprisoned until several theological faculties could be asked for appropriate penalties. The mildest verdict was lifelong incarceration at hard labor, which sentence was imposed. The six were sent to the border fortress at Jülich, where they suffered severely until released at the end of four years through the intervention of some Dutch gentlemen who heard of their plight. Another brother, Christian Liebe, was sentenced to the galleys for preaching in Bern, but was also eventually released through Dutch assistance.

The Krefeld congregation provided the first contingent to migrate, leaving for Pennsylvania in 1719. Some internal problems over church discipline contributed to the economic and religious pressures the Brethren experienced. The first considerable party of Germans to go to Pennsylvania had also been from Krefeld, and it is not surprising that the Brethren turned to the Quaker-directed colony in the pursuit of religious freedom and economic independence. The Reformed ministers from the Moers district reported the Brethren departure. The General Synod noted its satisfaction that the departure had taken place and cautioned the pastors "to be very much on guard lest similar enthusiasts should insinuate themselves in the future."[5]

The original Schwarzenau Brethren left Wittgenstein in 1720, but whether because of religious suppression or the lack of economic support is not clear. They went to Friesland, where they settled in a marsh colony called Surhuisterveen. Members of the Dutch Collegiants aided them in going to the Netherlands, and some of this conventicle-type association joined them. In 1729 Alexander Mack led a large party to Pennsylvania, at the urging of the Krefeld group which had emigrated earlier. Others left Europe in the 1730's, so that by 1740 most of the Brethren had departed. There are some slight references in the 1740's to Brethren remaining in Europe, but the remnants seemed either to have relapsed into complete separatism or to have joined a congenial body such as the Mennonites.

There are no definite figures on the size which the Brethren attained in Europe, but it could hardly have been more than several hundred. One list drawn up in 1899 totaled about 250. Be that as it may, the Brethren turned their backs on the inhospitable Old World and sought their future in the New.

Colonial America

Christmas Day, 1723, marked the reactivation of the Brethren movement in America. After the arrival of the first group of migrants in 1719, the newcomers busied themselves in establishing a livelihood in and around Germantown and further inland. Some were craftsmen — especially weavers — and many became farmers because of the cheap land available. In 1722 Peter Becker (1687-1758) and two others visited the scattered Brethren and informed them of their intention to begin regular meetings that fall. The suggestion found immediate acceptance and meetings were held in Germantown until bad winter weather made travel too difficult. This renewed interest continued in 1723, and soon some of those attending asked to be received into the group by baptism.

The Pennsylvanians wrote to Friesland to secure advice on what to do;

the answer was that they should choose some apt person as their minister and proceed with the baptism. Becker, noted for his piety and fervent prayers, was chosen as the first minister in America, and the baptism and accompanying love feast was then held on December 25, 1723. This caused a remarkable awakening, especially among the young people, of revival proportions. The occurrence was shortly before the noted Great Awakening which swept through the American colonies with such lasting effects for the course of religion in North America. An informed observer writing later suggested that the Brethren activity represented the first of the many waves of revivals which were to affect the German population in the colonies.

In the autumn of 1724 the entire male membership (fourteen in number) of the Germantown congregation set forth on an evangelistic tour in the wilds of "Penn's Woods." Their expedition led to the formation of two new congregations, at Coventry and at Conestoga. The future seemed bright for expansion of the Brethren witness, but serious division was in store. One of those baptized at Conestoga was Conrad Beissel (1690-1768), who thought himself a religious genius, which in some ways he undoubtedly was. A native of Eberbach/Neckar, Beissel had come into contact with Pietism as a journeyman baker in the Palatinate and the Wetterau. He came to the American shores in 1720 in the hope of joining the Kelpian community known as the "Woman in the Wilderness" (Revelation 12:6). To his disappointment it had been dispersed before his arrival. He spent a year as a weaving apprentice of Peter Becker's before going with a companion into the forest to live as a hermit.

Following Beissel's baptism, his evident gifts made him the obvious choice as the leader of the new Conestoga congregation. Unfortunately for the Brethren, Beissel was determined to go his own way. He immediately introduced such emphases as direct revelation (superior to the scriptures), the necessity of celibacy, and certain Jewish practices, including the observance of Saturday as the day of worship. These innovations quickly caused friction with the Germantown Brethren, and led to a final split in 1728. Not even the reconciling efforts of Mack when he reached America in 1729 were successful in shaking Beissel from his purpose.

His new admirers followed him when he moved farther into the wilderness, into present-day Lancaster County. They built crude huts around his cabin, after the model of the early Egyptian monastic communities. By the late 1730's a full-fledged Protestant monastic establishment had taken form, with large buildings and three orders (monks, sisters, and "householders," that is, families who lived nearby and belonged to the congregation). Ephrata, as it was called, became famous not only for its monastic qualities but also because of its cultural achievements. Singing, printing, illuminating of manuscripts — all reached a high state of perfection. Ephrata's fame spread across the ocean, and accounts of it were printed in ecclesiastical journals in Germany. Even Voltaire heard of them and called them the most inimitable Christians of their time. At its height, Ephrata numbered as many as 350 members. Beissel's death, the increasing inroads of civilization around the monastery, and the self-sacrificial service of the community in turning their institution into a military hospital during the Revolutionary War, all played a role in the demise. The last monastic members died in the nineteenth century, but some of the buildings still stand today as a historic shrine.

Despite the massive defection caused by Beissel, the Brethren went on to plant other congregations in the colonies. By 1770 there were fifteen in Pennsylvania and one in New Jersey. Many of the Brethren or their descendants left to search for better land, and seventeen other congregations were founded before 1770 in Maryland (the first in 1743), Virginia (1752), North Carolina (1742), South Carolina (1748), and possibly in Georgia. A careful census compiled by the Baptist historian Morgan Edwards in 1770 listed over fifteen hundred baptized members and forty-two ministers. Edwards estimated that the numbers of individuals related to the Brethren would be five times the number of members. He pointed out that there were few meetinghouses, as they preferred to "meet from house to house in imitation of the primitive church." The first meetinghouse was that of Germantown, built two hundred years ago (1770) and still standing, although in altered form. The oldest unaltered structure is the meetinghouse at Pricetown, Pennsylvania, a severely plain stone building constructed in 1777.

Brethren and Mennonites often settled in the same areas, but relationships between the two sister groups were not always harmonious because of the tendency of some of the Mennonites to join the Brethren. According to contemporary reports, they found more spiritual life among the Pietistically tinged Brethren; the practice of immersion baptism was also appealing to the Bible-loving Mennonites. The Quakers, as the proprietors of the colony where most of the Brethren lived, had great influence upon them, as can be seen in the styles of dress and of meetinghouse architecture and in some parts of the church polity (the phrases "Annual Meeting" and "query" for items of business brought before the meeting are cases in point).

The immediate cause of regular Annual Meetings was provided by the synods held in 1742-43 under the sponsorship of Count Zinzendorf. The Moravian leader had come to America with the plan of uniting all of the German denominations into what he called the Congregation of God in the Spirit. Brethren delegates did attend the first sessions, but eventually dropped out. Their reasons were: they found the domination by the count too great, the use of the lot to decide all matters questionable, and the synod itself a covert attempt to make all of the German sects into Moravians. When Zinzendorf baptized some Indian converts by sprinkling, the immersionist Brethren withdrew permanently. A few individual Brethren were drawn to the Moravians, however. One, Andrew Frey, accompanied the count back to Europe, but later returned and wrote an often reprinted exposé of the conduct of the Moravians during the so-called "Sifting Time" at Herrnhaag near Büdingen.

Some of the Brethren publications of the eighteenth century were polemical in nature, invariably responses to attacks upon them. Alexander Mack, Jr., (1712-1803) was the most prolific writer among the colonial Brethren; his *Apologia* (1788) has been called the best defense of Brethren practice and thought of that period. He was also noted for his hymns and poems, which he wrote in great numbers, as did indeed several others. Some of these composisions were printed in hymnals such as the *Davidic Psalter* (1744), which was used by groups and individuals outside the brotherhood as well.

Historians have often counted the production of the press of Christopher Sauer (1695-1758) as Brethren publications, but this is wrong for two reasons. The press was a private enterprise, and Sauer was never a member of the Brethren, although very sympathetic to their point of view. His like-named son (1721-1784) did become a Brethren elder and did continue his father's printing establishment, one of the most important on the whole Atlantic coast. The Sauers have to their credit the first successful German-language news-paper and the first Bibles in a European tongue issued in the colonies, as well as the first religious magazine and the first type cast in America.

The younger Sauer became one of the wealthiest men in Pennsylvania, but he lost all his property in the Revolutionary War. He and the other Brethren were appreciative of the privileges and liberties afforded them under British rule and were not eager to see the political conditions changed. More importantly, the Brethren were pacifists or, better, nonresistants and could not make common cause with a violent revolution. Their position was not ac-cepted by the rebel side, and much suffering resulted. The Brethren stance is best expressed in the petition they sent to the Pennsylvania Assembly in 1775, along with the Mennonites:

> The [Assembly's] advice to those who do not find freedom of conscience to take up arms, that they ought to be helpful to those who are in need and distressed circumstances, we receive with cheerfulness toward all men of what station they may be — it being our principle to feed the hungry and give the thirsty drink. We have dedicated ourselves to serve all men in everything that can be helpful to the preservation of men's lives, but we find no freedom in giving, or doing, or assisting in any thing by which men's lives are destroyed or hurt. We beg the patience of all those who believe we err in this point.[6]

The Brethren were willing to pay taxes, but they brought church disci-pline upon those who allowed themselves to be forced into mustering or into taking the oath of loyalty to the new government. Although the impact of the Revolution has been overplayed in some histories, there is no question that the treatment suffered by many of the brotherhood reinforced them in their conviction that they should hold themselves aloof from worldly affairs.

Early Nineteenth Century

Far from being the "Dark Ages" or the "Wilderness Period" of Brethren history, as it has been called, the first half of the nineteenth century was a crucial era in the life of the church. The first half century of the National epoch saw the arrival of the first Brethren on the Pacific Coast, the first system-atic theological statement of Brethren doctrines, extensive publishing activ-ity, and the appearance of some of the most outstanding leadership in the entire Brethren existence. It was a major achievement just to keep the de-nomination together despite its scattering across the continent; this period saw the consolidation of the Brethren in the format which they kept until almost the close of the century, to be sure not without serious challenge. Mallott quite rightly observed: "There has been a tendency to apologize for the period, and to regard the greater urbanity and sophistication of the grandchildren of the period as indications of an improvement. We are confronted with the fact that the foundations of the existent church were laid during that period. It was the congregations planted then that have increased by division and extension; the membership on that soil has multiplied. The church of 1950 rests upon foundations that were substantially laid by 1850!'"[7]

The negative side of the consolidation was a certain reliance on legalism which threatened to equate sound faith with the avoidance of "the world." Many of the minutes of the Annual Meetings of the nineteenth century read like a catalog of prohibitions; among things to be spurned were: bells, carpets, life insurance, lightning rods, likenesses, liquor, musical instruments, salaried ministers, secret societies, shows and fairs, tobacco, and flowered wallpaper. Although such prohibitions may be easily satirized, they represent an attempt to live simply and decently as good stewards of material treasures. There is reason to believe that these Brethren led full lives, although more austerely than would now be considered necessary. Of key importance was keeping the unity of the brotherhood by mutual agreement.

Brethren expansion across the country followed, or on occasion even preceded, the general move westward. Some areas of Ohio, Indiana, and Illinois were first settled by the Brethren. Members were in Kentucky, Tennessee, and Missouri by 1800, Iowa by 1844, and as far as Oregon by 1850. Eight years later there was a congregation in California. Annual Meetings were held in Ohio by 1822, in Indiana by 1848, and in Illinois by 1856. There were three main routes taken by those moving west. One was in the north, by way of the Erie Canal and Buffalo. The most heavily traveled was through Pittsburgh, thence either by wagon or by flatboat down the Ohio. The third was through the Cumberland Gap into Kentucky and Indiana.

The story of the Wolfe family can stand for many. George Wolfe, Sr., moved over the Alleghenies to Fayette County, Pennsylvania, in 1787. In 1800 he and his family built a flatboat and traveled down the Monongahela to the Ohio and from there to Logan County, Kentucky. George Wolfe, Jr., with his brother Jacob explored the woods of Illinois and moved there, first to Union and then to Adams County. Wolfe, Jr., became an influential figure in Illinois affairs as well as a Dunker elder and played a role in keeping slavery out of that part of the territory. A nephew of Wolfe, Jr., also named George Wolfe, reached the west coast by way of Panama in 1856.

Quite often groups of Brethren settlers moved as units, settling nearby in order to help one another. They immediately began meeting for worship in their homes, which were often constructed so that large rooms could be converted by folding back walls. The Brethren way was to gain adherents by living their faith, not by overt evangelization. Their neighbors saw their sincerity and were sometimes impressed enough to join them.

Of course, much of the Brethren growth took place in the east, as families grew and most of the children entered into membership. Usually young people waited with baptism until they were ready to marry and settle down. As congregations grew larger, they would be divided, so that the original gatherings would have many daughter colonies. As it became common to build several meetinghouses within the congregational confines, it was easy to assign meetinghouses to the new groupings. The Conestoga congregation has often been pointed out as an example of how growth could occur by this method.

It was at this time that clearer identification of church offices came about. These offices included deacons (and deaconesses), ministers, and elders, who were sometimes called bishops. Church leaders were elected by the entire membership (male and female) of a congregation, in the presence of elders from adjoining congregations. This method usually produced the most able, or at least sincere, leadership. Congregations appreciated but did not demand eloquence. Since there were ordinarily several ministers in a congregation, different talents could come into play. Some were known as excellent counselors and administrators of church affairs while others were known for their preaching.

No salary was paid to ministers, and although expenses might be reimbursed, they seldom were asked for. Church officers were chosen for life. Eldership entailed an extra sacrifice, for this involved much traveling to other congregations. Most of these men had limited schooling, but they applied themselves to the study of the scriptures and used the books they did own to excellent advantage. They sometimes developed considerable polish of presentation and acquaintance with theology, to judge by the comments of visitors. Their moral exhortations were enhanced by their living with their flocks. They had no reluctance to speak a word of prophetic judgment, for they could not be relieved of nonexistent salary.

The widely dispersed Brethren were kept together as a denomination by two agencies — the traveling elders and the Yearly Meeting. Visits were made upon the initiative of individual ministers or upon the invitation of the local churchmen. Ordinarily several churches would be visited in the course of a journey. Elder Jacob Leatherman (1787-1863) walked more than ten thousand miles in performing his ministerial duties in Maryland. The most notable example was John Kline (1797-1864) of Virginia, who covered more than 100,000 miles by horseback during his lifetime, 30,000 of which were on the back of his favorite mare "Nell." As Kline traveled, he arranged business matters, healed the ill, and brought news as well as his edifying messages of the gospel. He became probably the most beloved figure of all of Brethren history. The story of his life can be gleaned from his published diary, albeit in heavily edited form.

The Yearly Meeting, held at Pentecost, brought together most of the elders and many of the other members. It was a time of much preaching (not unlike the contemporary camp meetings, but without their emotional excesses). Usually a large number of non-Brethren would also attend. All in attendance were given hospitality in food and shelter by the host congregation, which had to provide huge quantities of meat and staples to feed the guests. Meetings were often held in barns, as the largest structures available, although sometimes special structures were built or tents erected.

A committee of elders, which came to be called Standing Committee, prepared the business for presentation to the assembly. Decision was by unanimous consent. If there were differences of opinion, the matter would be set back for a year. The meeting was chaired by a moderator who was chosen both for his strong voice and for the respect he enjoyed among the brotherhood. In 1856 it was agreed that there should be district gatherings of five or more local congregations to decide matters of limited import, saving the time of the Annual Meeting for substantive discussion. More than anything else, this system of conferences helped to shape the identity of the Brethren. This was expressed by Henry Kurtz, who came to the Brethren from the Lutheran ministry:

> This (our yearly) meeting was altogether a new thing to us, if we except our common council meetings [congregational], with which we had become acquainted previously. These, our common council-M[eetings] I had learnt to consider as practical *Schools* of Christian Wisdom and Christian Morality, where the general principles of the Gospel were applied to individual cases; there every Christian virtue, such as love, humility, patience, forbearance, etc., was called into exercise and where every moral evil was to be set in its true light, in order to remove it. And such a school, I now found, was also the yearly meeting, only on a much larger and higher scale. . . . [8]

Brethren worship services were informal (low church) and lengthy. Men and boys, women and girls, sat on different sides of the plain meetinghouse, on low, backless wooden benches. Ministers faced them, seated behind a long trestle table which was on the same level as the congregation to demonstrate that there was no difference between clergy and laity. A deacon would ordinarily begin the service by announcing a hymn, which he proceeded to "line." This entailed the reading of the first line or two, after which the congregation would sing them. Then he read the next lines, with song following, continuing in this manner until the hymn was completed. The reason for this practice was the lack of hymnals, but it persisted even after hymnals were made available. After the reading of scripture and a long prayer (always concluding with the shared Lord's Prayer) it was time for the sermon. The ministers would extend the courtesy down their ranks, until someone rose to preach. It was felt that the Spirit would provide an appropriate text and also edifying comments upon it. Sermons consisted usually of exegesis and ethical application. Following the conclusion of the sermon, the other ministers would comment on the same text, endeavoring to reemphasize the good points made by the first speaker or bring other reflections of their own. The service was terminated by prayer and a hymn. The absence of musical instruments did not hamper the strong congregational singing and, if anything, enhanced it.

The love feast was the high point of the church year. It was always preceded by the annual visit of the deacons in each home. The following questions were asked: "Are you still in the faith of the Gospel, as you declared when you were baptized? Are you, as far as you know, in peace and union with the church? Will you still labor with the Brethren for an increase of holiness, both in yourself and others?"[9] If the visit brought any stress or disharmony to light, the love feast would be postponed until the problem was resolved.

Revivals or "protracted meetings" were not customary before the latter part of the century. It was felt that decisions made under emotional strain would not last when the pressure was removed. Joining the church was the most serious thing a person could do in his lifetime and should be soberly weighed. "Count the Cost" (Luke 14) was a favorite text. This reservation caused the loss of quite a number of Brethren to the revivalistic groups, which included the Brethren in Christ, the Evangelical Association, and the Church of God (Winebrennerian).

There were other significant losses experienced during the same period. Universalism, which was popular in America after the Revolutionary War, stressed the belief that a God of love could never condemn sinners to eternal punishment. The atonement of Christ was sufficient for all mankind. The more radical of their number denied the reality of any punishment or reward in an afterlife. As the Brethren had in their beginnings accepted a mild form of universalism, they were susceptible to the aggressive movement. Entire congregations in North and South Carolina went over to the Universalists. These families provided much of the leadership for the Southern branch of Universalism. In Kentucky, Indiana, and Missouri, it was the Disciples who made inroads. A theology which appealed to the frontiersman, articulate leadership by Alexander Campbell and Barton Stone, and an emphasis upon Christian unity were the chief characteristics of the Disciples. Hundreds of Brethren, indeed the entire Kentucky membership, went over to them. The most active leader in the process was the former Brethren preacher Joseph Hostetler (1797-1870).

An early doctrinal treatise was written by Elder Benjamin Bowman (1754-1829); the title was *A Brief and Simple Exhibition From the Word of God* (1823). This was read by a Lutheran-bred, Methodist class leader named Peter Nead (1797-1877), who was so impressed that he looked up the Brethren in Virginia and was baptized by them. He was convinced that they followed the New Testament ordinances more closely than any other church group. After becoming a minister he began to write on the Brethren doctrines in several volumes. These were gathered together in one book called popularly *Nead's Theology* (1850). It was influential in codifying the beliefs of the brotherhood and was much used for introducing the Brethren to newcomers.

With the outbreak of the Civil War (1861-1865) the Brethren were hit hard, but the conflict did not result in rupture, as was true of almost all other denominations which had membership on both sides of the Mason and Dixon line. This was attributable to two reasons: first, the Brethren had never allowed members to hold slaves, and secondly, great efforts were made to keep contact alive across the battle lines despite the war. John Kline, who was reelected moderator through these war years, played a major role in this regard. He made repeated trips from his home in Virginia to the Northern states. His journeys, though purely on church business, brought him under Confederate suspicion of being a Northern spy. He made no bones about abolitionist feelings, and it is perhaps not surprising that some hotheaded local Confederate soldiers waylaid and murdered him in 1864. He had earlier spent time in jail in Harrisonburg for his efforts in freeing Brethren and Mennonite young men from the military.

The churches in the South suffered more severely than did those in the North during the war. This was because of their antislavery views and because the Confederacy needed manpower more desperately than the Union. Although both in North and South it was possible to be freed from military service by paying a stiff (three- to four-hundred-dollar) commutation tax, administration of the exemption was more erratic in the South. Some Brethren were forced into the Southern army and were maltreated for refusing to fire on the enemy. Some others fled to the Northern states to escape this fate, and some hid away for long periods of time. On both sides congregations pooled their resources to help pay taxes for the poorer members. Some of the Southern Brethren lost their homes, barns, livestock, and crops when the Northern armies embarked on scorched-earth policies. Sums of money were collected after the war in the North to help destitute Southern Brethren.

The important point was that the Brethren came through the bloody struggle as a united people, and remained consistently loyal to their nonresistant principles. There is no doubt that church growth was hampered by the troubled times. By 1865, it is estimated that there were twenty thousand members in some two hundred congregations across the country. Great changes were in store for this brotherhood in the second half of the century.

---

1. Morgan Edwards, *Materials Toward a History of the American Baptists* (1770), quoted in D. F. Durnbaugh, ed., *The Brethren in Colonial America* (Elgin, Ill.: Brethren Press, 1967), 175.

2. H. Jung-Stilling, *Theobald, oder die Schwärmer* (Leipzig: Weygand, 1784), I:36; Max Goebel, *Geschichte des christlichen Lebens in der rheinisch-westphälischen evangelischen Kirche* (Coblenz: Karl Bädeker, 1852), II:816; Heinz Renkewitz, *Hochmann von Hochenau* (Breslau: Maruschke and Berendt, 1935).

3. D. F. Durnbaugh, ed., *European Origins of the Brethren* (Elgin, Ill.: Brethren Press, 1958), 115-120.

4. *Ibid.*, 216.

5. *Ibid.*, 283.

6. *A Short and Sincere Declaration* (1775), published in Durnbaugh, ed., *Brethren in Colonial America*, 363-365.

7. Floyd E. Mallott, *Studies in Brethren History* (Elgin, Ill.: Brethren Press, 1954), 133-134.

8. Henry Kurtz, "Our Late Yearly Meeting, & The Gospel-Visitor," *The Monthly Gospel-Visitor*, III (June 1853), 11.

9. Otho Winger, *History and Doctrines of the Church of the Brethren* (Elgin, Ill.: Brethren Publishing House, 1919), 206.

2

RECENT HISTORY

Donald F. Durnbaugh

The nineteenth-century Brethren were known as a "peculiar people" and found no offense in being thus labeled. Their distinctive manner of dress, restricted way of life, and vigorously defended cultic practices helped to keep them separate from the world. Like the early Christians whom they took as patterns, they thought of themselves virtually as a third race, in this world but not of it, as sojourners on their way to a better land. In the terminology of the sociologists of religion, the Brethren were sectarian.

Ellsworth Faris, a pioneer investigator of the concept of religious sectarianism, used the Brethren to illustrate the sect *par excellence.* He urged his colleagues to turn their attention to an examination of these Dunkers: "The religious sect, and particularly the modern isolated sect, has many advantages which ethnography does not afford. . . . If sociologists cared to give the same careful and detailed study to the foot-washing of the Dunkers . . . as they do the totem dances of the Australians or the taboos of the Bantus the material would not only be found equally interesting but in all probability more fruitful."[1] Faris was unaware that at the time of his writing (1928) the Brethren had already changed remarkably from their earlier character, but his reference to the Brethren as a "modern isolated sect" is an apt description of them during the previous era.

A sociologist visiting the Church of the Brethren today would probably still find feetwashing practiced (although some congregations have dropped it), but he would hardly find the isolated sect so intriguing to Faris. Contemporary Brethren live, dress, and conduct themselves very much like other middle-class white (there are a few minority group members) American Protestants, although largely still Germanic in ethnic background rather than Anglo-Saxon. If he were to observe more closely he could detect some continuing characteristics of the sectarian heritage: emphasis on the historic peace witness, sermons on the "simple life," familial feeling in the denomination, resistance to credal statements, and openness to social concerns. He would find some limited geographical areas (Eastern Pennsylvania, Maryland, and the Southeast) where older behavior patterns still persist and are, somewhat patronizingly, respected by the broader denomination. An articulate group of younger church members show signs of increasing appreciation for the viability of some of the traditional values in meeting current problems.

It is, nevertheless, obvious that a tremendous transformation has taken place within the Church of the Brethren in less than a century. Some observers have estimated that the Brethren have changed more in a shorter period of time than any other comparable communion. Whether this is strictly true or not, the most cursory glance at the recent history of the Brethren does indicate radical and rapid change. What were the influences which caused this shift?

Several sociologically oriented studies have been written to analyze the social factors involved. The greater density of population, enforced public schooling, marriage outside the church membership, the impact of informational media — these are said to be leveling agents in homogenizing particularist groups. The only religious communities successfully to retard the process, it is held, are the Hutterites and the Amish who have virtually withdrawn from society.

Others speak of the effect of the "sect-cycle." As sectarian groups mature, they tend to adopt the postures and practices of the church establishments from which they sprang. They become more concerned with nurture than conversion, with trained ministry rather than charismatic lay ministers, with involvement in society rather than fleeing from it. Strict discipline brings economic prosperity, and prosperity brings with it an advance in class standing, and changed class standing calls into question previously held church views.

Others have laid more stress upon economic determinants. The impact of industrialization is the key in the change, they say. As America became industrialized during and after the Civil War, all segments of the population were affected. A predominantly agricultural population (and the Brethren were almost completely rural in the nineteenth century) moved to the growing cities. As mass production made goods more plentiful, the old ways of living (and church rules about them) seemed to be passé. "The Dunker elder bought an automobile and stepped on the gas; out of the window went his broadbrim, followed by his wife's bonnet, followed by his whiskers."[2]

Perhaps it is possible to draw these several explanations together under the rubric *acculturation*. The immigrant religious fraternity, kept apart by its language, its demanding ethic, its close-knit family ties, its self-understanding as a "called-out" people, gradually came to feel at home in the American culture. It is generally accurate to say that all of the currents which swept through American religious and national life also affected the Brethren, but often after a lag of several decades. As we come closer to the contemporary scene, the lag becomes smaller and smaller. This would hold true for theological trends, architectural styles, liturgical developments, and social issues.

The Brethren missionary thrust of the late nineteenth century is a case in point. The Brethren involvement in missions went through the same tensions experienced by other religious groups at the beginning of the nineteenth century. Of course, the ways in which the Brethren responded to these various influences were molded by their own distinctive background. In certain fields, especially social concerns, the Brethren have not been followers only, but have been occasionally leaders for Protestantism. It is significant that the average American Protestant who hears of the Brethren would identify them by their innovations in social welfare.

A key to the question of acculturation was the process of transferring from the predominant use of the German language in worship and home to the American English of their neighbors. The change came rapidly and early in the few urban or suburban congregations of the Brethren, as in Germantown or Baltimore. Soon after 1800 church records in those places began to be kept in English. The switch came much more slowly in the country. One good way to follow the change is to notice the language of much used church publications such as hymnals. By mid-century, it was common to have English and German hymnals published and bound together, for there would be only German-speaking and only English-speaking members in the same congregations. In the "free ministry" system of the time, some would preach only in German, some only in English, and some were fluent in both. With the dwindling knowledge of German in the later nineteenth century, its use in public observances diminished rapidly. The gateway was thus opened for the introduction of the ways and values of the surrounding society. It is noticeable that some of the sharpest criticisms by the "Progressive Brethren" prior to the schisms of 1881-1883 were leveled at the "ignorant" elders who could not write and speak English correctly. The language shift heightened tensions inasmuch as language became a symbol for openness to new ideas or stubborn clinging to old traditions.

The process of change can also be followed in the official designations of the Brethren. It was not until 1836 that an official name was provided by Conference action; this was *The Fraternity of German Baptists*. In 1871 that was modified to *The German Baptist Brethren*. After lengthy discussion, in 1908, the bicentennial year of its founding, the Annual Conference acted to change the name to *The Church of the Brethren*. One of the arguments given for the new title was that the use of the word *German* in the designation was no longer accurate, as German was no longer used in public meetings and membership was by no means limited to this ethnic background.

Second Half of the Nineteenth Century

The westward movement of the Brethren which was so prominent in the first half of the nineteenth century continued strongly in the latter half. The process generally was to fill in the gaps left in the push to the West Coast. In 1856, the same year that a congregation was planted in Oregon, the first church was organized in Kansas. This state saw rapid church extension, especially in the years after 1883, when in six years the number of congregations increased fourfold. Nebraska had its first church in 1872, Washington in 1876, Colorado in 1877, Idaho in 1878. During the 1880s some congregations were established in the Southwestern states including Texas and Louisiana, but these have always remained isolated. North Dakota was settled in the 1890s. By 1908 there were 298 congregations, 816 ministers, and some 15,500 adult members in nineteen of the twenty-two states west of the Mississippi River. Much of this membership, however, represented a migration from Brethren congregations in the East and Midwest, rather than new converts.

A novel element was the role of the transcontinental railroads. Having successfully pushed their tracks across the continent, the companies were now eager to attract settlers. These newcomers would provide business as they moved and become customers for shipping farm produce to markets. German religious groups were especially courted, for they tended to move in large numbers and had the reputation of being stable personalities and good farmers. As for the church leadership, they were able to find spiritual motivation to buttress the economic appeals made by the railroads. Colonization in the West could be and was interpreted as a means of extending church witness; they also thought that islands of morality could there be established to continue the narrow way of religious truth. The overpopulated East was full of many distractions. When increasing criticisms of the colonization efforts were being made, the mind-set of some Brethren leaders was revealed in an editorial in a church paper written in 1906:

> The railroads, though soulless corporations, are being used wonderfully by the Lord for the spread of the church. Even though it be true that the agents for the railroads have been active in urging people to go and see and believe and settle, from sinister motives, that does not keep God and His real children from taking advantage of these opportunities for the glory of His name. . . . Today these roads may be reaping rich returns financially for their aggressive work. Well and good. These arteries of our nation have made it possible for the hands of the church to operate where, had they not gone, the church could not now be.[3]

Another boom of the same period was the inauguration of schools of higher learning. Nearly forty institutions of academy (high school) level or above were started by Brethren between 1852 and 1923, most of short duration. Of these attempts, seven exist today. There were many reasons given for the development of Brethren-sponsored schools. Youth from Brethren homes were in fact attending schools, and it was argued that they would be lost to the church if no institutions were available in which they could receive education in an atmosphere conducive to Brethren values. Advertisements stressed the care to be taken to provide a wholesome situation which would reinforce the teachings of family and church. The Brethren by this time were increasingly accepting (although there was stubborn resistance) the pervasive belief in the nation that education provided the key to future happiness and social usefulness. Interestingly enough, at first the Brethren were scrupulous in keeping religious education as such from the school curriculum, for this was held to be solely the prerogative of the church and home. Bible courses, it was held, would be the opening wedge for the creation of a seminary, and then the path to a "hireling" ministry would be open.

Another reason for the surge of schools was that they provided an acceptable avenue for financial investment. Prosperous Brethren could participate in what was hoped to be a profitable undertaking and be doing good at the same time. In fact, very few of the schools flourished in any business sense, and many supporters lost heavily. Chronicles of the schools recount the sacrifices of founders and faculty. They had been encouraged in these ventures by the desire of many of the small towns where Brethren lived to secure schools. Usually land and often buildings were made available for this purpose by the town fathers.

Accompanying the development in education and usually involving the same people was the upsurge in periodical publication. Although started and continued as private business ventures, these papers were published on behalf of the denomination and were subject to its criticism and semicontrol. Henry Kurtz (1796-1874) was the pioneer Brethren publisher, with his *Monthly Gospel Visitor* in 1851. Formerly a Lutheran pastor in Pennsylvania, the German-born and well-educated Kurtz had moved to Northeastern Ohio in 1827. For Kurtz a church periodical was essential to safeguard the unity of a widely scattering brotherhood and was a practical way to solve doctrinal and practical problems by providing a sounding board for insights and conclusions. He also saw in the paper a means to promote certain values and ideals he felt were important. In this he had great success, for he was ordinarily tactful enough to avert strong opposition. Scholars have seen the Kurtz press as a pivot point in the history of the Brethren. The causes of higher education, missions, theological literacy, reform in polity, aid for needy in faraway places, and a less parochial vision all found their first advocacy in the columns of the *Gospel Visitor*.

Kurtz found an effective associate in his publishing venture in James Quinter (1816-1888), who went on to become the owner of the *Visitor* and the leading educator and church statesman of his time for the Brethren. In that day of popularity for debating as a way of airing if not solving controversial issues, it was Quinter who, reluctantly, became the champion of the Brethren cause, traveling the country to debate the distinctive Brethren doctrines and practices with churchmen of other persuasions. Stenographic records of many of the debates were taken so that they could later be published.

The *Gospel Visitor* was not long the only Brethren journal. Many others were begun. Nearly sixty different publications have been identified between 1851 and 1900. A steady process of merger took place, however, so that the principal organ was Quinter's publication, which after several mergers was known as the *Gospel Messenger* in 1883. In 1897 it came under direct church control and has continued as the official house publication until this day. It is now called the *Messenger*, published in Elgin, Illinois, the location of the Brethren Press.

Another sort of journalism was introduced by a Kurtz employee, Henry R. Holsinger (1833-1905). He began a weekly, the *Christian Family Companion* (1864), and a paper for young people (1870), issued full reports of Annual Conference discussions, and printed the first hymnal with notes. Holsinger had a more aggressive approach to his publishing enterprise than either Kurtz or Quinter. These men were eager to see the church move, but were willing to suggest steps and cultivate support. Holsinger wanted to push the church into reform, and used polemics, satire, and personal criticism to accomplish his purposes. He opened up the pages of his publications as a forum for comment and criticism from his readers. Holsinger focused his impatience also on the dominance in the Conference of the older leadership. He, therefore, argued for a thoroughgoing congregationalism in polity, which would allow more rapid change. New methods for church work including revival meetings, salaried pastors, Sunday schools, and lively literature, he maintained, were needed.

These views alarmed a number of conservative elders, many of them residents of Southern Ohio, who decided they needed to organize for the preservation of the "old order" of church practice. They were led by Elder Peter Nead, the foremost Brethren theological writer of the mid-century, and by Nead's son-in-law, Samuel Kinsey (1832-1883), the editor of the conservative journal, *The Vindicator* (1870). The conservatives, who were called the Miami Valley Elders, were frankly concerned about their loss of leadership and control in the denomination. They sent repeated petitions to the Annual Conference calling for a halt to innovations. Although they met with early successes, those on the other side, the "Progressives," kept active as well, so that issues remained alive. In 1880 the Conference replied to a petition of the conservatives: "While we declare ourselves conservative in maintaining unchanged what may justly be considered the principles and peculiarities of our Fraternity, we also believe in the propriety and necessity of so adapting our labor and our principles to the religious wants of the world as will render our labor and principles most efficient in promoting the reformation of the world, the edification of the church, and the glory of God. *Hence while we are conservative, we are also progressive."* [Emphasis added.]'

This seemed to be the last straw for the conservative faction, and they sent a near ultimatum to the next Annual Conference, which was rejected on a technicality as not having come through the regular channels. The "Old Order" faction of about four thousand therefore pulled off and organized in 1881 what is known as the Old German Baptist Brethren. The name is to signify their conviction that they represent the true continuation of the original Brethren. The schism brought with it anguished splits within congregations and individual families, and some contention over control of church property.

The pain was to be compounded by a corresponding exodus from the progressive side. Many in the center party had become exasperated by the prodding for reform by Holsinger and his friends and called for an Annual Conference committee of elders to visit Holsinger in his home congregation, Berlin, Pennsylvania. Because of a dispute about procedure, the committee never did come to a discussion of the real issues with the congregation, but nevertheless announced that Holsinger should be considered disfellowshiped until the next Conference could pass final decision. The committee action was sharply attacked and defended during the months before the 1882 Conference, which began in a state of high tension. Many voices called for patience and mercy in deciding the issue, and Holsinger himself extended an apology, but the mood of the majority was for censure. The committee was upheld and Holsinger's expulsion confirmed.

Those who rallied to the Progressive leader at this point decided to organize a new branch of the church, which was called the Brethren Church. In this they waited until 1883 to see if a reconciliation could be effected with the main body, but this was not forthcoming. Perhaps six thousand members sided with Holsinger, as most of those wishing for reform thought it could still be implemented within the church structure and were hesitant to cause more disunity than had already happened. In fact, most of the changes for which Holsinger contended were soon introduced, leading to the conclusion that the second schism could have been avoided, given more tact on the part of the Progressives and more forbearance on the part of the Conference leadership.

The Brethren Church became, over the years, more conservative in theological position than the main body, perhaps because it was at first more open to modern currents of theology, including fundamentalism, than the Church of the Brethren. Between 1936 and 1939 a sharp doctrinal struggle took place, resulting in the formation of the National Fellowship of Brethren Churches (Winona Lake, Indiana) and the Brethren Church (Ashland, Ohio). The two groups have separate colleges, seminaries, mission boards, and publications, and are actually two separate bodies today although officially still one denomination.[6]

Surprisingly, despite the internal upheaval of the early 1880's, the parent body experienced remarkable growth after the schism. Its greatest numerical increase came in the period between 1890 and 1930. It can perhaps best be explained that as both the conservative and progressive extremes left, the fairly homogeneous group which remained was free to turn its interests outward. Evangelists such as I. J. Rosenberger (1842-1923) were known for their many converts at this time.

The developments in the area of foreign missions demonstrated this renewed vigor. Missions had repeatedly been raised earlier as a concern for the Brethren, but without much response until 1876, when a Macedonian call came from Denmark. (Henry Kurtz had preached and baptized in Switzerland during a visit to Europe in 1839, but this was purely a personal initiative.) A Dane named Christian Hope (1844-1899), who had come to America to find religious freedom, read about the Brethren, sought them out, and joined them. They seemed to him to be the closest he could find to apostolic Christianity. He wrote back from his new home in Illinois to friends in Denmark and arranged for the publication of some tracts translated into Danish. Those in Denmark whom he reached asked that someone should come to baptize them. Hope took the challenge to the local district, which ordained him as a minister and decided to send him, with two others, to Denmark in 1876. This, however, was a district endeavor, and the brotherhood gave little response to their call for further financial support.

Following 1884 the mission interests of the Brethren were reorganized, and support increased. When the mission board began its work in 1884 it had a sum of $8.69 to work with. By 1913, the annual receipts were over $100,000 and the assets amounted to nearly one million dollars. Missions as "the great first work of the church" became the slogan for the denomination. This was the title of a book by Wilbur B. Stover (1866-1930), an indefatigable promoter of missions and first Brethren missionary to India. As other fields opened, missionaries who volunteered became the heroes of the denomination and were received with acclaim upon their return on furloughs. The 1919 Annual Conference at Winona Lake, Indiana, alone received a collection of $150,000 for missions. D. L. Miller (1841-1921), a wealthy merchant and educator, was a stalwart in broadening the vision of the Brethren by his reports of his world travels and his service on the mission board.

The Twentieth Century

The twentieth century brought yet more changes to the Brethren. Of more than symbolic significance was the "dress question"; by this is meant the controversy over the wisdom of the denomination's continuing to enforce the wearing of the plain dress. The matter had been repeatedly raised, even after the three-way split of the 1880's. A representative committee was asked to bring a "clear, concise restatement of our position on this vexed question" to the 1910 Conference. A carefully worded and closely reasoned report was brought back which the Conference accepted, but another committee was asked to prepare a supplementary report. The second report reiterated the strong recommendation for a uniform manner of dress set forth in the 1910 statement, but failed to make dress a matter of church discipline. Congregations could decide to disregard the previous Conference rulings. This opened the way to the rapid rejection of the distinctive garb. A small faction under the leadership of B. E. Kesler (1861-1952) withdrew in 1926 as a protest against this trend.

One of the arguments for discontinuing the peculiar dress was to free the Brethren to involve themselves more in the needs of the world. There is a clear trend toward greater public participation in the first decades of the twentieth century, centering first on support of such causes as temperance and international arbitration of disputes. Church leaders were eager to throw the weight of the membership behind those agencies and movements working for social uplift and moral improvement. Brethren were urged to be good citizens and make their voice heard on public issues. A Brethren minister, Martin G. Brumbaugh (1862-1930) became governor of Pennsylvania in 1915.

This served to complicate the Brethren reaction to the demands brought by World War I. In previous wars the Brethren position was clear-cut; members could pay taxes if demanded by the government; they could even pay a commutation fee, if imposed upon them, to free themselves from military service; but they could not enter military service. When the United States began drafting men in 1917, some of the church leaders took the position that consistent nonresistance was no longer tenable. They argued that as the Brethren participated as citizens and enjoyed the privileges of the nation, they could not now completely refuse a call to serve the country in wartime. They recommended that the Brethren draftees enter the army as noncombatants, a category provided by the draft law for those religiously opposed to killing.

The federal government delayed for a year in determining what kinds of duty in the armed services were considered to be noncombatant. The final delineation included the expected medical corps and also the quartermaster and engineering units as noncombatant. This was unacceptable to many conscientious objectors. During the period between the declaration of the war and this administrative ruling, many young Brethren were called into the army. Most of them had to decide for themselves how far they could go in cooperating with the army, although some effort was made to send Brethren elders to the military camps as visitors and advisers. Those Brethren who refused to wear the uniform and to carry out military orders often underwent harsh treatment. Camp officers tried to break their wills by harrassment and brutality, and sometimes met with success. Those remaining firm were court-martialed. Many of the conscientious objectors asked for overseas assignments in civilian capacities as ambulance drivers and the like, but few succeeded in this attempt. Some were given farm furloughs, which provided an acceptable alternative.

In the meantime, a special Conference was called in Goshen, Indiana, in January 1918. The purpose was to reach consensus on the Brethren attitude to the world conflict and the military demands. Those attending drew up a comprehensive statement, which consisted of resolutions to be sent to the heads of the government, a strong theological justification for the refusal to bear arms, and a procedure for organization to represent the church in these matters. The Goshen statement was printed and distributed to the churches. It soon found its way to the offices of the War Department in Washington as draftees produced it to answer the question why they would not fight. The federal government threatened prosecution of the Conference officers for treason, which was successful in forcing the withdrawal of the statement. Trial and possible imprisonment of church leaders were thus averted, but at the price of the virtual rejection of the official peace position.

Some of the younger men who went through the problems of the war experience determined to give their lives to the cause of peace, beginning with the strengthening of the peace position among Brethren. Notable among them were Dan West (b. 1893) and M. R. Zigler (b. 1891). They involved them-selves deeply in the life of the denomination, Zigler especially serving in major leadership roles. They found many who supported them in their peace en-deavors. Owing to these efforts, when World War II came the Brethren were more clearly prepared and united in their attitude, even though not all of the constituency held to the strict pacifist line. There was, in fact, a minority who held a consistent conscientious objector position during World War II.

These peace leaders could be classified as liberals in theology, as were others who held the key positions in the denomination during the interwar period. Many had secured advanced education at schools such as Crozer, Yale, and Vanderbilt, and had caught the vision of a church engaged in social mission. This created counterpressures, from both the conservative Brethren who wished to remain more withdrawn, and those who had been influenced by a resurgent fundamentalism.

Middle Pennsylvania became the center of this theological conservatism. Juniata College, under the presidency of Charles C. Ellis (1874-1950) set up its own seminary, of a more conservative tone than Bethany Bible School in Chicago (later Bethany Theological Seminary). Bethany was founded in 1905 by Albert Cassel Wieand (1871-1954) and Emanuel B. Hoff (1860-1928). A possible church division was avoided when the Chicago school was accepted in 1925 as the property of the denomination and the Pennsylvania seminary was terminated. Under the leadership of Wieand and D. W. Kurtz (1879-1949), the seminary developed as a moderately liberal institution.

The fundamentalist issue came to a head after 1941, when the Brethren became members of the Federal Council of Churches by Conference action upon the recommendation of the Council of Boards, a coordinating group of

Brethren boards. Approval was also given for membership in the World Council of Churches upon its organization. Calls came for a reconsideration of the decision, as it was felt in some quarters that the Conference had approved the affiliation without sufficient study. Since that time a vocal minority has protested the conciliar affiliation, charging modernism and unpopular political viewpoints in the leadership of the councils. Two Pennsylvania congregations underwent serious divisions over the fundamentalist issue, though the courts ruled that property should be kept in the hands of the parties remaining loyal to the denomination.

Although, since they began to become active in political affairs, the Brethren have tended to vote for the Republican ticket, the throes of the depression of the 1930s brought some changes. A survey made by the liberal Kirby Page in 1934 on questions of a military, a political, and an international nature, included a large sampling from the Brethren. One fifth (over five hundred) of the Brethren ministers to whom he sent the questionnaire answered. About one half of these called for a "drastically reformed capitalism" as the most effective way to achieve a cooperative commonwealth and fully one fourth favored socialism. Individual Brethren became more concerned with questions of economic justice, although as late as 1941 the Annual Conference suggested that members should be cautious in their union activity.

This period saw great involvement of the Brethren in the Sunday school movement. Only reluctantly accepted in the nineteenth century, this form of Christian education came into its own following the creation in 1896 of the denominational Sunday School Advisory Board. By 1921 an enrollment of 139,915 was reported for the church schools. The *Brethren Teacher's Quarterly*, which began in 1899 and attained broad circulation, was based on the International Lessons. Cooperation with other denominations was earlier and stronger in this field than in any other. The term *Evergreen* was used for those congregations which included all age groups in their school programs and continued throughout the year.

Another influential innovation in the life of the denomination was the beginning of the camping movement. The first Brethren camp was perhaps that held in Nebraska in 1916, although other camps in Indiana and Pennsylvania were among the early permanent sites. Soon most of the districts of the denomination sought to develop their own camps as a place for intensive education. Visiting leadership awakened many of the children and young people to the possibilities and challenges of church vocations. This seemed more effective in changing values and forming commitments than the Christian education taking place in the home congregations. By 1939 there were twenty-nine different Brethren camps in thirteen states and Canada.

Mid-Twentieth Century

The impact of World War II intensified the tendencies of the Brethren to become more deeply involved in society. This can be seen in the lives of a few Brethren who achieved national prominence at this time. Two stand out in this respect, Kermit Eby and Andrew Cordier.

Eby (1903-1962) became well known as an educator, labor leader, and intellectual gadfly, and also as the most articulate interpreter of the Brethren heritage. Born and bred in a rural area of northern Indiana near Elkhart, he attended Manchester College and the University of Chicago, before becoming a teacher in Ann Arbor, Michigan. There he became acquainted with leaders of the Congress of Industrial Organization, which was unionizing the Michigan auto workers. He was called to Washington in 1942 by the labor movement as national educational director, but eventually came to feel that the unions were becoming insensitive to the needs of the rank-and-file. As a free-wheeling professor at the University of Chicago after 1948, Kermit Eby was known as a voice of conscience speaking out on all the current issues. Everywhere he went he called for the introduction of the virtues of honesty, integrity, industry, and human relationships which he had been given by his Dunker background.

A personality with similar beginnings is Dr. Andrew W. Cordier (b. 1901), former president of Columbia University, and longtime official of the United Nations. Born into a Brethren family in Ohio, Cordier attended Manchester College and the University of Chicago before returning to Manchester as professor of history and political science for nearly twenty years. During this period, he became an expert on international relations and an adviser to the influential United States Senator Arthur Vandenberg. Cordier was brought into the State Department as a planner for an international agency for international peace after the end of the war. When the United Nations was formed, Cordier went into its service as a senior American official, becoming the executive assistant of the first two secretary-generals and undersecretary for general assembly affairs. As such he was often sent to trouble spots around the world to direct the UN presence. Some Brethren felt that in this role he was departing from the original peace teaching of the church, but Cordier himself indicated that he saw himself practicing the teaching of reconciliation learned at Brethren conferences and at their love feasts.

Even before World War II the Brethren had been associated with attempts at alleviating world problems, although usually oriented toward the relief of sufferers. Following World War I the Brethren sent a large amount of money to help the Armenians. Civil war in Spain and the Japanese invasion of China called forth Brethren aid. There was close cooperation with the American Friends Service Committee on several of these projects, and the Brethren seemed to be following in Quaker footsteps in broadening the arena of their activities.

It is, therefore, not surprising that when the Brethren organized their own agency for relief and rehabilitation, they took the name Brethren Service Committee (1939). The onset of World War II made impossible much work overseas, although preparations went forward. Major Brethren Service Committee attention was centered in the Civilian Public Service program. This represented a cooperative program of the historic peace churches (Brethren, Mennonite, and Quakers) and the federal government to provide civilian work "of national importance" for religious objectors. The peace churches had lobbied to get total exemption for all conscientious objectors, whose sincerity would be established by civilian tribunals after the British example. They were unsuccessful in obtaining this, and therefore agreed to help run camps for this civilian service. Young men entering CPS would spend as much time as men in military units, and their support would be provided by the churches. The government undertook to provide work, largely in the Park Service and conservation agencies, and supervisory personnel.

The agreement represented a tremendous undertaking for the three small denominations, especially as they were expected to support all conscientious objectors, of whatever background. The Brethren alone expended more than $1,250,000 between 1942 and 1946 to administer the CPS program for three thousand men, who worked more than 2,500,000 man-hours. The difficult administration of the program was largely in the hands of a young former pastor from West Virginia, W. Harold Row (b. 1912). There proved to be many problems in the base camps, but the initiation of "detached programs" of mental hospital attendants, dairy testers, and control patients, which were mostly self-supporting and socially more meaningful, proved helpful. They also brought a generally favorable public response to the plan.

Following the end of hostilities, BSC took on new life and the church threw itself into the supplying of needed materials and foodstuffs for millions of war sufferers around the world. It is fair to say that the Brethren Service interest displaced missions as the chief focus of the denomination although support still ran high for the latter. In 1948, the Brethren had work in Austria, China, Ecuador, England, Ethiopia, France, Germany, Italy, Japan, Poland, and several other countries. Young college graduates spent several years of voluntary service in these foreign countries, administering programs and representing the church people at home, who were the donors of the relief goods. Some Brethren-sponsored agencies won interdenominational support, and many Brethren personnel were brought into ecumenical organizations as staff workers. New Windsor, Maryland, the site of a former Brethren college, became the center of a relief operation of vast proportions. The program continues today, although the areas of need have shifted from Europe to Africa and Asia.

The postwar period was also a time for reorganization and reform in polity and church administration. The pattern during the 1920's and 1930's had been the creation of independent boards, of which the General Mission Board was by far the most powerful, to carry on the work of the denomination. The areas of competence of these boards tended to conflict, and they sometimes found themselves competing for funds. There was thus interest in creating a unified plan which would make for greater efficiency in operation and better use of church funds. A committee of fifteen developed a comprehensive report on church polity which was accepted in 1946 and implemented in 1947. There was created a General Brotherhood Board of twenty-five members, which incorporated the former boards within its five commissions. The board acted as the administrative arm of the church under policies set by the Annual Conference. Denominational employees were under the supervision of the board, whose members were chosen among five geographical regions defined by the report. This introduced another level of polity in addition to the districts, created in the mid-nineteenth century.

This organization prevailed until the summer of 1968, when a restructuring plan was adopted. The new scheme called for a General Board, divided into three commissions — World Ministries, Parish Ministries, and General

Services. Three associate general secretaries head these commissions, with overall coordination coming from a general secretary. Two underlying principles of the new plan are that the work of the denominational officials should be on a team basis with the possibility of shifting assignments as problems change, and that the general offices of the church should be concerned with consulting with local congregations rather than developing programs for handing down to the local areas. Denominational headquarters will provide resources to aid congregations in carrying out their mission locally.

The mid-twentieth century has been marked by virtually complete utilization of full-time pastors by all congregations able to afford such leadership. Intensive efforts have been made to provide these men with more adequate compensation (according to a salary scale adopted by the denomination but not binding upon congregations) and more professional status. The current shortage of trained pastors has led to quite a few multiple parish situations, with one pastor serving several congregations. Increasingly, Brethren congregations are also being "yoked" with congregations of other denominations.

In the last two decades observers have noted an increasing emphasis upon local concerns with congregational needs tending to supplant earlier concentration on missions or Brethren Service. The introduction of the unified budget at the time of the reorganization in 1946 was in part an effort to control the popular appeal of these two causes. Pastors played an increasingly large role in the determination of policies through the General Brotherhood Board after 1947. From the 1930s to the 1950s it had been predominantly educators who had been elected to the moderatorship of the denomination. After 1960 pastors dominated this office, which is considered to be the highest at the disposal of the church.

With the increasing centrality of the role of the salaried pastor, there was a corresponding decrease in the importance of the traditional eldership. This function was accordingly called into question and, after several years of study and debate, was abandoned at the Annual Conference of 1967. Those men who had been ordained as elders for life retained that status.

Major denominational attention and support in the 1950s and 1960s were devoted to the relocation of both the general offices or headquarters of the denomination and the seminary. The offices and publishing house moved to a modern new plant on the outskirts of Elgin, Illinois, in 1959. The seminary sought a more spacious site for its campus in Chicago's western suburbs in Oak Brook, Illinois, and moved into the new setting in 1963. Some opposed the latter move as an evasion of the needs of the inner city, but the majority of the denomination followed the recommendation of the seminary board in upholding the wisdom and necessity of relocation.

Great emphasis was placed during these years on church extension, with attempts to begin new congregations in the growing metropolitan areas. A statement on church extension adopted in 1958 pledged the Brethren to cooperate on a comity basis with other churches. In order to attract those from other denominational backgrounds, Brethren should receive them by transfer of letters without requesting baptism and should also provide Sunday morning communion services after the usual Protestant pattern. This marked a major step away from traditional Brethren practice and was accepted only on the basis that the action was permissive and would not be binding in all congregations.

Following World War II there was a boom in new church building construction. This often brought with it a change from the former pattern of the pulpit in the center of the chancel, which had in turn supplanted the old meetinghouse style of a preacher's table along the long axis of the house at the same level as the congregation. The newer tendency was for a divided chancel, with lectern on one side, pulpit on the other, and communion table and/or cross as a worship center in the middle. Architects, borrowing from traditional Protestant style, often fenced off the chancel. Little attention was given to architectural accommodation of the Brethren practice of the love feast, which was, therefore, often relegated to the basement or "fellowship hall." Gleaming kitchens provided the opportunity for meals for the entire congregation on social occasions. The outer appearance of the buildings often incorporated real or suggested steeples, reminiscent of the New England Congregational churches.

This change in architecture represents change in the self-understanding of the denomination which was more felt than articulated. To help clarify its position two carefully planned theological conferences were held, one in 1960, the second in 1964. The topic for the first consultation was the "Nature and Function of the Church." It included position papers, outside speakers, and intensive discussions. The mood of this first conference might be summed up in the statement that the Brethren should be more clearly identified with a "transformationist strategy in relation to the world." The second conference, which set its theme as "The Meaning of Membership in the Body of Christ," was composed of a broadly representative group, which both furthered discussion and hampered satisfactory resolution of the problems which presented themselves. The report of the conferences found no unifying theme which could encompass the diverse Brethren membership. A commentator spoke of an "identity crisis" as the Brethren recognized the extent of their change from an earlier sectarian posture without being able to achieve clarity or feasible future options.

The same ambivalence surfaced on a denomination-wide level with the issue of full participation in the Consultation on Church Union. The consultation (COCU) represented the most serious effort of the twentieth century to unite major Protestant bodies in the United States in a church "truly reformed, truly catholic, and truly evangelical." From 1963 on Brethren attended yearly COCU meetings as "observer-consultants." In 1965 a specific invitation came to the Brethren to become full members. After a year of intense discussion in congregations, districts, and periodicals, the Annual Conference of 1966 voted decisively to abstain from full participation. At the same time the delegates strongly reaffirmed their attachment to the ecumenical principle as practiced in conciliar relationships and cooperation among Christian churches. In 1968 the Conference decided against reopening the question.

During this period diversity began to take on organized forms. A conservative element founded the Brethren Revival Fellowship in 1959. This largely eastern group has urged the Brethren through literature and meetings to place more emphasis upon evangelism, scriptural authority, and doctrine, less on social witness and action. Membership in the National Council of Churches and liberalism in denominational publications and curriculum materials have been heavily criticized. Of quite different temper are the Brethren Action Movement and the Brethren Peace Fellowship which coalesced around 1968. They desire more vigorous activity in peace education and antiwar projects. They form loosely linked fellowships across the country to accomplish these goals, with special attention to reaching Brethren students.

Although these groups considered the denominational program to be inadequate in the area of social action, it is clear that as a church body the Brethren are moving toward a more activist stance in relation to current social issues. This may be illustrated by comparing the denominational themes in the post-World War II period. The theme for 1946-1947 was "Christ the Hope of the World"; for 1949-1950, "Deepening the Spiritual Life." By 1962-1965 the theme had become "To Heal the Broken," and for the period 1965-1970, "God Loves the World So . . . ." Interpretation of the themes left no doubt that the intent was to turn the attention of Brethren churches to the needs of the world about them. A denominational drive to effect this goal was given the name "Mission One" and church literature highlighted social action congruent with the theme. In 1969 a Fund for the Americas was created to raise major sums of money for minority groups.

At the same time there was great interest in the development of persons within the church. Many of the techniques of group dynamics were used in workshops, "group life laboratories," and retreats. The Mission Twelve program has brought together small groups from several congregations in a retreat setting over a period of three weekends for intensive training in interpersonal relations. It was hoped that as these teams returned to their local churches they could serve as resources for renewal and greater congregational vitality.

A matter for concern has been the leveling off in church membership since 1945. In fact, after 1963 totals for membership and church attendance receded slightly. The only area of real growth was Nigeria, where the years of patient work since 1922 were repaid by a flood of Africans seeking admission to the church. Some of the reasons given for the decline in membership in the United States were: Conference actions which encouraged the removal of the names of inactive members from the rolls, the increased activity of the church in controversial areas of civil rights and peace, the greater mobility of families, the migration from the rural areas to the cities, and the overall lessening of religious interest in the United States.

A third theological conference was held in July 1969. The theme, "Faithfulness in Change," took as its focus the diversity and pluralism found both in the denomination and the surrounding society. An observer noted that, unlike the 1964 conference, there did not seem to be the same unease regarding the identity of the church. Pluralism was accepted as a fact, without embarrassment. There seemed to be more looking to the future, rather than dwelling upon the past.

The conference theme may well serve as a summary of both the problems and the hope of the Church of the Brethren as it enters the last third of the twentieth century. There is a sense of realism in accepting the fact of change. There is evidence of dedication to the quality of faithfulness among the Brethren. How faithfulness in the face of change may best be expressed finds different answers in the church today. The future will reveal both the answers which the Brethren will give and the extent to which they were the right ones.

---

1. Ellsworth Faris, "The Sect and the Sectarian," *American Journal of Sociology*, LX (May 1955), 75-89; originally published in 1928.

2. Quoted in Floyd E. Mallott, *Studies in Brethren History* (Elgin, Ill.: Brethren Publishing House, 1954), 264.

3. *The Missionary Visitor* (February 1906), 97.

4. *Minutes of the Annual Meetings of the Church of the Brethren* (Elgin, Ill.: Brethren Publishing House, 1909), 382.

5. For a brief description of the history of the Old German Baptist Brethren after 1881 see John M. Kimmel, *Chronicles of the Brethren* (Covington, Ohio: Little Printing Co., 1951), 254-324.

6. For histories of the two branches of the Progressive Brethren movement see Homer A. Kent, Sr., *250 Years . . . Conquering Frontiers* (Winona Lake, Ind.: Brethren Missionary Herald Co., 1958) and Albert T. Ronk, *History of the Brethren Church* (Ashland, Ohio: Brethren Publishing Co., 1968).

3

BELIEFS

Vernard Eller

It would be expected that this chapter deal with the doctrine and theology of the Brethren. In one sense it will do so; yet the topics treated here will not constitute what we normally think of as a theology. The central factor in Brethrenism, we will suggest, is a commitment to follow Christ in "radical discipleship." This thrust immediately skews Brethren thought away from the conceptual, the theoretical, the systematic, the theological, and toward the practical, the applicable, the existential.

The Brethren tendency agrees with Kierkegaard: "The truth, in the sense in which Christ was the truth, is not a sum of sentences, not a definition of concepts, etc., but a life. . . . And hence, Christianly understood, the truth consists not in knowing the truth but in being the truth. . . . Only then do I truly know the truth when it becomes a life in me. . . . "[1] "What I am concerned about is the 'how,' the personal enforcement of the proclamation; without that, Christianity is not Christianity."[2]

In consequence, the Brethren never have shown much interest in theologizing. Pretty much as a matter of course they have accepted the general doctrinal stand of orthodox, evangelical Protestantism, but within those limits they have allowed considerable flexibility and divergency. On many theological issues it is simply impossible to speak of a "Brethren" position; the question, rather, has been, "What is the quality of your commitment and discipleship?"

This is not to say that the Brethren have been doctrinally careless, taking the position that it makes no difference what one believes or that any understanding of the gospel is as good as any other. Theirs has not been an irrationalism or obscurantism. The attitude perhaps can best be characterized as anti-"intellectualism," a desire that the Christian faith be kept life-centered (centered in the total involvement of an intensely personal relationship, disciple-to-Lord) and not allowed to become merely thought-centered (intellect-to-doctrine).

An immediate result of this emphasis has been the Brethren refusal either to subscribe to the historic creeds of the church or to formulate credal standards of their own. The insistence has been that the New Testament itself is a sufficient definition of faith and that the attempt to regiment men into the closer and finer definitions of the creeds is a distraction from the true work of Christianity.

In the first place, the thrust toward credal orthodoxy tends to distort faith from existential venture into mere intellectual cognition. In the second place, creeds tend to divert the Christian away from the New Testament call to discipleship and to focus his attention simply upon later stages of the church's development and thought. In the third place, creeds presume a finality of understanding that undercuts the Holy Spirit's work as continuing teacher and encourages the believer to settle for past formulations of the faith rather than to strive for even deeper understandings and such as are uniquely relevant to his own time and condition. And in the fourth place, throughout Christian history credalism has been the occasion and excuse for some of the church's most shameful acts of bigotry, regimentation, even bloodshed.

With the Brethren, the stress on discipleship also imparts to the faith something of an eschatological perspective — as it seems to do for radical Christian groups generally. This perspective is not always (perhaps not usually) explicit, but we will spot its effects at different points in the discussion to follow. The correlation is a natural one: Discipleship is a following after the Lord as he goes on his way. And when the Lord is Jesus, the end of his way, obviously, is the kingdom of God. The eschatological orientation of Jesus himself inevitably becomes the orientation of the follower.

An Epitome of Brethren Beliefs

As we come now to make a listing of those things that the Brethren most surely have believed, we present an outline — and a diagram even. Although the drawing upon which the diagram is based does have some significant historical associations, it is used here merely as a convenience for organizing our thought. There is nothing established, official, traditional, or approved about this arrangement; it represents the sheer invention of the author. And even at that it is somewhat misleading in that it suggests that Brethren thought is much more fixed, neat, and systematic than ever has been the case in actuality.

The drawing is adapted from a seal, the first known impression of which is dated 1753. The evidence is that it was designed by Alexander Mack, Jr., and that he intended it in some sense as belonging to the Church of the Brethren as a whole. In any case, in recent years some Brethren have revived the emblem and used it in this way.

The central element is a cross, the universally recognized symbol of the Christian faith, of Jesus Christ and his way. Superimposed upon it is a heart which speaks of devotion, commitment, a total giving of oneself "from the heart." The third element, the fruit of the vine, recalls the passage: "I am the true vine. . . . Abide in me. . . . By this my Father is glorified, that you bear much fruit, and so prove to be my disciples" (John 15).

We, then, have added the lettering that transforms the drawing into an outline of Brethren belief and practice. In the center, at "the heart" of the faith, lies the commitment to radical discipleship, which is obedience to Christ. *Radical* we understand in its etymological sense as "that which drives dras-

DISCIPLESHIP: antiintellectualism; anticreedalism; voluntary personal decision; inward commitment; devotional immediacy

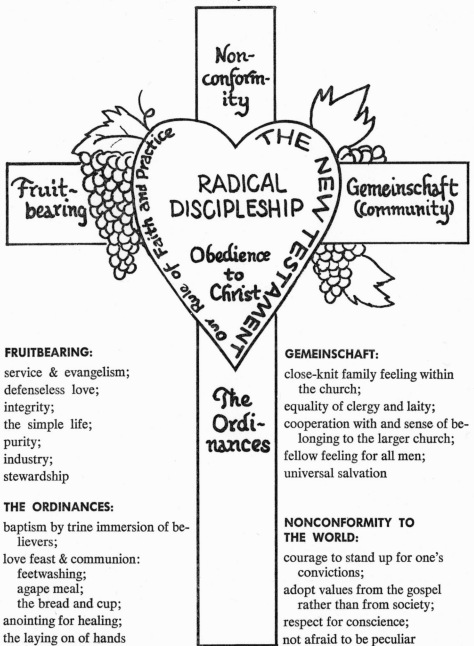

FRUITBEARING:

service & evangelism;
defenseless love;
integrity;
the simple life;
purity;
industry;
stewardship

THE ORDINANCES:

baptism by trine immersion of believers;
love feast & communion:
  feetwashing;
  agape meal;
  the bread and cup;
anointing for healing;
the laying on of hands

GEMEINSCHAFT:

close-knit family feeling within the church;
equality of clergy and laity;
cooperation with and sense of belonging to the larger church;
fellow feeling for all men;
universal salvation

NONCONFORMITY TO THE WORLD:

courage to stand up for one's convictions;
adopt values from the gospel rather than from society;
respect for conscience;
not afraid to be peculiar

tically toward the root"; and *discipleship* is "following after" (the German word *Nachfolge* puts it better than any English word can). It is our following after the Christ who is the leader-Lord making his way (and a way for his people) through the world toward the kingdom of God.

It must be noted that in the thought of the founding Brethren this discipleship was not what one does in order to be saved (that would be works-righteousness) but is the consequence of the fact that he has been, or is being, saved. Salvation is the act of God, freeing people, enabling them to form a new community, providing them a leader-Lord, and setting them upon a way. Discipleship, then, is the response that God's salvation makes possible and not man's effort to gain salvation. If, as we quoted Kierkegaard, "The truth, in the sense in which Christ was the truth, is a life," then to be following after Christ is to be in the truth, and to be in the truth is what we mean by salvation.

Several first-ranked implications of radical discipleship are listed at the top of the chart. Two of these — anti-"intellectualism" and anticredalism — we have discussed already. A third and very crucial implication is that any commitment as far-reaching and stringent as that of radical discipleship surely must be based upon the voluntary, deliberate, fully conscious decision of the believer. Although the Brethren would be the last to deny that Jesus Christ has a love that can care for infants and children, they would insist that New Testament Christianity (which is the call to radical discipleship) can concern only those who have reached the age of accountability. Thus they consistently have practiced believer's baptism and have understood that baptism is an initiation into the covenant of discipleship, the way of dying with Christ and being raised with him to newness of life.

Such commitment, too, must involve what Kierkegaard called "inwardness," or "subjectivity." It is a venture of such risk, consequence, and irrevocability that it must capture a person totally; it must be the total act of a total person, "from the heart" as the diagram would suggest. Clearly, commitment of this order dare not be equated simply with affirmation of a creed, membership in an institution, the making of a verbal confession, the undergoing of a rite, or anything of this sort. It is the voluntary giving of one's life into the hands of another.

This sort of relationship can happen, obviously, only as the disciple has a lively sense of the actual, effective, and abiding presence of the one who is his leader-Lord. This we call "devotional immediacy," and Brethrenism — as an inheritance from the Pietist movement out of which it sprang — has been marked by such awareness. It shows up particularly in the worship tradition — the hymns, prayers, and poems — of the church, but it also has been a very strong concomitant of the church's sense of fellowship (*Gemeinschaft*) and even of its works of service and ministry.

The New Testament Basis

Around the border of the heart, enclosing the center of radical discipleship, the chart carries the words, "The New Testament — Our Rule of Faith and Practice." Radical discipleship is the effort to discover and practice the mind of Christ. The mind of Christ is most clearly revealed, is given its normative expression, in the pages of the New Testament. The New Testament, then, becomes as it were the mediatory factor between the commitment to discipleship and the specific acts of the life of discipleship. It is this relationship the chart is intended to convey.

The Church of the Brethren was founded out of Bible study and remains true to its essential character only as it continues to be grounded in Bible study. However, there is more that must be said regarding the nature and procedure of that study. In the first place, the fact that our rubric states "The New Testament" rather than "The Bible" is significant. The Brethren consistently have defined their focus this way. In no sense has this been intended as a rejection of the Old Testament. The intention, rather, has been to affirm that the mind of Christ is the believer's norm, center, and authority; that the New Testament is the site at which the mind of Christ comes to the clearest expression; and that the value of the Old Testament lies in its providing the context and background for this mind of Christ. The Bible itself has a center, and it falls within the New Testament.

Another very important implication follows from this line of thought. The basic relationship that constitutes a Christian is the intensely personal and lively one of follower to Lord and not the dead legalism of nit-picker to statute book. The scripture must be read in such a way that it can act as a mouthpiece for the living Lord, in such a way that the Word become flesh can speak through the word become print. Each reading must take place in the context of commitment; the disciple reads not so much in order to know as to do; even before reading he has obligated himself to obey whatever of the mind of Christ he might discover. Each reading must be a fresh one in which the reader is seeking Christ's will for himself; he dare not lean upon traditional interpretations and understandings — even if they carry "official" sanction. Each reading must depend upon the help of the Holy Spirit as the interpreter, the one who leads into all truth.

This thought infringes upon our next topic, but the Brethren have been convinced that the best situation for the sort of scripture reading we have described is the *Gemeinde*, the intimate community of faith. Of course, such an emphasis is not intended to belittle the importance of the person's private, highly individual reading in which he seeks to discover God's will for his own life. It is to say that even this sort of reading is enhanced when there is opportunity for one to share with his brethren, check his insights against theirs, join in a common quest, and invite the communal action of the Spirit.

Gemeinschaft

As the Brethren committed themselves to radical discipleship and went to the New Testament to discover its content, they found teachings which can be grouped under the four general topics which we have listed on the four arms of the cross. We look first at the right arm and the subtopics listed below it. *Gemeinschaft* is a German term for which there is no adequate English equivalent. It denotes the intimate sense of union that comes as a group shares some deep commitment in common. The Brethren experience has been that banding together as the people of the Lord following him on his way to the kingdom is the profoundest commonality possible and so the source of the greatest *Gemeinschaft* men can know; that the Brethren have been known as "the Brethren" is not entirely coincidental.

This *Gemeinschaft* has carried something of an eschatological orientation, because the *Gemeinde* (and the church as a whole) has been conceived as a "caravan," i.e., an intimate company of travelers banded together to make common cause in seeking a common destination, rather than as a "commissary," i.e., an institution licensed to dispense certain benefactions to the constituency. The *Gemeinschaft* of the Brethren, then, is that of the *viatoris,* those who are together on the way. And thus it has been marked by an intensified sense of interdependency and each person's being an integral part of this "mission of God."

The Brethren emphasis on *Gemeinschaft* has been demonstrated foremost as a family feeling with the *Gemeinde.* This feeling has not been confined simply to the congregational meetings of worship, fellowship, and business but has included broader aspects of life together (visiting in one another's homes, neighborly helpfulness, prayer and Bible study groups, etc.).

And this *Gemeinschaft* has acted as a source not only of mutual enjoyment but of mutual discipline as well. During periods of Brethren history, it must be confessed, such discipline degenerated into a rather inhumane legalism — and at present the use of congregational discipline has disappeared almost entirely — but at its best the close-knit *Gemeinde* was the situation in which Christian brethren truly could be counselors and pastors one to another, even in the extreme situations where overt discipline was the thing needful.

The fact that among Brethren so little has been made of the distinction between clergy and laity (the difference being merely one of function) is a strong evidence of what *Gemeinschaft* has meant. Many other items to be discussed in the succeeding chapters on liturgy and polity will underline the point even further.

This family feeling has extended beyond the local congregation to include the denomination (the brotherhood) as a whole. As the chapter on polity will make clear, the brotherhood itself has been structured as a family of congregations, but, more than this, individual Brethren have demonstrated a strong sense of fraternity with those from widely scattered areas of the brotherhood. The Annual Conference takes on the flavor of a large family reunion. Of course, the relatively small size of the denomination helps make this sort of *Gemeinschaft* possible, and some have maintained that the very enjoyment of it has made the church complacent in its smallness and lax in the work of evangelism. Whether or not such an analysis can be supported, the Brethren sense of brotherhood has had some wider repercussions that should be noted.

Surely it is a broad concept of *Gemeinschaft* with other Christians that has made the Church of the Brethren more active in the ecumenical movement than most other denominations its size have been. The Brethren are charter members of both the World and National Council of Churches, and a recent study indicates that proportionately the Brethren are supplying more executives and staff personnel for ecumenical work on the local, state, and national levels in the United States than any other denomination. Also, they introduced the practice of open communion and transfer of membership by affirmation of faith ahead of some other denominations of their type.

Further, *Gemeinschaft* with all men is reflected in the long-standing emphases of refusal to participate in military service and of the positive duty of serving one's fellowmen (both topics to be given more extended treatment under another heading). But perhaps most impressive in this regard is the fact that at the church's inception in the eighteenth century the Brethren held a doctrine of the ultimate restoration of all men — a view held by few except for Radical Pietists in that day. Although the idea was later lost to the church, there is evidence that subconsciously there has been a move back toward such an understanding. All things considered, it seems clear that by and large the Brethren have attempted to practice an open rather than a closed *Gemeinschaft*.

Nonconformity

On the head of the cross our diagram displays the major rubric, "Nonconformity to the World." This follows as a direct implication of radical discipleship. Because the way of the world obviously is directed by motives other than the desire to be wholly obedient to Christ, those who follow the way of Christ are going to find themselves in tension with the world. Nonconformity is simply the principle that in all such situations we must obey God rather than men; above all, radical discipleship implies that no man can serve two masters.

There also is a tie to our preceding topic that should be noted. If a person is to stand out against society, resisting all its pressures toward conformity, it is almost necessary that he have a *Gemeinde* of brethren to support and encourage him in this effort. And conversely, the opposition and disdain which they receive from the world inevitably drives deeper the sense of *Gemeinschaft* among those who stand out against it.

Nonconformity to the world can be read as implying withdrawal from the world, a retreat into cloistered piety. And it must be confessed that at times in their history the Brethren have fallen into this misreading. The protection against this, however, is the realization that the way of Christ necessarily leads one into the world as servant, neighbor, witness, and evangelist. Further, the eschatological orientation of the faith makes it evident that the way of Christ is a leading of humanity as a whole, of the world itself, into the kingdom of God. Thus the topics under our next heading, "Fruitbearing," stand in dialectical tension with "Nonconformity" to preserve it from becoming a withdrawal and an escape.

Another temptation into which the Brethren at times have fallen is the legalistic one of reducing nonconformity to a series of proscribed externalities. Here nonconformity was defined as not smoking, drinking, dancing, playing cards, attending the theater, using cosmetics, ornamenting one's home, or having one's picture taken. For a period, even nonconformity centered in one's wearing the peculiar clothing ("garb") that visually differentiated him from those of the world. Although some of these items may be proper manifestations of truly Christian nonconformity, it must be evident that the orientation of legalism is something quite different from that of the dynamic relationship of being disciple to a living Lord.

For modern Brethren, however, the temptation goes the other way. Partly as a reaction against earlier misapplications of the doctrine and partly because of the contemporary emphasis on "turning to the world" (which emphasis, it can be argued, has missed the point of what Bonhoeffer had in mind), the very concept of nonconformity has been lost to a considerable sector of the church, and the doctrine is looked upon as a quaint relic. There is some evidence that the church may be on the verge of rediscovery of the original intention, but it is too early to speak with confidence.

The balance between being in the world but not of the world is a far from easy one to maintain, although in their origins — and as an ideal — the Brethren seem to have discerned the New Testament concept. Nonconformity means that the Christian (and the *Gemeinde*) derives his norms and values by looking to Christ and the gospel rather than to the culture in which he finds himself. As it was put by the anonymous father of the early church who composed "The Epistle to Diognetus": "They [the Christians] live as luck will have it either in Greek or non-Greek cities; they follow local usage in their dress, food, and way of life; and yet they manifest a marvelous and admittedly strange way of life in their society. They live in their own native cities, but as though they were strangers. They participate in everything as citizens, and yet carry out their obligations like aliens. Every foreign city is their native land, and every native city a foreign country."[3]

From this position, the Brethren derived a strong conviction about the right of Christian conscience and, along with the Friends and Mennonites, were influential in winning from the state the different rights of conscience that are recognized in America today. Along with such appeal to conscience there must go, of course, the courage of conviction that makes one willing to take the consequences of his nonconformity. Brethren history includes a number of heroic examples in this regard. Above all, nonconformity demands a willingness to be looked upon as "peculiar," to follow the Master in "enduring the cross" — not so much in the sense of withstanding the pain but in the perhaps even more difficult demand which Hebrews 12:2 describes as "despising the shame."

Brethren nonconformity does have at least something in common with the contemporary nonconformity of student protest and the new left. The crucial distinction, however, comes in the answer to a necessary question, "If you refuse to conform to a corrupt society, to what then do you conform?" The Christian responds, "I strive to conform to the mind of Christ," whereas the secular nonconformist can say only, "I conform to what I find within myself at the moment."

Fruitbearing

The topics we have covered thus far — anti-"intellectualism," anticredalism, inward commitment, devotional immediacy, the study of the New Testament, *Gemeinschaft*, nonconformity to the world — all these represent the necessary *conditions*, the setting and prerequisites, of radical discipleship. Now, under "Fruitbearing," we come to the emphasis which our emblem itself picks up under the symbol of the grapes, namely the actual product or "fruits" of discipleship.

In one sense we have here arrived at the heart of Brethrenism, have gotten down to what the faith is all about. Yet it must be recognized that fruit cannot be harvested unless attention first is given to planting and vine tending. What we have discussed earlier cannot be discounted in the eagerness to get at grape picking, and to the extent that modern Brethren show an inclination to do this, they are short-circuiting an essential insight of their forefathers.

Actually, we have not even left our discussion of nonconformity, for now we will encounter the specific activities in which Brethren have found Jesus' lordship to lead them contrary to the currents of society.

The first topic on our list is "service." The fact is that three succeeding chapters of this book, those on Educational Activity, Social Involvement, and Missions, develop this theme — although it is regarding the second of these, Social Involvement, that the Brethren emphasis has been more unique and is what most people think of as "service."

This theme comes strong in Brethrenism through the fact that the Master who is the focus of radical discipleship is also the one who "took the form of a servant," who came "not to be served, but to serve," who "gave his life for the many," who "girded himself with a towel and began to wash the disciples' feet" — which act the Brethren have perpetuated in their practice of the love feast as recognition that the way of Christ is the way of self-giving service. Also, reinforcement of the emphasis has come through the eschatological understanding that humanity is helped toward its true destiny and the kingdom of God actualized as Christians lend themselves as instruments of God's servanthood in the world.

The early Brethren sought to minister to the poverty of the German immigrants arriving at Philadelphia, provided a home for the aged, and were very early on the scene as opponents to the slave trade. This tradition has continued through the years to become a rather farflung program of Brethren service — including the activities channeled through the agency which bore that name and many others outside it. Also, the Church of the Brethren was among those churches who saw that the foreign mission program should proceed under service motives (even as regards evangelism, the greatest service one can perform for his fellowman) rather than the imperialistic desire to spread the domain of the church.

Finally, Brethrenism has included a thrust which is very real and yet difficult to document, because it does not take the form of explicit projects and programs. However, the understanding has been that the entire career, work, and activity of the individual Christian is to be dedicated to the service of his fellows. The Brethren, with Bonhoeffer, have seen that their Lord and Master essentially was "the man for others" and that discipleship to him demands the same quality in themselves.

Nonresistance

Defenseless love, or *nonresistance* (recalling Jesus' command to "resist not one who is evil"), are earlier and more accurate terms to describe the Brethren teaching which today commonly is known as "pacifism." The terminology is important in that it implies rather different motives and dynamics.

Since its beginning in 1708 the Church of the Brethren has registered its opposition to violence and to militarism and warfare in particular. Pacifism (in general usage and dominantly in modern Brethren usage as well) tends to denote a societal technique prudentially calculated to resolve conflict situations and enable one to achieve his chosen social goals; it becomes a means of manipulating society — toward good ends, it goes without saying.

Defenseless love points to a very different economy, one that is much more theological and thus vastly more radical than that of pacifism. In the first place, the essential motive now is discipleship, i.e., obedience to Christ and obedience of a most radical character. There may well be situations in which the Christian has some visible hope and confidence as to how his non-resisting love might operate to bring about the desirable outcome, but under the dynamic of discipleship he is committed to follow the way of nonresistance even when he cannot calculate the outcome — and even when his calculations would project the undesirable outcome.

The paradigm, of course, is Jesus' death on the cross. That death proved to be a conclusive defeat of evil, as desirable an outcome as can be envisioned. But it took a resurrection to make that death a victory — and the resurrection marked the introduction of a qualitatively new element which could not possibly have been calculated on the basis of the cross itself, could not have been calculated on any human basis. Jesus did not go to the cross as a calculated means of becoming victor; he went to the cross out of obedience, and God crowned that obedience with victory.

The case is the same with nonresistance as with all discipleship, although the radicality of refusing to defend oneself makes the economy more apparent: Christian defenselessness proceeds from an eschatological faith. The future in store for humanity is the kingdom of God. That it is the kingly rule of God means that it is ordered according to his calculations and not ours. For him to bring that kingdom, then, requires that we renounce our own calculations and step out in simple obedience — obedience that leads even to death on a cross — in the faith that God can and will use that obedience even though as drastic an overriding as a resurrection may be required in appropriating it.

The way of Jesus was to frustrate and close off evil by opening himself defenselessly to it and absorbing its assaults into himself rather than either by hardening himself or by fighting back and thus reflecting the evil back into the world. This is the way of the cross, but by the grace of God the cross can itself become the way to resurrection. This is Jesus' way to the kingdom, and it must become the way of the disciple as well.

In this light it can be seen that nonresistance is much more than a position regarding only military service. It is the overall stance of the Christian and the church toward the world and all of the evil met therein.

Integrity

Illustrative of the Brethren concept of "integrity" is the slogan that was popular during the period that Brethren were identifiable by their special garb: "A Dunker's word is as good as his bond." This was more than mere slogan; in communities where Brethren were known, bankers and other businessmen did in fact accept a Dunker's say-so in lieu of bonds, notes, contracts, etc. One of the truest and most helpful ways of being a man for others and of fostering *Gemeinschaft* is by being entirely trustworthy, forthright, and aboveboard in all one's dealings. Thus the Brethren saw their discipleship as demanding.

A direct corollary of integrity has been the Brethren effort to follow Jesus' prohibition regarding the swearing of oaths. The Brethren teaching has questioned: (1) whether the state has either the competence or authority to administer oaths in the name of God (and that without regard as to whether either the administrator or the taker of the oath believes in God); (2) whether an oath commands any power either to help one tell the truth or to guarantee that what he is telling is the truth; (3) whether what oath-taking implies is legitimate, namely, that integrity is obligatory only under special conditions. The Christian's commitment to integrity is part and parcel of his commitment to discipleship, and the integrity he shows he credits to the help of Christ; to grant status to an oath is to confuse the truth of this situation. Brethren, in court, always have been happy to affirm that they will strive to tell the truth; they have refused to concede that oaths can play any role in the matter. "Let what you say be simply 'Yes' or 'No'; anything more than this comes from evil" (Matthew 5:37).

"Simple Life"

The simple life is a Brethren phrase describing the Christian's relationship to the world of things and particularly to his possessions. It marks the effort to find that standard of living which recognizes the blessing God intends for man through the goods he has created but which also strives to keep these goods from obscuring the higher values of faith. To the extent that the necessities of life are necessary, they are valid gifts of God; as soon as they threaten to dominate a person's interest they encroach upon his commitment to discipleship.

Also, the simple life involves the desire to practice a standard of living that can be common to the mass of humanity, involves the willingness to sacrifice one's own luxuries so that the brother might have necessities.

Obviously, this doctrine is not an asceticism that sets out to punish the body for the good of the soul, and neither is it a glorification of the sort of poverty that cheapens and degrades life. Rather, it attempts to hit a balance that cannot be defined or legislated, a balance that gives spiritual values the preeminence they deserve and retains the good of what God has created without losing the good of God himself.

During the nineteenth century the Brethren corrupted their teaching by attempting to enforce the simple life through legalistic prescription. In the twentieth century there is danger that the teaching will be lost altogether. The answer, of course, can come only as part of an overall movement toward radical discipleship.

Purity

If a man is truly to be "for others," then obviously he has no more right to squander, dissipate, or cut short his own life than he does theirs. A man is not his own possession; he belongs to his Lord for the good of his brethren. "Purity" designates the Brethren desire to avoid anything that would detract from the Christian's ability and effectiveness, whatever would make him anything less than he could be.

Theoretically, then, the standard of purity should apply even to such commonplaces as overeating, overwork, lack of recreation and exercise. Historically it has been applied much more strongly to such things as liquor, drugs, tobacco, pornography, profligacy.

As with the simple life, purity is one of the Brethren emphases being eroded by modern life. The use of beverage alcohol is an example. In times past the church took pride in being known as "the oldest temperance society in America." That feeling has changed. But whether or not the church's defense of total abstinence always has been set upon the strongest basis, the argument from radical discipleship is just as valid as it ever was. If the overall effect of the liquor traffic is detrimental to man's life in society — as statistics regarding alcoholism, automobile accidents, absenteeism, marital breakups make obvious, then it is every bit as valid for Christians to protest this evil by refusing to participate as to protest militarism by refusing to participate there — and so on down the line.

Industry

"Industry" denotes the values of hard work, responsibility, initiative, and thrift. These long have been prized by the Brethren as part of the good life that God intends for man and as a further means of being useful to one's fellows. Beyond doubt there is considerable Christian validity in this teaching. However, the problem that the Brethren (along with the church and the world) now face in this regard is how to retain these values in a technological age that is forcing us to redefine work, prohibiting many men from exercising responsibility and initiative in the ways to which we have been accustomed. It remains to be seen whether the teaching can be adjusted to the context of leisure, avocations, cultural pursuits, the arts.

Stewardship

"Stewardship," man's making proper and careful use of the physical resources God has put at his disposal, is another Brethren emphasis that calls for critical adjustment.

Stewardship often has meant simply the giving of one's time, energy, and particularly finances in the service of the church and one's fellowmen, and this is proper, of course. However, for Brethren, stewardship has carried another thrust as well. Up until quite recently the Brethren lived predominantly in an agrarian economy, and Brethren farmers were aware that their commitment to discipleship implied responsibility — yes, even loving care — for the soil that God had entrusted to them. They were conservationists on religious principle, this interest relating very closely to our earlier discussions regarding the simple life and industry.

If the Brethren are to be consistent, their teaching now must be opened up to include other areas of conservation such as the pollution of air and water, city planning, the depletion of mineral, forest, and recreational resources. Because the entire earth is the Lord's and the intended site of his kingdom, the concept of Christian stewardship must be as broad as the earth itself.

Ordinances

In our diagram we move now to the trunk of the cross to pick up the last major heading, "The Ordinances." Under this rubric appear what customarily would be called the sacraments, yet the shift of terminology points directly to one of the great distinctives of Brethren belief. Because the matter comes in for detailed examination in the next chapter of this book, we shall here say only enough to ensure that these ordinances are recognized as an integral and vital part of the overall picture we are drawing.

The switch to the term *ordinances* was a step taken by the Brethren forefathers expressly to avoid some implications of the churchly term *sacraments*. In the first place, they denied that the elements used in these rites carry any inherent sacramental value. The Brethren thus have had no place for any *ex opere operato* doctrine (the belief that the rite has an effect simply in the performance of it), for any doctrine of a real presence of Christ's body and blood in the bread and cup, for any doctrine of baptismal regeneration that attributes efficacy to the water.

In the second place, Brethren have resisted the "religious" implications of sacrament, denying that the performance of these rites has any intention of influencing God, of causing him to dispense his grace differently than if the rite had not been performed.

Rather, in Brethren thought the performance of the ordinances is an act of obedience (of discipleship), a drama enacted by the *Gemeinde* for its own edification as it were. God has acted graciously in Jesus Christ and in the sending of the Holy Spirit. His kingdom is at hand, it is becoming actualized in our midst, and its powers are available here and now. It hardly is in place, then, for man to perform rites with a mind to exciting God to act; what is needed is for man to become more aware of, more open to, and more ready to appropriate the grace which even now is freely available without system, without password, without priest, without sacrament.

The Brethren ordinances are communal dramas which the Lord inaugurated among his disciples that the *Gemeinde* might portray before its own eyes and for its own benefit the source, dynamic, and nature of its commitment to kingdom discipleship. In the ordinances, then, the Brethren seek to remind themselves who they are, who their Lord is, and where lies their kingdom goal; they seek to celebrate and give thanks for the grace they have experienced in discipleship; they seek to renew and deepen their commitment to their Lord and to one another; they seek to make themselves open to new light, to more power, to a closer following upon the Lord's way to the kingdom.

Our description of Brethren beliefs necessarily has been sketchy. Succeeding chapters of the book will put a little more meat on these bones. Yet, let us close as we began: Brethren belief never has designated a theological system but has marked an exploration into discipleship, the attempt to discover what it means to be a caravan following the Scout of the oncoming kingdom.

---

1. Soren Kierkegaard, *Training in Christianity*, trans. Walter Lowrie (Princeton: Princeton University Press, 1944), 200-202.

2. Soren Kierkegaard, *Papier*, quoted in Hermann Diem, *Kierkegaard's Dialectic of Existence* (Edinburgh: Oliver and Boyd, 1959), 145, n. 30.

3. "The Address to Diognetus" in *The Fathers of the Primitive Church*, ed. Herbert A. Musurillo (New York: New American Library, 1966), 147.

4

LITURGY

Dale W. Brown

The Brethren style of liturgy is similar to a New Testament usage of the word, which denotes not only the style of worship of the Christian community but also encompasses good works and acts of charity (2 Corinthians 9:12; Philippians 2:30). The sacramental life has been the daily walk. The true mystery has been the presence of the Spirit of Jesus Christ in the total life of his people. Symbols, ordinances, and practices are celebrated both in and outside of church buildings. For example, the rite of baptism has been moved indoors, but the earlier practice of baptizing in rivers, creeks, and lakes remains as a legacy. The anointing service takes place in a home or hospital. The refusal to swear an oath becomes visible in relationship to civil government.

Today, edifices for worship and fellowship are called churches, but when earlier generations moved from homes to simple buildings, they used the term *meetinghouse*. They avoided the terms *church* and *sanctuary* because they wished to reserve these words to designate the activity of the people of God. The people of God do not go to church; they are the church. This theology of the meetinghouse pointed to the affirmation that all of life is sacred; the meeting in a house was for the purpose of celebrating this truth. The Brethren were slow to adopt the pattern of the Christian year. Their reaction against a sharp separation between religious celebrations and appropriation in life led to a bias against the customary observances of advent, Christmas, saints' days, and Lent. A noticeable exception was Pentecost, which early was chosen as the time for the great yearly meeting (Annual Conference).

It has been conjectured that though the Catholics and Anglicans attend church for reverent worship of God and members of the Reformed tradition gather to be instructed from the Word of God, the Brethren assemble to see one another. It is recognized that this is an oversimplification of each of the traditions, for in the case of the Brethren there has been a concern for the Pauline injunction to gather both for corporate acts of worship and correct biblical interpretation and instruction. It has been felt, however, that a special sacramental quality often seems to be present in face-to-face relationships. Because of this warm informality and the "low church" nature of some of the

Sunday services, the impression has often been given that the Church of the Brethren is not very liturgical. A closer examination will reveal a rich liturgical tradition with a unifying dynamic in the midst of a variety of forms.

Ordinances

The Brethren departed from sacramental terminology to speak of ordinances in referring to their many covenantal acts. This may have resulted from their attempt to follow the New Testament, which does not use the words *sacrament* or *means of grace,* but which does refer to acts instituted by Christ and commended by the apostles. In their desire to obey the commandments of Jesus and to follow the patterns of the New Testament church, they understood ordinances to be acts of obedience. Liturgical practices inside or outside of the church building have had special status if they are in some way related to a New Testament reference.

Though not always successfully, the Brethren have attempted to avoid a slavish legalism. Alexander Mack, the leader of the early brotherhood, taught that "eternal life is not promised because of baptism, but only through faith in Christ." Nevertheless, a believer will automatically wish to be obedient to the commandment of baptism.[1] A nineteenth-century writer, in speaking of the biblical admonition to greet one another with the holy kiss, maintained that the kiss of formality would never be a fulfillment by itself of the apostle's injunction. "There must be something connected with it more than form to make it holy."[2] Nevertheless, sterile formality and legalism have sometimes plagued the brotherhood. At times, the teaching has been explicit that the commands should be obeyed simply because they are in the New Testament. At other times, the message has implied special rewards for this type of faithfulness.

But the Brethren have not been legalistic in determining an exact number of ordinances. They have been Protestant in emphasizing baptism and the love feast (which includes the eucharist) more than other rites. But they have been similar to the Roman Catholics in adopting many other practices. These have included feetwashing, the agape meal, anointing, laying on of hands, the holy kiss, covered and uncovered heads, nonswearing, and nonlitigation. They have also emphasized the sacredness of the family, fidelity in marriage, and strictures against divorce.

Because of the reaction to legalism, the decreasing emphasis on some of the above practices, and a growing kinship with other Protestants, many contemporary Brethren have appropriated the word *sacrament* for baptism and the communion service. Many still refer to these acts as ordinances, while many others are searching for a more appropriate designation. As contemporary Brethren vary in their nomenclature, so they vary in their theology of these practices. Practically all would deny any inherent sacramental value to elements such as water and bread. Many would be Zwinglian in feeling that the elements are signs to point to religious truths. Some would follow Paul Tillich in viewing these acts as powerful symbols which not only point beyond themselves but participate in that reality to which they point. Others would stress the real presence of Christ in his body, the people, rather than in the elements themselves. This pluralism of theological interpretation is somewhat typical of the Brethren who participate in corporate acts of the tradition without possessing dogmatic formulations.

Baptism

The names given the early Brethren — *Täufer, Neutäufer,* and *Tunck-Täufer* — point to their identification with the Anabaptist wing of the Reformation as well as to the immersionist mode of baptism. The typical Brethren practice of baptism would include the following acts. The believer assumes a kneeling position in a body of water in the presence of the *Gemeinde.* Following a public confession of faith and a promise to be faithful to Jesus and his teachings and the community, the baptizand is dipped three times, in the name of the Father, the Son, and the Holy Spirit. Then the hands of the minister are laid on the head for a prayer seeking the forgiveness of sins and the presence of the Holy Spirit.

Earlier Brethren literature is replete with references to baptism, much more so than in recent decades. A caricature of Brethren preaching in the nineteenth century has been that whatever the text, the exhorter would eventually come to baptism. On the American frontier, many schoolhouse debates between Brethren elders and spokesmen of other traditions focused on this rite. Brethren apologists vigorously defended believers' baptism against the pedobaptists. They quoted the church fathers and Luther in support of immersion instead of the sprinkling and pouring used by other denominations. And they marshaled many arguments to buttress the threefold forward action against other Baptist groups who dipped backward in one action. These debates over specifics often have buried the deeper meaning and issues.

More basic than the form has been the underlying theology of baptism. It has pointed to the relationship of the Christian and the *Gemeinde* to society. The Brethren were Anabaptist in their repudiation of any idea of the *Corpus Christianum* and any ultimate allegiance to other authorities than the Lordship of Christ and scriptural norms. Faith must be the free response of responsible agents. Alexander Mack, Jr., wrote that Baptist-minded people do not baptize their children because "they firmly believe that the covenant of God under the economy of the New Testament demands only voluntary lovers of God and of His truth."[3] In this espousal of voluntaryism, religious freedom, and separation of church and state, the Brethren have been a part of the larger Free Church tradition.

In this it has often seemed to others that the Brethren have manifested a one-sided individualism and works-righteousness. Their emphasis on the commitment and response of the individual has seemed to subvert the prior and more important emphasis on God's grace. How they answered these concerns may be seen in the similar feeling of Alexander Mack, Sr., about infant baptism: "Therefore, if a child dies without water baptism, that will not be disadvantageous for it. . . . The children are in a state of grace because of the merit of Jesus Christ, and they will be saved out of grace."[4] Brethren families have presented their babies to the Lord in the presence of the community to point to the priority of God's grace and its coming through the *Gemeinde.* In recent years church parents are increasingly being chosen to stand with the parents to represent this loving concern. In other ways there have been attempts to allow the love of the community to encompass their children through nurture, worship, and fellowship. But the act of baptism itself and the biblical metaphors of new birth, of dying and rising, are seen to point to the conjoining of God's grace with the faith response of the individual believer.

The voluntary faith response of the believer not only denotes freedom from political and ecclesiastical domination, but it points to a vital relationship with the *Gemeinde*. Before baptism the sections from the eighteenth chapter of Matthew which deal with the method of settling differences and the necessity for forgiving the brother have often been read and stressed. Following the action of baptizing, there occurs Brethren "confirmation," the laying on of hands. Though rejecting any notion of baptismal regeneration, namely, that the rite of the church saves, the Brethren, nevertheless, did stress an intimate connection between baptism and membership in the *Gemeinde*.

A point of difference with the River Brethren (the present Brethren in Christ denomination) in the late eighteenth century may help clarify the ecclesiological significance of baptism. The River Brethren emerged from revivalistic and evangelical Pietism in colonial America. They adopted the Brethren form of baptism but refused to practice the laying on of hands for the coming of the Spirit. For them the most mighty working of the Spirit was in the conversion experience which preceded and led to baptism. But the predecessors of the contemporary Church of the Brethren followed the story of the eighth chapter of Acts and Paul's own conversion experience, in which the laying on of hands came after baptism and the vision of Christ on the Damascus road. Without denying the working of the Spirit prior to baptism, they felt that there was a special manifestation of the Holy Spirit in relating to the community of faith. The church is not simply a volunteer association of converted Christians; it is an agent of God's saving work. The laying on of hands points to the coming of the grace of God through the lives of other people, through the *Gemeinde*.

Increasingly, there is a growing recovery of the theology of baptism as ordination for the general priesthood. The model is the baptism of Jesus which coincided with the beginning of his public ministry and his real identification with sinners. Peter Miller, who was close to the colonial Brethren, defined the baptism of Jesus as "an ordination to His office as mediator."[5] We are called to participate with Jesus in this task. In baptism we take on what we have been elected to be. Here, instead of thinking of baptism as saving for heaven, we are saved from self-centeredness to be persons for others. This is to be the beginning of public ministry.

Today, there is less emphasis on the form of baptism, though it is rarely changed in actual practice. The Brethren hold an open membership, one which receives persons from other communions on the basis of their previous baptism and confession of faith. Some feel that most basic differences have disappeared as the Brethren dedication of babies corresponds essentially with infant baptism, and Brethren baptism is the same as confirmation in other traditions. Others criticize the movement toward virtual infant baptism in progressively lowering the age of baptism from late adolescence to twelve years of age or in some cases to even younger ages. They feel that this violates the principle of voluntaryism in urging baptism at a time when one may gain an easier acceptance. They would like to return to the earlier practice of believers' baptism which corresponded in most cases to the identity crisis of late adolescence. The current practice most often involves church membership classes preceding baptism at pre- or early adolescence.

The Love Feast

Historically the love feast has been the high point of Brethren liturgical life. In preparation for the love feast the deacons would conduct the annual church visit to each home of the congregation to ask whether the members were still in the faith, in peace and union with the church, and still willing to labor with the Brethren for an increase of holiness. Opportunity was given for the family to bring any matter to the attention of the church which they thought might serve its welfare and ministry. If the members were in sufficient harmony, the date for the love feast was announced. Large crowds, including Brethren from neighboring and distant congregations and often many visitors, would gather for the free hospitality of food and lodging offered by the host congregation. The preaching held on Saturday was preparatory for the three-to five-hour love feast beginning Saturday evening. The weekend concluded with singing, prayers, and exhortations Sunday morning and a common dinner.

The love feast weekend was an opportunity for a youth gathering, a great social occasion for the Brethren, a frequent attraction for the activities of rowdy young men who disrupted the activities, and an opportunity for witness by the community to children, visitors, and hecklers. In the twentieth century the weekend love feast has been replaced by shorter meetings, often on World Communion Sunday and Maundy Thursday of Holy Week. In addition to two love feasts, many churches have additional communion services, similar to other Protestant services, partaking just of the bread and the cup during a Sunday morning church service. The annual deacons' visit has been replaced by a brief self-examination service preceding the love feast.

These services have attempted to dramatize anew the central events of the Upper Room. The love feast is based on a literalistic piecing together of the biblical narratives concerning the Last Supper. The first part of the service is based on the thirteenth chapter of John. Jesus washed the feet of his disciples and commanded his disciples to do the same. The second part comes from the primitive practice of an agape meal, a common meal around the tables. In the Brethren heritage men have gathered around one group of tables, the women around the others. (In some instances it is now arranged so that families might sit together, in which case the feetwashing service might take place in adjoining rooms.) It is in a table setting that they eat together of the bread and drink of the cup in continuity with the practices of much of Christendom. During the entire love feast, hymns are sung, prayers are offered, silence is observed, scriptural passages are read and interpreted, and confessions and exhortations are offered by the minister or various members of the community. The total experience is called the love feast. The Lord's Supper usually refers just to the meal. Holy communion and eucharist are the most common designations of the service of the bread and the cup.

The general structure of observing feetwashing, the meal, and communion has known basic continuity. But the variations concerning the specifics have been legion. Alexander Mack, Jr., recounted how the Brethren originally practiced feetwashing following the meal and communion, then following the meal, and then changed to feetwashing first when instructed by a brother who knew Greek.⁶ For several decades the Brethren living in the eastern part of the United States differed from the "Western Brethren" in that the former practiced the "double mode" (in which one washed and another dried the feet of several Brethren), while the latter adopted the present practice of having one's feet washed by a neighbor at one side and in turn washing the feet of the brother at the other side. Generally, it has been the practice to greet one another with a kiss following the washing of feet. For some time a separate rite of binding the brotherhood together by the passing of the kiss of peace was practiced between the meal and the communion. This observance has disappeared except in the Old German Baptist Brethren branch of the church.

The agricultural style brought a change from the biblical mutton to the common beef of the American farm as the main substance of the meal. Today, the menus vary widely from congregation to congregation. The temperance movement in America brought a change from the biblical wine to the use of grape juice, and medical hygiene became the rationale for the substitution of individual communion cups for the common cup or glass. Occasional experiments have included the shining of shoes instead of the feetwashing service or the clearing away of the dishes of another as a symbol of service. Instead of the traditional unleavened bread and grape juice, a few services have attempted to appropriate whatever may have been used for the meal such as tea, milk, coffee, rolls, or crackers. Though there are frequent attempts at novel experimentation and a widespread freedom to attempt the new, the usual love feast still involves the washing of feet, a common meal, and specially baked unleavened bread and grape juice.

Theologically, the Brethren have seen in the liturgy of the love feast the visible manifestation of one of their fundamental emphases, the inseparable relationship of the two great commandments. God's love for us and our love for one another belong together. This Johannine theology has been basic: "If we love one another, God abides in us . . . " (1 John 4:12). The feetwashing rite and meal point to the love for the brother, the neighbor, and the world. The eucharist symbolizes the suffering of God through Christ for the world. But this neat distinction is difficult to maintain, for all three parts manifest the reality of the presence of God in the midst of his body. In the love feast the people celebrate, witness to, and participate in the fellowship and mission of the body of Christ.

The reading of the thirteenth chapter of John introduces the feetwashing service. It has often been referred to as the symbol or sacrament of servanthood, but the Johannine reference to washing as cleansing has likewise been a part of the basic meaning. As baptism refers to our justification and regeneration, the washing of feet becomes for many Brethren a continuation of the cleansing without which we, like Peter, would have no part of Jesus. A new forgiveness, a new purification, or a new sanctification is always needed.

Moreover, each person should be open to be served as well as to serve in order to combat the sin of self-sufficiency, pride, and the striving for power. For this reason each person should have his feet washed. We need also to wash one another's feet, for this act participates in the egalitarianism of the body of Christ as well as the necessity to adopt the servant role in relation to the world.

As liturgy, the washing of the feet of the brother may sometimes be crude, awkward, and lacking in aesthetic finesse. Yet the washing of feet may lead to acts, such as the changing of bedpans, feeding the hungry, clothing the naked, or binding raw wounds, which have the same characteristics. Some Brethren are embarrassed to identify with such a service in twentieth-century America; others feel that the attitude and manner of practice often lead to more pride than humility. But for many Brethren the rite of feet-washing remains an integral, meaningful part of the total love feast.

The Lord's Supper for the Brethren has been the agape meal based on the last meal of Jesus with his disciples and admonitions concerning it given by Paul (1 Corinthians 11:20-21). Again, this meal represents more than a legalistic attempt to duplicate literally the biblical references. This becomes clear in a statement by Alexander Mack, Jr.: "For Christ did not say that one should recognize His disciples by the feetwashing or the breaking of bread, but He said that by this shall every man know that you are my disciples, that you have love for one another.'" For this reason the meal has often been referred to as the symbol or sacrament of brotherhood. The meal represents more than a mere togetherness; it it togetherness as a divine gift and an eschatological expectation. Some Brethren homilies before and during the meal have interpreted the meal as a foretaste of the messianic banquet. By grace the community is granted a foretaste of the bond of peace which God wishes ultimately for all mankind.

In the breaking of bread for a brother, the eating together, and drinking of the cup, the Brethren share more in a commonality of practice and theology with other churches. Here are both memory and participation in the death, redemption, and resurrected body of Jesus. The breaking of bread expresses brokenness in the midst of a community which is open to healing love. The true mission of the church lies in its identification with the body and blood of Christ given for the world. The Brethren have believed neither in the transubstantiation of the elements nor in the complete absence of the real presence of their Lord. Increasingly, a feeling has been articulated that in the communion we do have the real bodily presence of our Lord in the lives of the people.

Other Ordinances

There are other traditions which have been derived from New Testament admonitions. A literalistic following of some of these has prompted some to see in the Brethren a New Testament Phariseeism, the making of a new law out of the commandments and practices of the early church. But a deeper examination may reveal symbolic meanings comparable to the significance of liturgical colors, orders of worship, and special costumes in other traditions. If religion is life, liturgical acts will be found in ethical contexts. Many twentieth-century Brethren feel that some of these practices should be regarded as *adiaphora,* acts which have no special merit or demerit. But others would regard them more highly because of their symbolic and pedagogical value and biblical rootage. There is no longer extensive preaching and teaching supporting some of these practices. Many youth and members only learn about them through their homes or real life experience.

The anointing service finds a rootage in James 5:14-16. After the manner of the biblical admonition, the initiative, for the most part, comes from the person who is ill. The condition usually involves more than a minor illness, though the person need not be critically ill. Sometimes, the service is called for before surgery. Traditionally, two elders or ministers have administered the anointing; today the patient often receives a pastor and a deacon or another member. The service is conducted in a simple fashion in a home or hospital, often in the presence of a few intimates or members of the family. The passage from James is read; an opportunity is given for confession of sins and of faith; a brief hymn, prayer, or scriptural passage may follow; then, the pastor places oil on his fingertips and anoints the person on the forehead three times — for the forgiveness of sins, the strengthening of faith, and the restoration of wholeness to the body. Then, both ministers lay hands on the head of the one who has been anointed and both offer prayer. Brief parting words of love and encouragement usually conclude the service.

For the most part Brethren have attempted to avoid making faith a work which will insure physical health or the service as a manipulative act to use God for our own purposes. On the other hand, the Brethren have not held to a naturalism which would close the door to the possibilities of a miraculous working of God. The prayers have tended to be in the name and spirit of Him who prayed, "Nevertheless, not as I will, but as thou wilt" (Matthew 26:39). The Brethren have not highly publicized healings. They have perhaps followed too literalistically the command of Jesus: "Tell no one" (Luke 5:14); so much so, many feel, that they often have failed sufficiently to inform the membership and larger community of the nature and availability of the anointing service.

We have noted the practice of laying on of hands after baptism and the anointing of the sick with oil. The practice has also been used in the service of ordination for preaching or pastoral ministry beyond the initial one-year licensing. It has also been appropriated for special acts of commissioning service, missionary, and pastoral ministries at a closing convocation of the Annual Conference. In the nineteenth century where was a question whether deacons should be received with the laying on of hands or simply with the kiss and hand. In recent years there has been a plurality of practice in the use of the laying on of hands in relationship to special gifts and tasks in the life of the church and the world. Following the theological clues of the Book of Acts, the rite has symbolized the enabling power of the Holy Spirit to be present with the one commissioned for ministry. And for the Brethren this power is related to the love, choice, and support of the community. For many decades it was not considered in good taste to desire to become a minister. It was felt that the Holy Spirit worked more effectively through the wishes of the church. In recent decades, however, the call of the individual and the choice of the congregation have both been regarded as valid contexts for the working of the Spirit.

Because of the many biblical references to the posture of kneeling in prayer, the Brethren have often assumed this position, much more so in earlier times than in recent decades. They also sought to follow the special instructions of Paul (1 Corinthians 11:3-15); while prophesying or praying, women should have their heads covered, and men should appear with un-covered heads. In some parts of the brotherhood, one will still find uniformity in that all of the women of a particular congregation wear for worship the traditional small white lace caps or veils. In other places there will be only a few thus attired, and in many other congregations the practice is extinct. At present, there seems to be a great latitude of freedom and respect for the feelings and practices of others in reference to this custom. In some congre-gations prayer veils appear in greater numbers during the observance of the traditional love feast. In the Pennsylvania Dutch country, which includes Mennonites, Amish, and other plain people, one may still find the prayer veil and other plain clothes worn for all activities during the week. The observance of the covered and uncovered heads has not only represented an attempt to take seriously the instructions of Paul, but also has symbolized reverence for God and life. Likewise, it has often pointed to an interpretation of the proper or Christian vocational roles for men and women.

To a great extent, the religious costume, which was characteristic of the members of the *Gemeinde* during the late eighteenth, the nineteenth, and early twentieth centuries, is disappearing. Successive Annual Conferences see fewer and fewer bearded tieless Brethren with their broadbrimmed hats and straight-cut coats and plainly dressed sisters in black bonnets, sober-colored dresses, and black stockings. In actuality such garb at one time was a power-ful symbol which not only pointed to but participated in the Brethren emphases on nonconformity, simplicity of life and dress, and the priesthood of all believers. The origin of the costume is uncertain. Some have speculated that it was borrowed from the early Quakers in order to identify with them in the peace movement of the commonwealth of Pennsylvania. Today, the Brethren dress as other people. In a society of dominant militarism, however, some of the youth, often to the chagrin of their parents, are again identifying with the peace movements of the times by adopting a different style of hair and dress.

As with other New Testament instructions, the Brethren took seriously the five references in the epistles to greet each other with a holy kiss. The exchange of a kiss accompanied by a warm handshake of brother to brother and sister to sister in meeting has been indicative of the intimate nature of the brotherhood. In the nineteenth century it was taught that the kiss is a confirmation of baptism, feetwashing, and ordination. A person who had just been baptized or ordained would be greeted with the kiss and a handclasp or by just the handclasp by the members of the church. The following ex-planation was given in the *Monthly Gospel Visitor* in 1852: "We meet in baptism our brother for the first time upon the heavenly road, as a member of the body of Christ; . . . in feetwashing we show by the kiss, that love prompts us to perform this lowly service; . . . in establishing a deacon, a teacher, etc.,

we salute a brother for the first time in that capacity, and show our willingness, in laying on him a burden, also to help him [in] bearing it."⁸ To a great
degree the kiss has been replaced by a friendly handclasp as the customary
form of greeting, but the practice of exchanging the kiss survives as a part of
the feetwashing service. The warm greetings by members to new members
and ministers often remains as a legacy to the spirit of the practice.

From the Sermon on the Mount and the letter of James (5:12) the
Brethren appropriated the prohibition regarding the swearing of oaths. Not
only was profanity forbidden, but other civil oaths were not allowed. When
called to a court of justice, Brethren historically have shared the mood of
Quakers and Anabaptists who have felt it foolish to swear on the Book which
commands one not to swear. For this reason civil practice in many places
recognizes those who affirm or promise to tell the truth instead of swearing
an oath in relation to signing legal documents and appearing in courts. Again
more than literalistic adherence to the letter has been involved. More basic
has been the pedagogical and symbolic value of pointing to a style of basic
integrity, a higher allegiance than civil authority, and the refusal to dichot-
omize the sacred and the secular.

The strictures against oaths led naturally to a prejudice against secret
oath-bound societies. Though Christians are to be in mission to all men, it
was emphasized that they were not to be "unequally yoked together with un-
believers" (2 Corinthians 6:14). Christians are to be completely open; they
are to hide nothing; they are not to acquire allegiances which would interfere
with their being completely honest with their Brethren. Of all the reasons
proposed against the oath-bound societies, probably the most basic was the
reluctance to relinquish a style of community life which was primary in terms
of allegiance and was regarded as a paradigmatic community to point to
God's intention for all of humanity. Perhaps the Brethren have been too
suspicious of divided loyalties. Today, belonging to oath-bound societies is
no longer a test of membership, though the teachings remain against such
allegiances.

The church regarded the methodology in Matthew (chapter 18) as normative for the settling of disputes. One was first to confront the brother, then
others, and if necessary the entire church. In this context the Brethren
stressed the principle of nonlitigation spelled out by Paul (1 Corinthians 6:
1-7). A brother is not to go to law against his brother. He may go to court
when called to be a witness. He may even appear to defend the rights of
others. But he is not to take to civil authorities what should be settled in the
life of the *Gemeinde*. Insofar as possible he should attempt to live at peace
with all men. Here is a small incarnation of the role of the suffering servant.
The chief posture in life is not that of defending one's own rights and interests,
but one of service.

Gathering for Worship

Though the early Brethren emphasized the necessity of prayer and instruction in the home, they did not intend to neglect the regular assembling
of themselves for corporate worship. They were not as strict in their observance of the Sabbath or Lord's Day as their Puritan neighbors, but habits

of faithfulness emerged in setting aside special times for church meetings and fellowship. In the colonial period and into the nineteenth century, the members rotated from house to house for worship in many parts of the brotherhood. Some members built their farm homes with sliding doors between some of their rooms in order to accommodate the gathering of the community for worship. Larger gatherings such as love feasts and annual business meetings often had to be held in large barns. The first church building was erected by the parent congregation in Germantown in 1770. In other areas the first buildings were called love-feast houses with kitchens for the purpose of preparing the agape meal and upper lofts designed for sleeping guests, a wall dividing the women's quarters from those of the men. The necessity of providing a kitchen has caused some to speculate that this Brethren innovation might have been a contributing factor in the unique American phenomenon of the centrality of the kitchen and fellowship dinners in the life of Protestants.

The stark simplicity of the architecture and the designation of meetinghouse for the building reflects the egalitarian ecclesiology of the *Gemeinde* as well as their disaffection from the more institutional and formalized modes of worship of the mainline churches. The meetinghouse usually had two doors, the men entering through one and the women coming in the other side. The uncomfortable benches were frequently made with a back which could be lifted to serve a dual purpose as a tabletop at the time of the love feast. The walls were barren except for hooks on which rows of broad-brimmed black hats or black bonnets were placed at the time of meeting. Wood stoves often occupied the center of the room. There was no pulpit, no lectern, and no altar. There were long tables placed along the broad side of the room around which sat the elders and ministers who were in charge of the meetings.

On the American frontier the Brethren borrowed schoolhouses for the purposes of engaging in public debates with others on doctrinal questions, conducting singing schools, and holding preaching missions. As they settled in communities, however, their meetinghouses evolved into churches which in architecture began to resemble those of their Protestant neighbors. With the advent of the paid pastor in the twentieth century, the central pulpit on a raised chancel replaced the long table. Increasingly there has been the adoption of an open chancel with a pulpit on one side, a lectern on the other, and often a table in the center which is sometimes called an altar, sometimes a communion table, and sometimes a worship center. The introduction of Sunday schools in the last part of the nineteenth century led to the provision for classroom space for Christian education and often a fellowship hall for special assemblies and dinners. In the post-World II period many Brethren communities have erected beautiful edifices, churchlike in appearance and reverent in mood. The chief characteristic of contemporary Brethren architecture is variety in style and in size of buildings. Many small plain meeting places remain to provide a sense of continuity with the past. A continuity in atmosphere is also in evidence in the many large church kitchens, fellowship halls, and large foyers for the purpose of conversation following the worship services.

The early order of worship gave an appearance of spontaneity as the elders would exhort one another to "be free, Brethren." But often planning took place through a prior huddle of ministers or through preparation of exhortations on the part of the individual ministers. Often a text would emerge as a theme on which several ministers would speak, referring to the remarks made by a previous brother. An American Baptist historian, Morgan Edwards, gave this description of the early Brethren (1770) which contains some hints as to their manner of worship:

> Their church government and discipline are the same with those of the English Baptists; except that every brother is allowed to stand up in the congregation to speak in a way of exhortation and expounding; and when by these means they find a man eminent for knowledge and aptness to teach, they choose him to be a minister, and ordain him with imposition of hands, attended with fasting and prayer and giving the right hand of fellowship. They also have deacons; and ancient widows for deaconesses; and exhorters; who are licenced to use their gifts statedly. They pay not their ministers unless it be in a way of presents, though they admit their right to pay; neither do the ministers assert the right, esteeming it more blessed to give than to receive. Their acquaintance with the Bible is admirable. In a word, they are meet and pious Christians; and have justly acquired the character of the *Harmless Tunkers.*[9]

Nineteeth-century worship probably became more ordered and controlled by the ministers than would be indicated in the above passage. In 1887 Henry B. Brumbaugh compiled *The Brethren's Church Manual containing the Declaration of faith, Rules of Order, how to conduct Religious Meetings, etc.*[10] The last such manual, *Book of Worship: Church of the Brethren*[11] focuses more on liturgical helps and less on doctrinal statements. Today, one finds a wide appropriation of resources from other denominations and a freedom to use books of prayers and liturgical manuals from many sources. The most consistent characteristic of Brethren worship today is its growing variety. It is true that some congregations may be enslaved by the necessity to maintain the typical Protestant style of worship of several decades ago. Others may be faddish in the compulsion to experiment with new. For the most part, however, there is a growing freedom to appropriate from others, and to experiment with new forms. In some congregations there has been a movement to high liturgy with congregational participation and great choral music. The informality and face-to-face style has been maintained, however, through the popularity of Brethren summer camps, the small-group movement, and opportunities for "talk-back" sharing after the sermon.

Some observers in colonial America regarded the Brethren to be among the more zealous and spirited of the sectarian groups. Since the Brethren were peaceful and orderly in daily life, such references no doubt referred to their singing. They shared without question in the Pietist legacy of devotion, edificatory writings, and the composition of new hymns. The Solingen Brethren composed many hymns while in prison. From the preface to the first Brethren hymnal, *Geistreiches Gesang-Buch,*[12] we discern the purpose, namely, that "these hymns will be able to serve them to the awakening and joy of their hearts to look even more steadfastly to Jesus."[13] The first hymnals published and widely used in America were *Die Kleine Lieder Sammlung* (1826) and the English hymnal, *A Choice Selection of Hymns* (1834). The latter points to the necessary adjustment which came from a change from the German to the English language in the nineteenth century.

The Brethren originally sang *a cappella;* organs and pianos did not come into church buildings until the early decades of the twentieth century. The large selection of hymns and worship resources in the present *Brethren Hymnal* indicates the ecumenical nature of contemporary Brethren worship, for the present hymnal is replete with social-gospel hymns, classical hymns of Protestantism, gospel songs from revivalism, and older and newer selections from Brethren authors and composers.[14]

The poetry and hymns written by Brethren have contained many references to Jesus. Phrases such as "looking to Jesus," "lover of Jesus," and "Jesus' beauty" may indicate a Jesus mysticism. The most common christological title used by Alexander Mack, Sr., was "Lord Jesus." Such a devotion does not imply a repudiation of beliefs in the divinity of Christ, but it does indicate a strong emphasis on his lordship. In one way or another the Brethren have often identified with the *imitatio Christi* motif of Christian piety. Such identification with the mind and spirit of the Jesus of the Gospels may be one of the basic theological deductions which can be made from the documents of Brethren devotional and liturgical life.

It has been noted that the Brethren are not united by common credal affirmations or a book of prayer and liturgical instructions. They have possessed a common tradition of rites or ordinances, common ethnic bonds, and an annual meeting for fellowship, inspiration, and business. Their communal feeling and style has been basic to their theological and liturgical life. But basic to the tradition has been a spirit of openness to changing forms and practices and to new light as the consensus of the community develops in relation to the Word. And in the midst of the resultant plurality of practices and beliefs, one finds both the tensions and unity of the brotherhood.

1. Alexander Mack, Sr., "Basic Questions," in D. F. Durnbaugh, ed. *European Origins of the Brethren* (Elgin, Ill.: Brethren Press, 1958), 331-332.

2. *The Monthly Gospel Visitor,* II (October, 1852), 103.

3. Alexander Mack, Jr., "Apologia," in D. F. Durnbaugh, ed., *The Brethren in Colonial America* (Elgin, Ill.: Brethren Press, 1967), 483.

4. Durnbaugh, *European Origins,* 352.

5. Durnbaugh, *Brethren in Colonial America,* 510.

6. *Ibid.,* 467.

7. *Ibid.*

8. *Monthly Gospel Visitor,* II (October, 1852), 104.

9. Durnbaugh, *Brethren in Colonial America,* 175.

10. (Huntingdon, Pa., and Mt. Morris, Ill.: Brethren's Publishing Company, 1887).

11. (Elgin, Ill.: Brethren Press, 1964).

12. (Berleburg: Christoph Konert, 1720).

13. Durnbaugh, *European Origins,* 407.

14. (Elgin, Ill.: Brethren Press, 1951).

5

POLITY

Warren F. Groff

The Church of the Brethren has recognized the need for definite structures of church government. These structures must be faithful to the New Testament guidelines. They are also required to serve the church's life and mission. Organizational patterns are important, but they are not so sacred as to be above criticism or change. Procedures are clearly subordinate to the worth and needs of persons. They are always to be measured by the yardstick of God's purpose which was set forth in Christ "as a plan for the fullness of time, to unite all things in him, things in heaven and things on earth" (Ephesians 1:10).

Definitions

Polity refers to the ways the church is equipped for mission, in obedience to Christ and in an effort to render its fitting service in the world. It connotes those organizational procedures which stem from what the church is and from what the church is called to do. Jesus himself appointed disciples to share in his ministry (Mark 3:13-19). He also commissioned them to their life of servanthood (Luke 10:1-12).

Polity includes both formal and informal elements. There may be assemblies with delegated representatives, as well as elected boards and commissions. Some personnel serve on a voluntary basis. Others hold salaried staff positions. In addition a particular tradition is usually held together and united for given tasks through the impact of charismatic individuals and *ad hoc* groupings. Such centers of spontaneous leadership are often routinized and made part of official structures.

We can approach our theme in a related way. Polity has to do with the exercise of authority within and on behalf of a group. Who has the power to make and carry out decisions? This is the authority question. All participants in the church have an important contribution to make as living limbs of the "body of Christ" (John 15:1-11; Romans 12:4-5). There are various "gifts" which strengthen the total organism and which help equip the believers "for the work of ministry" (Ephesians 4:12). Each gift is essential for the support of faith and the life of discipleship in the world. In both formal and informal ways the community acknowledges these gifts, and the authority of individuals and groups who carry specific responsibilities on behalf of the whole fellowship (1 Corinthians 16:15-18).

We can distinguish the following major types of church organization: *Congregational:* the local unit is the highest authority under God. *Presbyterial:* representative individuals and groups of designated leaders are the highest authority under God. *Episcopal:* the bishop is the highest authority under God. Living traditions seldom embody these types in pure form. Usually all tendencies are present in varying degrees. In each case there is an intermingling of individual and communal aspects of authority.

Historical Insights

Those looking in from outside used to attribute strict congregationalism to the Brethren. But the polity of the Church of the Brethren has consistently combined diverse tendencies. Spokesmen for the group have been quite specific on this matter. I. D. Parker puts it this way:

> What then is New Testament Church Polity? . . . It may be called an Ecclesiastical Democracy, a government of the people, by the people, and for the people. It comprises a combination of forms:
>
> 1. It is Democratic in the sense that the highest authority is vested in the membership.
>
> 2. It is Republican in the sense that the church chooses representatives to execute her will.
>
> 3. It is Congregational in local matters, but general on all questions of doctrine and matters of a general character.
>
> The Church of the Brethren has taken this view of Church Polity . . .[1]

Even episcopal leanings have sometimes been present. Especially during the nineteenth century influential elders were occasionally called bishops. From the sphere of their own local congregations their influence extended over neighboring churches. Quite regularly they served as moderators for different gatherings. In the twentieth century the office of the elder has considerably less authority, with the wider use of lay moderators and the enlarged role of local pastors. Even the practice of ordaining persons to the eldership has been terminated, with only two stages of the set-apart ministry remaining: 1. the licensed minister; 2. the ordained minister. However, one continues to observe the presence and authority of particularly gifted persons whose sphere of influence in the brotherhood is quite broad. At the same time the Brethren have been moving as a denomination toward more rationalized or formally structured patterns of leadership.

From the very earliest beginnings there are evidences of a brotherhood consciousness. Even in 1723 the Brethren in Germantown, Pennsylvania, sought the counsel of their fellow-believers still in Europe before proceeding with a service of baptism. There were regular visits among congregations for mutual edification, advice, and discipline. It was the custom to invite elders from adjoining churches for such important occasions as the election of ministers, council meetings, and services of love feast and communion.

Throughout the years the distinctive characteristic of Brethren polity has been the rhythm between local initiative and brotherhood accountability. As early as 1742 definite brotherhood structures were formalized. That year the practice began of holding an Annual Meeting (more recently this has been called the Annual Conference, which is the nomenclature we shall use hereafter). It soon became clear that the "Annual Conference is the final authority of the Church of the Brethren in all matters of procedure, program, polity, and discipline."[2] This guaranteed a dynamic interplay between local and brotherhood patterns of authority.

In 1856 the formation of districts was sanctioned "for the purpose of meeting jointly at least once a year, settling difficulties, etc., and thus lessening the business of our General Yearly Meeting."[3] This made it doubly sure that local units would be yoked together with other congregations of a given area for mutual admonition, nurture, and mission.

The extent to which the Church of the Brethren is committed to a polity which combines elements of local and brotherhood authority has itself been a matter of dispute. This issue figured importantly in one of the major splinterings within the denomination. In the nineteenth century the Old German Baptist Brethren ("Old Order") separated from the continuing group. Part of their dissatisfaction was the failure of brotherhood authorities to stand against such innovations as Sunday schools, emotionally stirring evangelistic meetings which threatened to coerce conversions, variations in religious dress, and the development of institutions of higher education. They insisted that Annual Conference decisions were to be enforced in a binding way, albeit in defense of the established order.

On the other hand, the Progressive Brethren, as they were called, felt that Annual Conference was too slow in pressing for change. They advocated an educated ministry. They also felt there should be less preoccupation with questions of dress and church ritual. Because of their desire for progressive reforms, this group tended to trust and uphold local autonomy. They became a separate movement know as the Brethren Church.

Each of these dissenting groups has been convinced that it is the true successor to the original intentions of the Schwarzenau Brethren. Also, each has struggled since the time of division with the relation between local and brotherhood structures of authority. Still, it would be fair to say that Old Order Brethren opted for strong centralized control with less freedom for local innovations. At least in their beginnings, Progressive Brethren emphasized local initiative with less regulation from the side of the larger gatherings. To what extent did this predispose the one group toward a posture of continuity with the past, and the other toward more radical departures from the tradition? This would be a question worthy of further research than is possible here.

The polity of the group we continue to identify as Church of the Brethren clearly has reflected a working give and take between local autonomy and responsibility to the brotherhood. What has since become prevailing practice had already emerged by 1911. In that year the question of uniformity in religious dress ("the garb") again came before Annual Conference. It was decided that the time-honored values of simplicity and nonworldly adornment in dress should be upheld. But there was a great deal of latitude given for local variations in the implementation of this directive. The Annual Conference was coming of age in its relationship to districts and congregations.

Corporate actions were to be adopted in openness to the scriptures and the leading of the Spirit without setting up rigid programs of enforcement and without becoming indifferent to what happens on the local level. Brotherhood decisions needed to carry their own intrinsic persuasiveness, and must accurately mirror realities in the life and work of the church. This was their true claim to authority.

That same spirit continues to prevail, as evidenced by several paragraphs from a statement on polity which was recently adopted by the brotherhood:

> Annual Conference is the final authority of the Church of the Brethren in all matters of procedure, program, polity, and discipline. The authority of Conference has its source in the delegates elected by the local churches and districts who come together as a deliberative body under the guidance of the Holy Spirit.
>
> The actions of Conference are directives for the whole life of the church and implementation is assumed to take place within a reasonable span of time. This implementation does not depend on acts of enforcement by decree. Rather, education, consultation, and patience are characteristics of Brethren polity. Groups and individuals have channels of review when decisions of Annual Conference are questioned. It is important that there be mutual trust and shared responsibility between local, district, and Brotherhood structures of church order.[4]

Guiding Principles

As conceived and implemented within the Church of the Brethren, polity is subject to certain basic guidelines. The following were formulated by a study committee and adopted by brotherhood action:

> 1. The highest authority is God, as revealed in Jesus Christ. All human authority is judged with reference to this ultimate standard.
>
> 2. Authority is exercised both formally through organizational structures and designated persons and informally through spontaneous groupings and natural leaders. This authority is to be implemented with respect for individual conscience, openness to new light, acceptance of criticism, and the willingness to allow decisions to persuade on the basis of their intrinsic merit.
>
> 3. Authority is held accountable within the community, which in turn diligently seeks the "mind of Christ" in study of the Scriptures, in dialogue with the brother, and in openness to the leading of the Holy Spirit.
>
> 4. The principles of "voluntaryism" in membership and belief and "no force in religion," which are firmly rooted in our tradition, make us avoid arbitrary patterns of enforcement which violate the freedom of individuals and local groups.
>
> 5. The practice of brother confronting brother is an essential part of our serving as a "priest to one another." Our Anabaptist heritage teaches that "no man enters the kingdom apart from his brother." This leads us to reject unqualified individualism which denies the place of the community in the shaping of one's life of discipleship.
>
> 6. Openness to the brother reaches from the local congregation to the district, to the Brotherhood, to the ecumenical church. Administrative structures must constantly be measured by this criterion: Do they make possible full and free interchange between brothers in Christ as the collective means for coming to know God's will for His church?[5]

A brief commentary in relation to each of the foregoing paragraphs will amplify the polity implications:

1. To recognize God as ultimate authority is a posture of faith which is shared by all Christian groups. This overarching principle sets the tone for all other considerations.

2. This recalls our earlier reference to formal and informal channels of authority. We may cite the Brethren Action Movement as a current example of spontaneous groupings which develop occasionally and provide important leadership for the whole brotherhood. This movement is of recent origin. It claims no membership list. It has no official status as part of regular denominational structures. A central purpose is to encourage various direct action projects and personal disciplines in the interest of making more visible the church's witness for peace and justice in today's world.

Whether more highly institutionalized or *ad hoc* in character, the authority of individuals and groups is to be disciplined by sensitivity to divergent points of view, openness to unfolding insights, acceptance of brotherly counsel, and the readiness to lead by example and the intrinsic persuasiveness of positions held.

3. Authority is to be checked and tested within the community of faith. But the fellowship of believers is not ultimate. That status belongs to God alone. The community is responsible to the extent it remains open to Christ and the leading of the Holy Spirit. In turn, such receptivity requires an honest confrontation with the scriptures and the concerned brother.

4. Faith is a voluntary act. It presupposes the formative power of Christ and his living Spirit. It is also nurtured by the community of believers, which serves as the historical channel of grace from one generation to another. In these terms faith is a gift before it is a task. But it is not an automatic possession. It cannot be conferred by magisterial decree. Faith is a free response of a responsible agent. That is why adult baptism and voluntaryism belong together. Baptism celebrates the prior work of Christ and his Spirit. It is a communal event in which a person covenants his intention to take on the disciplines of discipleship. It is an act of commissioning to that ministry which is shared by all believers.

Voluntaryism is intimately related to the guiding principle of "no force in religion." Therefore, it is especially urgent that we avoid infringing upon the freedom of individuals and groups. This regulative ideal is part and parcel of the determination that polity decisions should commend themselves on the basis of their intrinsic worth and capacity to persuade rather than by arbitrary forms of coercion.

5. The heritage of the Church of the Brethren strongly supports individual freedom and local initiative. At the same time unchecked individualism is called into question. How can a limb flourish except it share in the life-giving energies of the total body? We enter God's kingdom with our brother, not as isolated and self-sufficient entities. We are commissioned to be "priests on behalf of one another." This is a very active mandate. My brother is a chosen channel of God's grace to me. In turn, I am responsible to help my brother in his pilgrimage toward mature discipleship. Thus, individual freedom and life in community are not unmixable opposites like oil and water. They intermingle and support each other when Christ, the Head of the body, is truly served as Lord of his church.

6. Interdependence with the brother occurs in an ever-expanding rather than a closed circle. Because I find my freedom in relationship to other

persons for whom Christ also died it follows that my brother is the distant neighbor as well as the neighbor near at hand. This points the individual away from himself, toward all those for whom Christ has given his all. Also, the local congregation is turned toward the district, the brotherhood, the ecumenical church, and finally toward that larger world which God so loved that he gave his Son on its behalf (John 3:16).

Since Christ turns us outward, administrative structures are judged by a clear criterion. Do such structures relate us to our brothers in the widest possible context? Are they sufficiently tempered by the mind of Christ so that they break out of their built-in tendency toward narrowness and provincialism? Only then is one brother free to serve another as the means of grace on his behalf. Only then are we empowered to know and to obey God's will for his church and his world.

Structures of Church Polity

In outlining specific structures of polity within the Church of the Brethren it is fitting that we begin with the *local congregation.* Here the purpose and benefits of the church touch the lives of individuals most directly. Here the Word and the love of God are proclaimed and made available to needy persons. Here the disciplines of discipleship — such as caring, integrity, and trust — are taught and appropriated. Here the ordinances are enacted and participated in. Here persons are incorporated through baptism into the death and resurrection of Christ, and thus are ordained to the priesthood of all believers. Here the gifts of the Spirit are discerned and deployed as the whole community dedicates itself to a mission of servanthood in the world. Ministry is first of all a work that is shared by every member. As part of the process of discernment and deployment of resources for the sake of mission, some persons are acknowledged to have specialized functions on behalf of the whole church. Included perhaps are appropriate services of licensing and ordination to set-apart ministries.

We have seen how a local group is dynamically interrelated with larger brotherhood structures. Responsible listening is called for from both sides. Each congregation is encouraged to develop its specific organizational structures and procedures in harmony with district and brotherhood polity. There is no disposition to dictate a completely uniform constitution or set of by-laws upon all local units.

Congregations are advised to develop their own affirmation of faith and purpose. The Church of the Brethren has no official creed to which all must subscribe. In 1964 the Annual Conference approved some guidelines for organization of the local church. The following statement of belief was included for adoption or adaptation by given groups:

This congregation:

1. Is founded upon the faith that there is but one God who is a personal Father God who in holy love creates, sustains, and orders all.

2. Confesses Jesus Christ as the Lord of the church and of all life.

3. Believes that the Holy Spirit is at work in the hearts and minds of believers, creating and sustaining the church through the gospel, giving guidance and comfort, and uniting believers with their Lord and with one another.

4. Maintains the New Testament as its only creed and rule of faith. In the Holy Scriptures is recorded God's search for man which is climaxed in God's redemptive act in and through Christ. Through His holy Word God still speaks and continues to accomplish His redemptive purpose.

5. Believes that the gospel is the Good News that God was in Christ reconciling the world unto Himself. Through the gospel God's sovereign will and Christ's redeeming grace are revealed.

6. Holds that the church is the body of Christ and is under the Lord's mandate to be faithful in accepting and transmitting the gospel by word and deed.

7. Considers that all members of the congregation, of the body of believers, are responsible for the total ministry of the church.

8. Accepts the ministry of the church to be the proclamation and fulfillment of the gospel for all people both near and far, and the nurture of the individual believers in the Christian faith and life.[6]

Brotherhood guidelines also clarify the relationship between the congregation and the church universal. Efforts at the local level are integrated not only with the denomination, but also with all other Christian bodies. Here again the image of an ever-expanding circle has relevance. The individual follower of Christ is pointed outward, toward his near and distant neighbor. So, too, a given congregation is positioned by the Lord of the church in the direction of those other groups which belong to the ecumenical community of faith. Indeed, the posture of radical openness faces the congregation toward that world which Christ loved and died to save.

We need not sketch all the suggested articles and bylaws that might appear in a local plan of organization. However, one additional area is important. The Church of the Brethren today is basically committed to a policy of open membership. The following procedures are recommended: "Members may be received (a) by confession of faith and baptism by trine immersion as practiced by the Church of the Brethren; (b) by letter of transfer from another congregation of the Church of the Brethren or of any other evangelical denomination; or (c) by affirmation of faith. Membership in the local church shall be open to all persons irrespective of race, national origin, or status in life."[7]

Organization into *districts* is another item in present-day Brethren polity. Annual Conference authorized their formation in 1856. Ten years later the following principles were laid down for their constitution and operation: (1) an appropriate number of districts should be formed according to geographical proximity and requirements for effective mission (the number has varied throughout the years, with a recent trend toward consolidation and realignment of previously separated units); (2) each congregation is to be represented in proportionate numbers (at first the limit was smaller, but now there may be four delegates for each member church of two hundred members or less, with one additional delegate for each one hundred members or major fraction thereof); (3) district meetings are to be simple in design and patterned closely after regular church council meetings; (4) no business ought to come before the district gatherings before it has been processed through the congregation in which it originated; (5) districts are to settle as many questions of a local character as possible; and (6) matters that concern the brotherhood in general should be carefully framed into queries and forwarded to Annual Conference.

Each district is free to develop its own constitution and bylaws. It is expected that there will be a clear definition of goals, organizational forms, and operational procedures. These are to harmonize with the purposes and polity of congregations and the brotherhood. Even with freedom for varying developments among districts, there has been a growing trend toward basic consistency and simplicity of forms and nomenclature. This pertains especially to the makeup of the conference delegate body, functions of officers and committees, the naming of district members to the Standing Committee of Annual Conference, character of the district board, names and tasks of commissions and continuing committees, as well as the subdivision of districts into smaller working sections.

From 1932 until recently the brotherhood was further divided into five regional areas. Each of these regions had a functional organization, including a board, an executive committee, and employed staff personnel. The regional structure and program have now been discontinued, partly as a result of its own efficiency. There has been a strengthening of the district field effort throughout the whole denomination. Many districts have been consolidated or are now in varying stages of realignment. Nearly all have employed executive leadership. Regional lines continue to be observed for such limited purposes as the election of members to the General Board of the denomination, the location of Annual Conference, and college constituency.

Still another structure of church polity is the *Annual Conference*. The earliest brotherhood gathering of this sort was held in 1742. Following 1830 the recorded minutes become more complete. From 1877 on the names of all major Conference officers are known.

Annual Conference acts upon the queries that originate in the congregations and districts. It appoints committees and receives reports, dealing with general problems in the life of the brotherhood. It designates persons to represent the church to other bodies and councils of churches. It reviews the brotherhood programs administered through responsible boards and commissions.

The voting body is made up of delegates who are direct representatives from all member congregations. In addition, there are delegates appointed by the various districts. The latter constitute the Standing Committee, which is empowered to act for the brotherhood between Conferences in the event of special needs. The Standing Committee processes matters that are to come as business items to the larger gathering, offers recommended answers to queries, determines the issues that involve policy changes and thus require a two-thirds vote of the delegates, and functions as Conference nominating committee. An executive group known as the Annual Conference Central Committee works closely with the Standing Committee in carrying out its assignment. The Central Committee carries the primary tasks of program planning and general arrangements for the annual gatherings.

The Annual Conference fulfills important educational and motivational functions. It is by no means only the official delegates who attend, and attendance totaling ten thousand persons is common. All age groups are represented in the various activities of the week. These gatherings have the character of a large family reunion. Sermons, addresses, Bible hours, and numerous special interest groupings are included. All these contribute to the sense of belonging to a total brotherhood. The reports of persons who represent the denomination as fraternal delegates to other Christian bodies and as participants in national and world agencies of ecumenical cooperation nurture an awareness of oneness with the church universal. Many of the items in the Conference program also serve to uphold the mandate and requirements of effective mission in today's world.

The many facets of the brotherhood program are administered through a General Board of twenty-five members elected by Annual Conference for designated terms of service. In turn, the work of the General Board is carried on through the offices of a general secretary and three associate general secretaries. The latter also carry special executive responsibilities in connection with the major commissions: Parish Ministries; World Ministries, and General Services. The General Board is directly responsible to Annual Conference. It reports regularly on all aspects of the brotherhood program.

The Annual Conference is the basic instrument through which individuals, congregations, and districts are given a consciousness of also belonging to a total brotherhood. It would be difficult to overemphasize the institutionalizing impact of this structure upon the group throughout the years. The Church of the Brethren has not been united around a fixed creed, except through an open-ended appeal to the New Testament as the one "rule of faith and practice." The group has not persisted in time through the stabilizing effect of a sacramental priesthood or church hierarchy. Nor have Brethren been held together so much around the classical Protestant stress upon the Word rightly preached and the sacraments faithfully administered. Echoing the Free Church tradition, it is the meeting of brother with brother that is central. The community of believers receives historical continuity as a gift, even as it is called to serve obediently as the elected channel of love and grace to one generation after another. That is why the practice of assembling regularly as representatives of the larger church family has such theological and sociological importance. God communicates his life-giving power and will as brother confronts brother in an ever-expanding circle, in receptive openness to the scriptures and the "mind of Christ." In this way the believers are disciplined for effective service within and on behalf of God's whole creation.

---

1. I. D. Parker, "Church Polity," in D. L. Miller, ed., *Two Centuries of the Church of the Brethren* (Elgin, Ill.: Brethren Publishing House, 1908), 161.

2. *Manual of Brotherhood Organization and Polity* (Elgin, Ill.: General Offices, Church of the Brethren, 1965), 4.

3. Otho Winger, *History and Doctrines of the Church of the Brethren* (Elgin, Ill.: Brethren Publishing House, 1919), 200.

4. *Minutes of the 182nd Recorded Annual Conference*, Church of the Brethren, June 25-30, 1968, 79

5. *Ibid.*

6. *Manual of Brotherhood Organization and Polity*, 35.

7. *Ibid*, 36

6

EDUCATIONAL ACTIVITY

Desmond W. Bittinger

The educational history of the Church of the Brethren during its existence of more than two and a half centuries has been presented by most writers as an experience in oscillation. It is maintained that following a period of enthusiasm for education the Brethren turned a complete circle and became wary of and antagonistic to education. This negative attitude in its turn changed to one of overacceptance until the Brethren were burdened with educational institutions beyond what they were able to support. Dr. John S. Flory, one of the church's outstanding educational leaders for half a century, writing about 1925, said:

> Our educational history as a church abounds in paradoxes. At the beginning of our history we were among the most ardent advocates of higher learning, and possessed a liberal share of it in our own membership. We promoted educational institutions with an ardor that would do credit to any people. Later we descended to the opposite extreme, and placed ourselves on record as opposed to all forms of higher education. After a while we began gradually to recover our pristine ardor for intellectual culture, and today are again taking our place among the sane promoters of higher learning in this country.[1]

From its beginning until the present, the Church of the Brethren has had a continuum of educational emphasis which sustained and supported the overall mission and purpose of the church as it was understood. The method of education and the educational instruments changed as the cultural conditions which surrounded the Brethren demanded, but the basic intent of the education was not lost, nor was the force and thrust of education greatly abated.

One of the basic purposes of the church as conceived and taught consistently throughout the changing fortunes of its history centers in the sacredness and supremacy of the individual, his right to freedom of conscience, his right to use and to interpret the New Testament as his creed and his code of conduct, and the indivisible relationship between his religion and his daily life.

When he lived in an accepting cultural environment he could teach this to his children in one way; when, by his own choice or forced by circumstances or adversity, he moved into a different environment and cultural situation it was necessary that he teach it in a different way. His need for and attitude toward educational institutions, publications, and the paraphernalia of education changed, but the basic thrust of his education remained at its core relatively constant.

Early Educational Interests and Emphases

The actual educational achievement of the eight individuals immediately involved in the founding of the Church of the Brethren cannot be clearly compared to current educational patterns so that we can say they were high school graduates, college graduates, or the equivalent thereof in the German system. We do know, however, that they were a studious people who were willing to meet to study their textbook, the Bible, in depth and that they were sufficiently educated to make their own evaluations of what they studied. In the minds of leading current educators this indicates true education. Their leader and others who were with them in their early years in Germany did have an awareness of some of the significant scholarship of that area and time.[2]

While Alexander Mack, Sr., the first minister, was still in Germany, he published certain suggestions and guides. These were studied by the membership along with the Gospels, which continued to be their main guide. Among his writings were *A Short and Plain View of the . . . Rights and Ordinances of the House of God* and *Answers to Gruber's Basic Questions.* These were published in 1713 and 1715. Alexander Mack wrote and published other items, including poetry and hymns.[3] Mack's little booklet, *Rights and Ordinances,* was exceedingly popular during the early life of the church. Christopher Sauer, Jr., reprinted it in 1774 in America. English editions were printed in Philadelphia in 1810 and in Ohio in 1860. The latter edition was reprinted in 1888, 1919, 1939, and 1954. A new translation appeared in 1958.[4]

Others of that early group also were interested in education and in writing. Since they were under persecution while in Germany they did not reach their educational stride until after their arrival in America. Obviously, not all of those who came to America in either the first or second migration were educated people. However, those among them who were educated and were interested in education soon became involved in educational endeavor. After they had settled in Germantown and in the nearby environs of eastern Pennsylvania, evidences of such interest are manifested in publication, in the propagation of schools, and in other enterprises both for themselves and for others within the communities in which they lived.

Though not all of the early Brethren could write either beautiful prose or beautiful poetry, they highly respected their educated leaders and looked to them for direction and for the means to educate their young. They were interested also in drawing others into the fellowship with them. Consequently, they turned to whatever educational enterprises there were in their day, and where none were available they established their own. Among these were day schools and a great wealth and variety of publications from the printing presses.

Elhanan Winchester, writing in 1803, said of the Brethren: "They are industrious, sober, temperate, kind, charitable people; envying not the great, nor despising the mean. They read much, they sing and pray much; they are constant attendants upon the worship of God. Their dwelling-houses are all houses of prayer: they walk in the commandments and ordinances of the Lord blameless, both in public and private. They 'bring up their children in the nurture and admonition of the Lord.' "[5]

Among the leading German immigrants was Christopher Sauer (Sower), Sr. Although not a member of the Brethren, he was a close friend and had significant influence. His like-named son became a Brethren elder. In 1738 he established in Germantown the first German printing press in America. Through this printing press Sauer was able to transplant some of the German culture to the new world. He was the first to use German type, and he edited and printed the first successful German newspaper in America. Apparently, Sauer wanted his publications to reach deeply into a broad community. He printed his motto in the largest and best type he possessed and placed it as a decoration on the walls of his shop. It read, "To the glory of God and my neighbor's good."[6]

Martin G. Brumbaugh, one of the well-known writers on early Brethren history, noted that Christopher Sauer was a prolific writer. "His newspaper and his almanacs contain numerous articles on . . . topics relating to the religious, educational, industrial, social, and civic welfare of the Germans of colonial America."[7]

Brumbaugh goes on to say that Christopher Sauer, Jr., who followed in the footsteps of his father as an educator and a publisher, went even further in the subjects covered, writing "wisely and at length upon . . . themes of . . . current value."[8] In 1754 Christopher Sauer, Jr., published a treatise entitled *Christian Education Exemplified.*

In addition to these publications the Christopher Sauers published an almanac which predicted the weather, set forth times of planting and so on. This was begun in 1738 and was called *The High German American Calendar for the year 1739.* This was issued annually by Sauer, his son and his grandson, for forty-nine years. It became the ABC and spelling book of the Brethren and other Germanic people in America.

Their single greatest contribution, however, was the production of the German Bible. These Bibles have since become very valuable because of their rarity. The first volume was printed on paper made principally by Sauer and with ink manufactured by him. The first edition was printed in 1743 and became the reading book in many German homes. In 1763 Christopher Sauer, Jr., issued a second edition and in 1776 a third edition.

Christopher Sauer, Jr., was a pupil of the famous colonial schoolmaster, Christopher Dock, who developed a unique method of teaching. Sauer, Sr., was able to get Dock to submit this in writing; it was published on the Sauer press in 1770 and rates high among early educational publications. The younger Sauer was vitally interested in education as an adult. He was one of the staunchest supporters of the Germantown Academy when it was founded in 1759, donating funds liberally and acting as a trustee for twenty years.

Some have claimed that the Brethren were pioneers in beginning Sunday schools in America. Actually the meetings held by the Brethren in

Germantown on Sundays were Pietist conventicles for mutual edification and differed in purpose and form from later Sabbath schools. Ludwig Hoecker developed at Ephrata what could be called a Sunday school, but this cannot be called Brethren activity as such.

The leading Brethren writer in the colonial period was Alexander Mack, Jr. He was a poet as well as an author of doctrinal tracts; his writings were published during his lifetime and also more recently as manuscripts have been recovered. The most important work from his pen was his *Apologia* (1788), a defense of Brethren practices and beliefs.

The foregoing paragraphs have shown at some length that the early Brethren were deeply involved in education. Their intent was to keep themselves knowledgeable of and faithful to their teachings and to exert a wholesome influence on one another and on the community in which they lived.

All matters were not completely harmonious within the Brethren community, however. One of the major defections was led by Conrad Beissel who established at Ephrata, Pennsylvania, a society which he called Seventh Day Baptists. Beissel was a religious mystic, mathematician, author, composer of music, teacher of gothic and ornamental penmanship, and instructor in the art of self-production. He composed no fewer than one thousand hymns. His printed hymns number four hundred forty-one, and his printed discourses sixty-six. The printing establishment developed at Ephrata rivaled the Sauer Press. Some of the Brethren defected from Germantown to join Beissel. Thus two educational operations developed close to one another. With the death of Beissel this operation soon disintegrated. It cannot be called Brethren since it was a defection from the Brethren, but it influenced many Brethren in a theological and educational way.

Cultural Change Comes to the Brethren

This pleasant, thriving, brotherly community of the Brethren which grew westward from the Germantown center must have had more difficulties than history had recorded. But, withal, it seemed to have been a community or a series of communities of considerable cultural solidarity, educational enterprise, strong home life, and generally wholesome community relations. This must have been an encouraging and satisfactory release from some of the persecutions and tensions which had driven the Brethren from their original home in Germany. Geographical and numerical expansion within the church doubled in these early years.

Persecutions similar to those which had plagued them in Europe presently began to emerge here also. Some of the reasons were the same. The avowed opposition of the Brethren to war and their unwillingness to be quiet about it soon brought them to the notice of those who were a part of the growing spirit of revolt against England and the movement toward American independence. "Their refusal to engage in war brought severe censure of the Brethren by these English colonists, so that the cultural breach between English and German became deep and permanent."[9] During the Revolutionary War Sauer's printing press and his personal property were confiscated by the new American government because of his opposition to the war and his refusal to abjure allegiance to the English crown. Other Brethren suffered from the revolutionary upheaval, but none to the extent of the wealthy Sauer family.

Thus began a dispersion of the Brethren. Nonacceptance and persecution caused many of the Brethren to begin a move somewhat in the pattern followed later by the Mormons as they also sought religious freedom. The Brethren, being skillful farmers, sought areas of good soil. This led them into the Shenandoah Valley in Virginia, across the mountains to the valleys of Kentucky, into Ohio, Indiana, Illinois. When it was possible to go beyond the Mississippi, they found good land in Iowa and Kansas on which to settle.

Some historians who write of them call this period the "Dark Ages" for the church. F. D. Dove wrote: "For almost a century the Church of the Brethren was without any active educational influence within its own ranks and the longer it continued in this state the fewer trained ministers and teachers there were among them. Even the Sunday school idea was abandoned during this period of scholastic depression."[10] He maintained further that in due time as a sort of cultural reaction they even came to look with distinct disfavor upon higher education and the types of culture it produced. D. L. Miller, continuing in this emphasis, said: "They came to look upon higher education as a snare of the devil to entrap the humble followers of Christ and to lead them into pride and worldlyism." This period is supposed to have lasted for three quarters of a century, and during this time "the cultural loss sustained by the church during these 'dark ages' . . . is inestimable."[11]

Further reflection upon these years in the light of current understanding of cultural and educational processes can justify modified interpretations. In their years in Germantown the Brethren were an accepted and leading part of the German cultural community. They were in the midst of others who likewise had come to Pennsylvania for religious freedom. They continued and improved their educational undertakings and their community involvement.

Now, after the dispersal, the German community was gone. The German language was no longer appropriate in the new communities. Their neighbors who did not speak the German language were often suspicious of the German people or of any people from other countries who were not zealous in learning new ways. Other denominations were moving into the same valleys in which the Brethren were establishing themselves. Since the population was sparse each denomination sought to add to its number any newcomers whom it could so that they could build new churches and support them. The Brethren could lose even their own children as members. Some may have looked upon the Brethren with unusual suspicion because they had not participated in the revolution which had brought about the American freedom of which they all now were a part.

As a consequence, the Brethren now saw a need for a different educational emphasis. If they were to maintain even their own children as a part of their membership and not to lose their identity within the frontier communities and the changed cultural setting, then the nature of the education had to shift decidedly. It had to center in the home. It had to be managed and overseen by those who had come through the persecution, those who knew the teachings of the past as promulgated by Sauer, Mack, and others. They felt that they needed to keep themselves disassociated from "the world." In this sociological sense "the world" had become anyone other than the Brethren. This became true also for the Brethren who did not leave for the frontiers.

The educational emphasis and activity, therefore, became similar to the educational process of any nomadic people or any persecuted group. The process was similar to that which had been advocated for the Jews when they were traveling from one area to another. Education was to be continuous, home centered, and to proceed from early morning to late night. Parents were to teach their children from their "rising up until their laying down at night"; they were to write the understood teachings into the minds and hearts of the young at every opportunity; they were to prevent, as fully as possible, the writing of other kinds of teaching into the minds and hearts of their youth. All parents and older siblings, therefore, became teachers. Much of the teaching was informal, but each day had its time of formality also. Family worship was a time for Bible reading and teaching. The memorization of scripture was emphasized. The "Brethren understandings" were carefully taught. The Brethren were not alone in this manner of teaching. Other denominational groups in movement were following similar practices.

In order to augment their different teaching and beliefs and to make it easier for Brethren to recognize other Brethren, they continued to hold now to the manner of dress which was in vogue at the time they began the dispersion. Dress presently became one of the facets of their teaching and an evidence of their faith. The outward dress became identified with the inward spirit. To dress "worldly" was to put on "pride"; from this the Brethren wished to shy away.

The efficacy of this form of educational activity is attested to by the fact that the Brethren through these persecuted and/or isolated years, were able to remain alive as a church. Not only were they able to remain alive, but they managed to maintain some of their teachings relatively unchanged. Thus their desire for the simple life, their holding on to the accepted forms of baptism, of communion, and other church practices, their commitment to nonviolence, and their concept of religion and life as being inseparable were a result of this strenuous and continuous education. Though they may not have participated heavily in formalized community activities, it was said of them in communities where they settled that "their word is as good as their bond." In other words, the same manner of life which characterized them in the Germantown area characterized them also in Kentucky, Tennessee, Indiana, Illinois, Kansas, Iowa, or wherever they went. It took education purposefully and ardently pursued at home and in the church gatherings to make this possible.

Eventually the Brethren became less isolated geographically. Roads began to develop, and the Brethren sought out other Brethren even though great distances separated them. Occasions for this seeking out were first centered around the observing of the love feast. This came once or twice a year. Entire families would travel by wagon for many miles in order to be in fellowship for two or three days with the distant Brethren. Some Brethren leaders put in a goodly share of their time, without remuneration, in traveling on horseback from Brethren community to Brethren community, helping in the observance of these love feasts or officiating at weddings, burials, or other events necessary to the life of the church. Such meetings, which the children were required to attend, were not so much educational valleys or dark ages as they were cultural and educational mountain peaks. Some of the ministers were outstanding persons who had educated themselves in remarkable fashion and whose fluency of expression and oratorical skills have not been surpassed in the total history of the Church of the Brethren.

Within their own circle, therefore, and for their own cultural needs the educational processes were not at a standstill but at a high operational level during these "wilderness years." It was an education developed to meet the needs of this particular cultural phase through which a developing country and a developing church were passing.

These meetings for fellowship and love feast were supplemented by a growing sense of need to have the several church communities coordinate into a larger fellowship or brotherhood. Such a brotherhood could receive queries or questions from the churches and give answers back to the churches. This was the role of the Annual Meeting of the Church of the Brethren. To get to these meetings required a week or sometimes several weeks of travel. Such annual meetings lasted for about a week. The entire family group from child to aging grandparents were involved in the worshiping, socializing, and educational process.

An Enlarging Educational Emphasis

As the Brethren traveled more widely to visit one another and as the Annual Meetings enlarged acquaintanceship and common interest, a few leaders thought of using the printing press to strengthen further the bonds of fellowship. By the 1850s the Church of the Brethren had grown to three or four times its earlier size and up to ten times its earlier geographic area. A sufficient number of the Brethren had migrated beyond the mountains as early as 1822 so that the Annual Meeting was held for the first time beyond the Atlantic slope.

Several printers associated with the Brethren such as the Leiberts in Germantown, the Baumanns in Ephrata, and the Salas in Canton, Ohio, had published for the brotherhood. But it was Elder Henry Kurtz of Poland, Ohio, who began the first periodical published for the church, though it was a private venture. This was the *Gospel Visitor* (1851). When this monthly started production in the springhouse on Henry Kurtz' farm, there were those who opposed it, fearing that it might sponsor a form of education which would weaken the faith. Queries, therefore, were brought to the Annual Meeting concerning this publication, whether it should be allowed to continue and later as to whether it could be considered in any way an official publication of the church.

The Brethren struggled through these years of accepting educational processes which went beyond the congregation and the home. They came through the struggle rather quickly, though not without pain. A quarter of a century after Kurtz began, several printing presses were active within the church. It has been said that during the last quarter of the nineteenth century the Brethren witnessed a revival of educational and literary activity which has been rarely surpassed among any other people.

Among those who wrote prolifically at this time were such highly qualified persons as H. R. Holsinger, James Quinter, Henry Kurtz, Peter Nead, Abraham Cassel, Daniel Hays, Isaac Price, S. Z. Sharp, and D. L. Miller. Their writings varied from articles in the *Gospel Visitor,* or other periodicals which were now coming into being, to tracts and sizable books concerning theology, such as those by Peter Nead. The tracts were sometimes the published accounts of debates which were now being held between Brethren leaders and the leaders of other churches. Each was defending the particular doctrines of his church; these seemed worthy to be set forth in written form as educational material for all. Once again, therefore, a written word other than the Bible itself as the form of education began to be circulated in the church.

It did seem necessary for the church to caution the writers from time to time about their writings. The Annual Conference during this period said: "In reference to the controversial articles published in our religious papers, we counsel and advise our Brethren . . . to publish nothing in their periodicals that disputes the practice of the precepts and ordinances of the gospel, as handed down to us from Christ and the apostles. . . . Disregard of this counsel will subject a brother to the counsel of the church."[12]

Some of the periodicals which came out of this period were *The Primitive Christian, The Brethren at Work, The Pilgrim,* and *The Brethren's Messenger.* Eventually, these were merged into what was known as *The Gospel Messenger* (1883), which continues to be the official publication of the Church of the Brethren. Currently it is known as *Messenger.*

An important development of an educational nature during this period was the introduction of the Sunday school. Such schools were conducted at the discretion of the congregation. Likely some of the tract material and some of the church papers became a background and supplement to direct Bible teaching in these schools. The church, however, as a whole, felt that these schools should be kept under the surveillance of the total denomination. From time to time queries came to the Annual Meeting with reference to this. One answer of Annual Conference reads as follows:

> In relation to Sabbath-schools, we feel the great necessity of guarding against the prevailing manner in which these schools are conducted; of cautioning the brethren who take any part in them against having festivals, or anything of the kind that does not comport with the spirit of Christianity, which such schools are designed to promote; that care be taken lest pride be taught rather than humility, and that nothing be encouraged thereby that will conflict with the established order and character of the brethren, and that care should be taken that no offense be given to the brethren in these things.[13]

Prayer meetings also began to be an addition to the regular Sunday preaching services. Since this involved teachers other than the designated ministers and elders of the church, questions again were asked of the Annual

Conference concerning the attitude of the brotherhood with reference to prayer meetings. The Conference indicated in its reply that they approved such meetings but asked that they be focused upon biblical teachings rather than upon social gatherings and that care be taken to uphold the understandings and doctrines of the church. They cautioned against introducing these meetings too rapidly in places where their introduction would cause confusion or trouble in the churches.

It can be observed that the desire of the Conference was to have the church, which was scattered widely across the continent, modify its practices only at such speed as would find acceptance in any given area. This characteristic has been continued in the church. Within the last decade there has developed some impatience with the idea of area or regional speed in cultural change. In the last quarter of the nineteenth century sufficient change had occurred in American culture to draw the center of education from the home into a more formal setting. The Brethren began to turn quickly toward this kind of education. The way was open now for the introduction of church-operated schools of secondary and higher education.

Higher Education

Children and youth have always been central to Brethren. Their proper education has always held high priority in Brethren thought. When the public school system began to be established across America and when children were expected or required to receive part of their education outside of the home, it was natural that Brethren as parents and as church members should be concerned about the nature of this instruction. Moreover, as the Brethren began to be more economically established in communities, it became evident that not all of the young people were going to settle on the farms of their fathers. The vocation of schoolteaching seemed a natural one for Brethren young people. Thus interest in formal education achieved two purposes at the same time: Brethren were related to the teaching of their own children in the school system, and Brethren found another vocation with economic remuneration.

Institutional education was encouraged by those who were making use of the press which the Brethren had developed. Henry Kurtz, Abraham Cassel, R. H. Miller, S. Z. Sharp, James Quinter, D. L. Miller, and others became more and more vigorous in urging that educational institutions be operated by the Brethren. This interest in higher education soon found its way in a query to the Annual Conference. The Conference answer was: "It is conforming to the world. The Apostle Paul says: 'Knowledge puffeth up, but charity edifieth.' "[14]

This answer was not sufficient to discourage the beginning of schools, however. In 1852 Jacob Miller began a school in Buffalo Mills, Pennsylvania. In 1859 Cedar Grove Seminary was opened in Broadway, Virginia. In 1861 Kishacoquillas Seminary was opened in Mifflin County, Pennsylvania, and in the same year the New Vienna Academy was opened in New Vienna, Ohio. By 1870 these emerging schools began to be called colleges and normal schools. The first of the normal schools to have a continuing life was opened in 1876 and was called the Huntingdon Normal School and Collegiate Institute, Huntingdon, Pennsylvania. It has since become known as Juniata College, one of the outstanding Brethren institutions. Related to almost all of these were secondary schools or academies. The colleges tended to emphasize pedagogy or preparation for teaching; consequently the name "Normal School."

Biblical emphasis was supposed to be kept central both in the academy and in the normal school. The founders of the schools were deeply religious, highly unselfish persons. Often they served without salary or with very little salary, and those who worked with them followed the same commitment. Sometimes not only the founder of the school but his teachers as well lost all of their savings in these enterprises even if the enterprise succeeded in remaining open. Many of the early schools failed within a few years of their founding.

School expenses were kept very low, since it was hoped that all students who might desire to do so would be able to attend, even though their financial ability was minimal. Expenses for one year including tuition, board, and room ranged from $120 to $140. Jobs around the school provided students, in some cases, even with the major part of this amount. Students helped with the food preparation and looked after the buildings and grounds. They likewise were employed in the construction of new buildings as these came into being. The college facilities were minimal and plain; the classrooms were multipurpose. Some teachers were called upon from time to time to teach almost every course which the curriculum offered.

Nearly forty different educational institutions of one kind or another were opened in the years 1852 to 1923. Seven of these have survived as institutions of higher education.

As mentioned above, Juniata College was the first to have a continuing life. In 1879 Ashland College, Ashland, Ohio, was started. (It later went with the division of the church known as the Progressive Brethren. This occurred in 1882.) In 1879 Mount Morris Seminary and Collegiate Institute was founded at Mount Morris, Illinois. It merged with Manchester College in later years. In 1880 the Spring Creek Normal and Spring Creek Collegiate Institute was founded in Virginia and has since become known as Bridgewater College. In 1888 McPherson, Kansas, was begun and has continued under the same name until the present time. In 1891 Lordsburg College in California was founded (now La Verne College); in 1895 Manchester College and Bible School, North Manchester, Indiana (now Manchester College); and in 1900 Elizabethtown College, Elizabethtown, Pennsylvania. In 1905 Bethany Bible School was established at Chicago, Illinois. It has since become Bethany Theological Seminary, Oak Brook, Illinois.

In addition to these educational institutions within the United States the Brethren founded institutions on elementary, secondary, teacher training, and, in some instances, higher educational or theological training levels in other areas of the world in connection with missions. Some of these have grown and have been turned over to the national states. Areas where such educational institutions have been founded are China, Africa, India, and South America.

It was inevitable that concern would arise about what was being taught in these emerging schools. As this concern was felt it followed also that the church would wish to know about the textbooks and curriculum and to have some control over what was taught and who was doing the teaching. If this was to be done some machinery would need to be devised to do it. The whole question of the relationship of the church to these emerging colleges or institutions was discussed through the publications, in special tracts or fliers, on the floor of Conference, and in congregational and district meetings. In 1890 the Standing Committee of the Annual Conference proposed the appointment of three elders for each Brethren school who would live nearby and be charged "to watch over the moral and religious influence of the schools." These elders were to serve for three-year terms.[15]

By 1900 these elders were asked to become general advisers to the schools and to help them with problems which might arise out of their church affiliation. By 1908 it became apparent that this was too loose an organization and that instead of having a separate committee for each college it would be better to have an overall advisory committee for all of the colleges. Consequently, the Annual Conference of 1908 established an Educational Board of seven members to take over the supervision of the educational work of the church. They were to serve for five years each. H. C. Early became the chairman of this educational board and served on it with significant leadership for many years.

It soon became evident that if the board was to coordinate the work of the colleges with any significance or effectiveness, the presidents of the several colleges would also need to be members of the board. This later became the action of Conference. The president of the theological seminary also served on this General Education Board. Questions concerning teachers, textbooks, courses of study, athletics, church government, morals, and religion were to be handled by the board. Its major duties were broader and more significant than this, however. They were defined by the Annual Conference:

(1) To devise ways and means whereby our educational institutions may recruit and educate an adequate lay, ministerial, and missionary leadership for the Church of the Brethren.

(2) To develop and nurture among the churches a higher Christian educational consciousness.

(3) To encourage closer cooperation and harmony of action among our institutions of learning.

(4) To assist all of our institutions of learning in promoting endowment and betterment campaigns so as to bring them up to the highest educational and spiritual efficiency.[16]

This assignment by Conference to the General Education Board brings into focus some problems which were developing in higher education. It indicates also that the church was eager to help with them. One of the problems was an oversupply of colleges for the population of the Church of the Brethren. Were there both an adequate student body and sufficient financial support? Another problem concerned the recruitment of faculties whose members were academically trained and at least a majority of whom were

Brethren or understood "Brethren ways." Another needed emphasis was the academic upgrading of the colleges.

The General Education Board during its existence was able to achieve much for higher education within the church. Prior to the emergence of this board there had been rather rigorous competition among the colleges for the rather scant student supply. Now general agreements were reached concerning the areas from which each college should seek church support and from which it should solicit students. This division covered the entire United States from the Atlantic to the Pacific and from the North to the South. When H. C. Early retired from the board, D. W. Kurtz, president of McPherson College, succeeded him. He also served with vigor and distinction through many years.

J. S. Noffsinger became secretary of the General Education Board in the 1920s. In 1925 he completed a Ph.D. dissertation and published it under the title, *A Program for Higher Education in the Church of the Brethren*. His research presented evidence that there were too many institutions of higher education within the church for the Brethren to support adequately. He compared the Church of the Brethren with other denominations in this respect, and suggested Brethren institutional mergers. About this time, F. D. Dove, also writing a doctoral thesis on a similar topic, said: "Either there must be further consolidation among the Brethren colleges to increase the efficiency and strengthen the support of a few schools advantageously located; or as the natural result of the increasing pressure of competitive standardization, some of them will be of necessity forced to discontinue."[17]

Mergers or some alternative seemed inevitable. Through the years until the 1950s conferences were held by the colleges and with church leaders to see how the work of the colleges could be advanced. Some consolidation did occur. Mount Morris merged with Manchester; Daleville became part of the Bridgewater system; Blue Ridge terminated in 1937, with its patronage divided between Elizabethtown and Bridgewater. The various alumni groups and the college area constituencies were reluctant to see any colleges close, however, and made strenuous efforts to continue each one.

An alternative to institutional collapse was sought. The colleges began to look beyond the church for students and for financial support. When this took place the colleges soon became "regional colleges." The percentage of Brethren students in the colleges began to decrease; church support was no longer the major income base. With this development church supervisory responsibility became less appropriate. Indeed, some of the "Brethren patterns" had to be modified as a major percentage of the student body began to come from non-Brethren backgrounds. As the colleges became accredited in their states and regions and offered teaching certificates, premedical, prelaw, prejudicial, predental, and many other preparations, the possibilities of having the denomination even nominally determine the curriculum diminished.

Without really intending to do so the colleges moved from denominational curricular control into the more general curricular controls exerted by the laws of their several states and by the requirements of professional and accreditation agencies of their regions or of the nation. The colleges were very much aware of these changes. They sought to keep contact with the church so that they could effectively prepare students to serve the needs of the growing and changing denomination. Likewise, they not only welcomed continuing support from the churches of their immediate area, but also hoped for a general financial support from the denomination as a whole such as was common in some other denominations.

When the General Education Board along with the other boards of the church were merged into the General Brotherhood Board (1947), the relationship of the church to its institutions of higher education was allocated to the Christian Education Commission, one of the Board's five commissions. It became a relatively minor responsibility of this commission. Two general higher education meetings were held each year; these included the six college presidents, the president of the seminary, and the secretary of the Christian Education Commission.

The availability of money from the federal government for the construction of buildings and of government loans and scholarship aids for students moved the colleges further away from the absolute necessity of a continuing major denominational support. Token support was given through the General Brotherhood Board and more substantial support continued to come from the churches of each college area. When the budget of the colleges moved from thousands of dollars to hundreds of thousands and then into millions, the percentage of the total support given by the churches became less.

As the Church of the Brethren concludes its two hundred sixtieth year and moves forward into the last third of the twentieth century it can be said that all of the Brethren colleges seem to be growing in enrollment, in academic performance, in the breadth of service they seek to render, and in increased recognition of their importance and status in the total community of higher education.

An additional word should be said with reference to the seminary. This institution, conceived in the minds and hearts of A. C. Wieand and E. B. Hoff, was founded in 1905 in Chicago as Bethany Bible School. Its purpose was to train leadership for the Church of the Brethren in all of its ministries, including Sunday school teaching, the pastoral ministry, mission work, and any other phase of life where Brethren might serve better by having biblical instruction. The seminary had its ups and downs just as the colleges did. It sought for recognition by and support from the church; it achieved this in 1925. In 1963 it moved to a new campus at Oak Brook, Illinois, where it operates in beautiful new buildings located in delightful surroundings. It has moved from a simple Bible school emphasis to broader studies in theology, to its present accredited status as Bethany Theological Seminary. Among seminaries it is highly regarded; the scope of its training is wide; the preparation of its teachers is outstanding. It has generally elicited the favorable support of the church throughout all its years; it has significantly served not only the Brethren but the ecumenical, theological, and worldwide community.

Other Educational Developments

It was stated earlier that Sunday schools came into the life of the church together with the revival of the press, the emergence of printed tracts, the prayer meeting, and the general move toward a system of schools.

When the church assumed some responsibility for the Sunday schools it wished to supervise the literature to be used by them. This responsibility was placed in the hands of the Missionary and Tract Committee. In 1895 the Annual Conference appointed a committee of five to assist the Missionary and Tract Committee in its growing responsibilities. This enlarged committee was asked to obtain statistics and information with respect to the needs of the Sunday school work of the church. They were to supervise the production of literature and to see that it contained sound doctrinal teaching.

In 1911 the Tract Committee was replaced by the Sunday School Board which was comprised of five members. This board was to oversee all literature for the Sunday schools and to help develop training courses for Sunday school teachers. These training courses were to be held in local congregations. They were asked to coordinate with the colleges in seeking to train young people for Sunday school work.

This board later was called the General Sunday School Board. Gradually it sought to coordinate the many educational movements which began during the first third of the twentieth century. Among these were vacation church schools, special work with young people, church leagues, mothers and daughters associations, fathers and sons associations, leadership training groups, Christian workers meetings, and similar organizations. By 1926 there were 1,180 Sunday schools with 2,121 organized classes supporting an enrollment of 131,000. The leadership training schools gave recognized credits and certificates for courses pursued. In 1930 alone, 1,788 credits were recorded by the brotherhood. During that year also 193 vacation church schools were conducted.

In 1924 a General Welfare Board was organized to promote peace, temperance, child rescue work, and similar concerns. (A peace committee had been named as early as 1911.) In 1917 a music committee was appointed to compile church hymnals, arrange singing classes, and provide for the music at Annual Conference. In 1928 these various boards were merged into one board, the Board of Religious Education, which was made responsible for supervising or combining the work which previously had been done by these several committees or boards.

The young people's department of the church presently became known as the Brethren Young People's Department (BYPD). It developed rapidly; in the 1930s a national youth secretary was appointed. The youth department moved enthusiastically into the camping movement. Camps were rented or purchased and outfitted in forested or lakeside areas from one end of the United States to the other. By 1920 there were twenty-six of these camps. Camp sessions ran from five to ten days and had a total attendance of several thousand youth. The camping movement broadened itself until it included not only the youth but young married people and adults. Leadership groups, family camps, intermediates, juniors, and even children's camps came into being. Some of the campsites have grown through the years and have become large institutions including dining halls, dormitories, lakes, campfire areas, swimming pools, libraries, etc. Other camps have continued as open forest areas without many buildings or much institutionalization.

The youth movement with its camps and its weekly meetings, its work camps, and other activities has functioned very significantly as a part of the total educational offering of the Church of the Brethren. Its direct effect upon the youth of the church may have replaced or supplemented the former major role of the colleges in inspiring youth to church vocation.

The Brethren Volunteer Service movement grew from this high interest of the youth and their parents in the work of the church. It has been enthusiastically sponsored and financed by the church since its formal beginning in 1948. Through Brethren Volunteer Service, young men and women have volunteered one, two, or more years of service to the church without remuneration. The church maintains them, trains them for specialized services adapted to a variety of types of volunteer work, and sends them to various parts of America and of the world to render humanitarian service. This became acceptable to the government for conscientious objectors in lieu of military service. The movement reached its highest impetus following World War II, when youth went all over the world in rehabilitation work. Part of the service was the physical clearing up of war rubble, but part of it was the rehabilitation of those damaged by war and the impacts of war.

Brethren Volunteer Service has become one of the most significant educational enterprises conducted by the church. It has paralleled the colleges in the early training of those who later became leaders in the church. Pastors, teachers, headquarters staff workers, and missionaries have received beyond-the-home training through BVS. Brethren Volunteer Service later broadened from a youth movement to include those who were older. The volunteer movement continues and by the end of 1970 had enrolled more than 3,000 persons.

Still another significant educational enterprise of the church is its exchange program. Youth and adults of other countries have been brought to America to spend a year in Brethren colleges or in Brethren homes or both. Some of this has been directly financed by the church, some of it through cooperation of the church and other agencies. There has been a similar sponsoring of Brethren youth and adults abroad. Brethren Colleges Abroad for juniors, first in Germany and then in Germany and France, has been sponsored jointly by the colleges since 1962. These ventures have broadened the outlook and deepened the sensitivities of the church to the needs and thoughts of other peoples. These enterprises continue as parts of the service and educational work of the Church of the Brethren.

Conclusion

The educational movement within the Church of the Brethren as presented in this chapter can be summarized in this manner. It began in the homes of people in Europe; it had its first formal meetings in the home of Alexander Mack where the founders of the church studied their Bibles and sought for enlightenment. It spread through personal teaching and through the writing of pamphlets and tracts.

In Germantown it continued its educational progress within the Brethren community and beyond it. It followed the same techniques: home teaching, preaching, publications. Its educational involvement at that time was wider than a strictly biblical interest; the writings and teachings dealt with the public interests of the day.

Owing to persecution placed upon the Brethren because of their nonviolent beliefs and their unwillingness to participate in war, there was a dispersion of the Brethren community into the valleys and plains of the south and west. Here, in isolation, the educational emphasis had to shift to the home and to the small local congregations. This was an effective education; it kept the church and its core of beliefs alive through nearly a century of pioneer frontier life.

As the frontier communities became better established and public schools emerged, the Brethren once again became involved in more formal outside-of-the-home education. By developing schools they sought to train their own leaders and their youth for schoolteaching and other professions. More colleges came into being than the church could sustain; a seminary developed. The necessity of accreditation and financial support as well as the entrance of many non-Brethren students have caused the colleges to become less denominationally centered. The seminary likewise has become deeply involved in the general theological community. These institutions are serving the church well, but they also serve in many ways beyond their own denomination.

The Sunday school, adult education, youth movements, Brethren Volunteer Service, and the student exchange have been other educational developments within the church to nurture its own membership, to train its leaders, and to involve its people in serving other peoples of the world.

The desire of the church to educate its youth has sustained an educational emphasis within the church which has adapted itself to the cultural changes of two and a half centuries but has remained constant in its commitment and intent. The prospect is that the educational endeavors of the church will continue this adaptation and growth.

1. John S. Flory, "A History of Education in the Church of the Brethren," in W. A. Cable and H. F. Sanger, eds., *Educational Blue Book and Directory of the Church of the Brethren, 1708-1923* (Elgin, Ill.: General Educational Board, Church of the Brethren, [1923]), 23.
2. Donald F. Durnbaugh, ed., *European Origins of the Brethren* (Elgin, Ill.: Brethren Press, 1958), chaps. 1-3.
3. Frederick D. Dove, *Cultural Changes in the Church of the Brethren* (Elgin, Ill.: Brethren Publishing House, 1932), 51.
4. John S. Flory, *Literary Activity of the Brethren in the Eighteenth Century* (Elgin, Ill.: Brethren Publishing House, 1908), 11; Durnbaugh, *European Origins*, 321-405.
5. Quoted in I. D. Rupp, *History of All the Religious Denominations in the U.S.* (Harrisburg, Pa.: 1844), 94.
6. Flory, *Literary Activity*, 37-67.
7. Martin G. Brumbaugh, *A History of the German Baptist Brethren in Europe and America* (Elgin, Ill.: Brethren Publishing House, 1899), 433.
8. *Ibid.*, 433-434.
9. Dove, *Cultural Changes*, 69.
10. *Ibid.*, 177.
11. Flory, *Literary Activity*, iv-v; Dove, *Cultural Changes*, 178.
12. Quoted in Dove, *Cultural Changes*, 77.
13. *Ibid.*
14. *Ibid.*, 177-178.
15. *Ibid.*, 182.
16. *Ibid.*, 105.
17. *Ibid.*, 185, 176.

7

SOCIAL INVOLVEMENT

Roger E. Sappington

The attitude toward social involvement in the Church of the Brethren has changed significantly during the first two thirds of the twentieth century. In order to understand this change, certain developments in the previous history of the church need to be reviewed briefly. From the very beginning of the church in 1708, its members were frequently on the defensive in their relationship to other segments of the society, especially the state, because of the opposition of the Brethren to some of the things which the state considered important. Also, since most citizens accepted and supported the laws of the state, the Brethren found themselves in opposition to the large majority of society.

As a result of this attitude of the Brethren toward society in general and toward the state in particular, the Brethren tended to withdraw and to become an ingroup. They took care of each other, and in the nineteenth century they believed that it was wrong to allow a Brethren to be sent to the state-supported poorhouse. Even earlier, the eighteenth-century Germantown congregation had collected offerings from its members to help meet the needs of its poorer members.

Because of the Brethren refusal to participate in military service during the American War of Independence, they were persecuted in various ways. As a consequence, many of them migrated from Pennsylvania to the south and the west, and they also withdrew as much as possible from participation in the normal activities of the state and of society. In a sense they developed an unwritten agreement by which they were to be left alone and they would leave others alone.

The Brethren Attitude Toward Prohibition

The Annual Conferences of the church spoke out on many occasions during the nineteenth century forbidding the Brethren to engage in any way in the traffic in alcoholic beverages. They were not to distill, sell, or drink such beverages. The policy seemed to be based on the idea that the church was responsible for its own members, for the Annual Conferences also refused to sanction any kind of cooperation with the organized temperance movement which developed in the years after the Civil War. In 1900 Annual Conference reaffirmed an earlier refusal "to petition the General Government to enact a law to prevent the manufacturing of ardent spirits, and to prevent the importation of the same into the United States."[1] As late as 1913 in response to a request to allow the Women's Christian Temperance Union to hold meetings in a Brethren church, Annual Conference warned the Brethren to "be very careful in our association with outside organizations, and the opening of our houses of worship for their use."[2] However, the church was willing to sponsor its own temperance movement, and in 1907 a Temperance Committee was established to disseminate information and to assist the local congregations.

From these actions which followed the Brethren policy of separation from society, the Brethren policy with regard to the prohibition movement (suppression by the government of the sale of liquors) made a dramatic change in the second half of the decade of the 1910s. The primary reason for the change seems to have been the election of Martin G. Brumbaugh, a prominent Brethren minister who had served as professor of pedagogy in the University of Pennsylvania, commissioner of education in Puerto Rico, and school superintendent of Philadelphia, as governor of Pennsylvania in 1915. Governor Brumbaugh supported many kinds of social legislation including a local option law "as a stepping-stone to the speedy elimination of the legalized traffic in intoxicating liquors from our nation." Annual Conference of 1915 commended him and his administration "for the high ground he has taken on all moral issues," including his policies on prohibition.[3]

The Brethren now moved in the direction of supporting the nationwide prohibition movement. For example, in 1917 Annual Conference adopted a resolution directly petitioning the government to take immediate steps "to prevent the use of all food products in the manufacture of intoxicants and also to prohibit the sale of such intoxicants during the existence of this crisis." Such restrictive action was taken by the government in response to widespread public pressure. Then in 1918 the Brethren pledged their "hearty support to the passage of the amendment to the Constitution for nationwide prohibition," and again this amendment was ratified and became the Eighteenth Amendment to the Constitution.[4]

Thus, through a series of steps in the years before 1920, the Brethren had taken a much more active role in society as manifested by their interest in prohibition. They were making the transition from a very narrow sectarian concern for the members of their own group to a broad concern for all of society. Furthermore, this concern led them to accept a policy of seeking needed social action by legislative means.

The Brethren and the State

Like the Brethren policy with regard to temperance, the Brethren policy regarding the state during the nineteenth century was based on the concept that they were to remain a separate community and to take care of all of their own needs. For example, the Brethren were forbidden to go to court, even to collect debts. Furthermore, they were not to participate in elections or to hold political office.

Although some of these policies had been liberalized in the late nineteenth century, as late as 1912 Annual Conference accepted the idea that the Christian was a pilgrim on this earth since his citizenship was in heaven. On this basis the Brethren were urged "not to allow themselves to become entangled in politics, nor even interested in a way that would lessen their zeal for the salvation of souls, or in a way that might militate against their usefulness in the church." They were advised neither to "vote nor accept an office of any kind unless they are convinced that by so doing they can more completely fill their mission in the world relative to themselves, to their fellowmen and to God." Finally, the Brethren were encouraged not to accept any office, "the performance of the duties of which would require the use of physical force or which might compromise in any way, the nonresistant principles of the Gospel of Christ."[5]

Such a conservative policy regarding the Christian's responsibilities to the state could not last for long in a day of rapid change, but it was 1918 before Annual Conference modified its policy. Conference reaffirmed its historic position on nonresistance and refused to "permit the holding of offices by the members, when such offices compel them to violate these nonresistant principles." Conference was ready to recognize, however, "that in a democracy, it is not wrong for Brethren to serve their communities and municipalities to promote efficiency and honesty in social and civic life, when the nonresistant principles and the New Testament doctrine on oaths are not violated."[6] This interpretation evidently settled the problem of Brethren participation in politics by voting and holding office, for there seems to be no further discussion of the matter on the floor of Annual Conference. Once again, it is clear that this policy had evolved from a very strict stand of forbidding or discouraging such participation to a very moderate position with few limitations or restrictions.

The frequently expressed Brethren pacifism which marked them as one of the historic peace churches was severely tested by the events of World War I from 1914 to 1918. Brethren pacifism had not been emphasized for fifty years since the end of the Civil War in 1865, and during that time the Brethren had been primarily interested in evangelism and expansion. The coming into the church of thousands of new converts had brought ideas which ran counter to the traditional Brethren separatism; one evidence was the change of the name in 1908 from German Baptist Brethren to Church of the Brethren because there were so many non-Germans in the church. One of the traditional tenets of the church which suffered accordingly was pacifism.

One result of the syncretism that had been taking place was that even the leadership of the church was confused about the proper policy for the church to follow in reaction to the American entry into the war in 1917 and the ensuing drafting of American men as soldiers. For example, Otho Winger, the conservative president of a Brethren college, Manchester College in Indiana, recognized that the Brethren had taken such an active interest in politics in recent years that there would be no "shadow of excuse or reason to be relieved" from violating church principles by entering military training camps.

Also, D. M. Garver, who was moderator of Annual Conference on three different occasions, believed that "our Brethren should accept when drafted, some noncombatant service." He believed that this was the only policy on which the Brethren could unite.[7]

On the other hand, the only official statement which the church issued during the war was the result of a specially called Annual Conference in January 1918: "We further urge our brethren not to enlist in any service which would, in any way, compromise our time-honored position in relation to war; also [we urge] that they refrain from wearing the military uniform." This statement was based on the fact that "the tenets of the church forbid military drilling, or learning the art or arts of war," or of participating in any kind of act which might lead to the destruction of human life.[8] Since the drafting of men had begun during the previous September, those Brethren who had refused to participate "in the acts of war" were commended by the Conference. Most of those Brethren who had refused to cooperate with the army had been imprisoned, although the treatment varied from camp to camp.

That the Brethren had waited until January 1918 to formulate their policy and that not all of the Brethren accepted that policy were evidence of the Brethren uncertainty; the Brethren confusion, however, was also matched by the confusion of the United States government about how to deal with pacifists. The Selective Service Act of 1917 granted exemption from military service to conscientious objectors, but it did not spell out the nature of this exemption. Consequently, when the first Brethren arrived in the military camps in September 1917, the commanders had no idea what to do with these pacifists. The government procrastinated in reaching a policy. In February 1918, President Wilson wrote in reaction to the statement which the Brethren had adopted in January that Congress was considering a recommendation from the Secretary of War to furlough all conscientious objectors to civilian occupations including farming and that the Secretary of War was "endeavoring to broaden the list of noncombatant occupations directly associated with the activities of the Army."[9] Both of these measures eventually provided some clarification of the issues, but the fact that it took the government about a year from the original enactment of the law to clarify its meaning with regard to the Brethren certainly contributed to the difficult situation in which the Brethren found themselves.

The final evidence of the government's uncertainty and procrastination with regard to the Brethren was the decision of the Judge Advocate General's office of the War Department to prosecute the Brethren under the provisions of the Espionage Act of July 15, 1917, and amended May 16, 1918. Evidently, the government believed that the statement issued by the special Annual Conference of January 1918 involved "treasonable intent of obstructing the operation" of the Selective Service Act by urging young Brethren not to cooperate. The case was dropped when the Brethren agreed to withdraw the statement from circulation.[10] In its urgent desire to wipe out German sympathizers in the United States, the government had also considered the prosecution of an innocent religious minority with long-standing views against participation in military service.

The threat of prosecution by the government knocked the props out from under the official policy of the church on military service. For the remainder of the war the drafted young men continued to make up their own minds concerning the type of service which they would accept; the majority went into the armed forces, although there were always some who refused to wear the uniform or to cooperate in any way with the military officials. In this way, the Brethren had changed, for the consistent refusal of the Brethren during earlier American wars to participate as soldiers had ended; they were no longer separatists, but people who wished to cooperate with their government.

By 1940 when the government again enacted a Selective Service law in preparation for World War II, both the government and the Brethren were able to profit from their earlier experience. Along with the Friends and the Mennonites the Brethren lobbied in Washington to try to prevent the enactment of any peacetime military conscription law and, if that proved unsuccessful, to secure the most favorable provisions. The evidence indicates that the pressure did result in the inclusion in the final act of a provision exempting conscientious objectors from any type of military service and establishing for them a program of civilian service as an alternative. M. R. Zigler, one of the Brethren group in Washington, spoke of "the tremendous change they were willing to grant." Certainly, the law in its final form was quite different from what it would have been if the Brethren, the Friends, and the Mennonites had not labored diligently to secure provisions more tolerant of the conscientious objector's position.

Not only was the government willing to allow the organization of a civilian program of alternative service, it also demanded that the churches take full responsibility for operating and financing such a program. M. R. Zigler, who was scheduled to take charge of the program for the Brethren, confessed that he was concerned about the church's ability to bear such great burdens. The government was willing to cooperate, however, to the extent of providing abandoned Civilian Conservation Corps camps,[11] tools and equipment, and supervisory personnel to enable the conscientious objectors to engage in nationally important programs of soil conservation and forest management. The churches were to provide for the maintenance and other needs of the young men as well as the general supervision and organization of the camps.

The result of this accommodation between the government and the churches including the Brethren was the establishment of the Civilian Public Service camps. The first Brethren camp, located at Lagro, Indiana, received its first draftees in May of 1941. During World War II the Brethren established a number of such camps to take care of the needs of those conscientious objectors who rejected all forms of military service. This unique program was administered by the Brethren Service Committee (BSC), later called the Brethren Service Commission. It had first been organized in 1939 and was officially approved by the Annual Conference of 1941.

In addition to the soil conservation and forestry camps, a number of other opportunities were provided for conscientious objectors to engage in civilian work of national importance. There was extensive interest among these men in serving overseas in relief and reconstruction projects, but the government never granted permission for such work. The Brethren were successful in sending a team which had prepared for overseas work to Puerto Rico, where they established a hospital and rendered a significant service in a depressed area on the island. Also, a number of detached service projects became available, and quite a number of men worked as attendants in mental hospitals. One of the more unusual projects in which these men participated was an experiment in human starvation at the University of Minnesota. The detached service projects were valuable to the church, because the men believed that they were really participating in a vital program, and this type of project also removed some of the financial pressure by being largely self-supporting. The Brethren spent nearly two million dollars on the total CPS program, two thirds of which was supplied by the church itself and the remainder by individuals or groups receiving services from Brethren Civilian Public Service.

The Civilian Public Service plan which the historic peace churches developed for their pacifists during World War II was certainly an improvement over the confusion and uncertainty of the period of World War I, but the Brethren in particular were resolved to make some improvements if the opportunity ever developed again. The Selective Service Act expired in 1947, but the advent of the Cold War led to the reestablishment of the draft in 1948. Conscientious objectors were exempted because of the limited number of men to be drafted. Brethren young people were disturbed by being exempted when others were being drafted and consequently exerted sufficient pressure on the Annual Conference of 1948 to secure the establishment of the Brethren Volunteer Service program for young men and women. A wide variety of projects was opened to these young people, including service in migrant camps, in inner-city areas, in homes for the elderly, in the processing of relief supplies for use around the world, and in various overseas areas in relief and rehabilitation. The program has completed its first twenty years and has rendered an immense amount of good both to those participating and to those being served. Some of its features were copied in the Peace Corps established by the United States government.

When the conscription laws were extended in 1951 to include conscientious objectors in reaction to the beginning of the Korean War the previous year, the church secured the approval of the government to open the Brethren Volunteer Service program to draftees. In addition, many nonchurch projects were made available to these men. During the first year of operation which ended in June 1953 the church had placed one hundred and sixty men in its own worldwide program and also had helped to place seventy-four Brethren men in other projects. This program seemed to have the advantage of greater flexibility than the program developed by the church during World War II. It has been continued by the Brethren in the 1960s to meet the needs of the relatively small fraction of Brethren young men who choose not to enter the military service. Certainly, for every Brethren young man who has served as a conscientious objector since 1940, at least three others have become a part of the military service. The evidence indicates that the separatism and distrust of the state which characterized the early Brethren have been abandoned by their descendants in the twentieth century.

Brethren Interest in Worldwide Relief

One of the most dramatic results of World War I for the Brethren was a newfound interest in providing for the relief of war sufferers regardless of who they were, where they came from, or what they believed. In other words, the postwar years saw a further development of a sincere concern for suffering people outside of the fellowship of the Brethren. In 1917 the attention of Annual Conference was directed toward the needs of the Armenians, and Conference approved the taking of collections in the local congregations "for the relief of these unfortunate sufferers."[12] These people had a special appeal because they were Christians suffering at the hands of non-Christians. Early Brethren missionary interest had been directed to that area.

The Brethren had great difficulty establishing a satisfactory organizational framework to maintain a program of overseas relief. Also, much time was consumed trying to determine where to carry on a project and with which other groups to cooperate, if any. Finally, early in 1919 under the leadership of J. E. Miller the Brethren decided to attempt to raise two hundred fifty thousand dollars for Armenian relief, since "our people give liberally to those people." Miller made an inspection trip in the spring of 1919 under the sponsorship of the American Committee for Relief in the Near East and returned convinced that the Brethren could perform a valuable service on a temporary basis. "We can do a wonderful work in a humanitarian way here. It would be doing what no other organization has attempted to do." The proposed project included the support of orphanages and schools, and the reconstruction of vineyards, gardens, buildings, and homes.

The members of the church responded enthusiastically to the challenge of this type of relief work. One of the reasons why the Brethren were eager to take on such a large project was that they had been heavily criticized for failing to do their duty in war work. As a result the Brethren were able to exceed their goal, and by the end of the campaign in 1921 they had contributed a total of $267,265.48 to Armenian and Syrian relief. Indeed, this was a substantial sum for a church that had never tried anything like this before. Also, the experience undoubtedly broadened the horizons of the Brethren. J. E. Miller typified this new attitude when he wrote that he now realized "as never before" the wide responsibility resting upon the church. Consequently, as he put it, the church needed to "recognize the work that others are doing and we have failed to do," both in church and national affairs.

Although the newfound Brethren interest in relief programs for war sufferers became a casualty of the general American return to "normalcy" in the 1920s, the crises of the 1930s again provided a challenge for any group interested in this type of activity. Also, the Brethren had given up some of the exclusiveness which had been manifested in their refusal to cooperate with the Friends in relief efforts during and after World War I; during the

1920s and the 1930s the two groups worked together in numerous programs to create a peaceful world. When the swords began to rattle again in Europe in the 1930s these groups redoubled their efforts to keep the United States at peace and also took steps to provide relief for the victims of the Spanish Civil War. During the first six months of 1937 the Brethren policy of cooperating with the Friends and the Mennonites, of sending Brethren relief workers to Spain, where they would work on both sides of the battle lines, and of providing the financing and the material to support such a program was developed and adopted.

The Spanish relief project proved to be a very valuable experience for the three cooperating churches, for it prepared them for the close cooperation which was needed during World War II in the establishment of the Civilian Public Service program. In addition, of course, the three churches rendered a valuable service to the victims of the bitter and bloody civil war in Spain. Dan West, who was a member of the church's national staff and who served as the church's first relief worker in Spain, reported after a visit in Washington in the fall of 1938 that the American Red Cross secretary was very delighted "at our cooperative work with the Spanish children," that the State Department officials "spoke in appreciative terms of our work in Spain," and that the Spanish ambassador insisted "that the work of our committee in Spain is the only piece of Christian action that has happened over there." Evidently, the work was very valuable for the Church of the Brethren, too, in creating good public relations with the society in which it lived and also in giving it confidence that it could do a good job in such projects.

At almost the same time that the Brethren were sending their first relief worker to Spain in September 1937, war broke out again in China between the Japanese and the Chinese. The Brethren had had missionaries in China continuously for nearly thirty years and were vitally interested in events there. Widespread agreement prevailed in the church that the Brethren ought to engage in the relief of war sufferers in China, and almost immediately plans were made to raise funds and to assign personnel for this task. Members of the mission staff who were already on the field and knew the language were used in this capacity. As the program developed in China the Brethren found opportunity to cooperate with the Friends and the Mennonites, who also had projects in the Far East, and with the Church Committee for China Relief, which represented all of the Protestant churches interested in China. Thus, the Brethren interest in cooperative action was being strengthened.

After World War II the Brethren had an opportunity to develop in China one of the most unusual of all of the many relief projects which the Brethren Service Committee maintained around the world. In cooperation with the United Nations Relief and Rehabilitation Administration (UNRRA) the Brethren sent fifty young men as tractor operators and mechanics to China to teach the Chinese how to operate American tractors provided by UNRRA and thus to replace the large number of draft animals which had been destroyed by the war. The idea originated in the mind of K. S. Sie, formerly dean of the College of Agriculture and Forestry of the University of Nanking and later the Chinese government representative on UNRRA.

The Brethren responded to Sie's idea with interest, and the lengthy negotiations among the Brethren, the Chinese government, and UNRRA began. Sie secured the final approval of his government by a trip to China in April 1946, and the Brethren began to recruit the fifty men that month. The statement announcing the project proposed that this project might be "the beginning of an undertaking which may well be a step forward in solving the famine problem which has menaced the Chinese for generations." The fifty men were readily secured, and after training in the United States they traveled to China in four groups between September 1946, and February 1947.

This project gave the Brethren an opportunity to emphasize their policy of rendering service to anyone in need regardless of political affiliation, race, creed, or national origin. Leland Brubaker, the staff member in charge of the project, emphasized that this policy had become "traditional with the Brethren Service Committee in their relief operations throughout the world." Furthermore, he indicated that the Brethren would withdraw either the whole unit or individual personnel, if any or all were "utilized in a political or controversial situation for the advantage of any one group against another" in the war between the Nationalists and the Communists. W. J. Green, the UNRRA official to whom Brubaker was writing, indicated that this policy of neutrality "fits in entirely with UNRRA's principles and policies," and he assured Brubaker that the unit would not be used in any political or controversial situation.

From the beginning to the end of the UNRRA-Brethren Service Unit in China, the UNRRA officials in China expressed their great appreciation of the men themselves and of the significant work they were doing. W. J. Green concluded that "the standard of work of the men is fine, their personality and purpose make them popular with all, and their behaviour, both individually and as a unit, is beyond reproach." Also, Harlan Cleveland, the director of UNRRA in China, seconded this impression of the men and recognized the significance of what they were doing by pointing out that 50 men and 1,136 tractors in one year had "succeeded in putting about 400,000 *mou* [six *mou* to the acre] of land under cultivation and training 1,000 Chinese." He was keenly aware of "the lasting benefits which hundreds of thousands of Chinese will enjoy for years into the future because of the painstaking and selfless efforts of a small group of men who traveled thousands of miles to an area of immeasurable need to bear witness to their conviction that all men are brothers."

A related Brethren project in China which also drew high praise from UNRRA was the sending of heifers. The Heifer Project was an idea of Dan West, who emerged from his Spanish Civil War relief experience believing that it would be easier and more practical to send cows than milk. The church supported his idea and thousands of cattle were (and continue to be) sent around the world. When he learned of the proposed donation of heifers by the Brethren to China, F. H. LaGuardia, director general of UNRRA, wrote that "this will be the first boat of cattle to go to China, and is one of the most important gifts that UNRRA has received." He recalled the thousands of

Brethren cattle in Czechoslovakia, Greece, Italy, and Poland which were helping farmers "feed the populations — rural and urban — of these countries which lost 50% of their livestock in the war." LaGuardia concluded that "the fine spirit of practical Christianity and the faith that your group has shown, are examples to us all in these days when, without faith, we can not progress." He knew that the Heifer Project had begun modestly, but now its spirit and work had spread around the world. "Transcending barriers of nationality and religious convictions, it has drawn to itself members of many denominations, and illustrated what can be accomplished when conviction and efficient enterprise and fine Christian generosity are combined."

As LaGuardia indicated, the Brethren were very much interested in conducting relief activities of various kinds in the European countries which had been ravaged by the war. In fact, the Brethren maintained projects in almost all of the war-torn countries which were not behind the Iron Curtain; even there, the Brethren had personnel in Poland until August 1949, when they were expelled. As the Brethren consolidated their efforts, the two countries in which they concentrated their work were Germany and Austria. These were also the two most difficult countries for volunteer relief agencies like the Brethren Service Commission to enter in the period immediately after the war, because the allied military authorities did not want such groups on the scene.

Finally, in February 1946, the constant pressure of the church agencies together with the realization by the military of the tremendous size of the job forced open the door to Germany. The Brethren got in on the ground floor as a member of the Council for Relief Agencies Licensed to Operate in Germany (CRALOG), which served as the coordinating agency for all church relief work in Germany. Most of the available relief supplies were used to help the refugees, who were entering the American zones from East Germany at the rate of ten thousand per day, to survive, since most of them were being turned away from the cities in West Germany without food.

Although the Brethren recognized the need for immediate material aid relief in Germany, they were also eager to develop some type of permanent rehabilitation project in Germany, as had been done in most of the other European countries where the Brethren had placed workers. The initial efforts were frustrated by the military authorities, but during 1947 the Brethren were able to assist the Evangelical Church in establishing a project near Bremen for the retraining of war cripples and expellees. This project was succcessful in teaching such trades as sewing, shoe repair, carpentry, weaving, and the making of artificial limbs, as well as dealing with the spiritual and educational needs of these people. In cooperation with the YMCA, with which the Brethren had worked during the war in a prisoner-of-war project in England, the Brethren provided limited personnel and material for the rehabilitation of a group of endangered youth at the castle of Kaltenstein near Stuttgart. Vocational, educational, recreational, and religious guidance was provided in this project.

The first of the many BSC-sponsored international work camps was held in 1948. These camps brought together young people, primarily students, from as many as ten or twelve different nations to engage in physical reconstruction projects on behalf of refugees and other needy persons.

One of the most dramatic of the Brethren projects occurred in the fall of 1949, when the Brethren made it possible for nearly one hundred German high school youth to spend a year studying in America. The American military government provided the funds and was delighted to have the Brethren provide the administration and the homes in America in which the students lived. This new program was widely acclaimed in both Brethren and non-Brethren cricles both in America and Europe for its value in overcoming international hatreds and differences. The Brethren themselves were impressed by the support of the military and governmental authorities in Germany who evidently had become convinced that Brethren Service was in Germany with purely service motives. In 1950 nearly two hundred German students were placed. This very successful program later became permanent as the interdenominational International Christian Youth Exchange.

Another aspect of the emerging program of Brethren Service in Germany was the utilization of participants in the new Brethren Volunteer Service program as members of the Brethren staff in Europe. Plans were developed to use a group of these volunteers in a project in the vicinity of Kassel, a city which had been seventy-five percent destroyed by American bombing raids during the war and was in desperate need of material aid relief and work among the thousands of refugees in the area. The first six volunteers arrived in the fall of 1949; among their first projects were assisting a group of refugees to complete an orthopedic clinic which included working on a children's ward for the clinic as well as recreational and social activities for the patients, and rebuilding a youth camp near the city. The program grew as additional volunteers arrived, and by May 1950 it was reported that "in a great number of areas in HICOG offices and among a wide circle of German people, Volunteer Service is not only recognized but is actually being requested." M. R. Zigler, who was now the director of Brethren Service in Europe, believed that "the volunteer movement is proving highly successful and is taking on a permanent nature that ought to be considered a program that will last through the centuries." Indeed, Brethren Volunteer Service has continued to render a significant service in Europe in the years since 1949.

The Brethren relief program in neighboring Austria came to include three different projects: cooperation in the distribution of material aid with the Reconstruction Committee of the Protestant Churches of Austria, an agricultural rehabilitation program, and material assistance and aid in resettlement of the *Volksdeutsche* refugees. The Brethren provided considerable assistance in material as well as personnel to the local relief committee. The leaders of the Augsburg and Helvetic Synods, which represented ninety-five percent of the Protestants of Austria, were most grateful for the work performed by the Brethren. They were especially appreciative because, as two spokesmen said, "your help so far has not only alleviated great need in many thousands of cases, but has also given us the feeling of brotherly unity. Your assistance has given us the courage to maintain our faith and our stand in this outpost of the Protestant Church."

To assist in the agricultural rehabilitation of Austria, the Brethren Service Commission helped to provide bulls for an artificial insemination program, which was part of the Heifer Project program. Also, BSC gave new life to the poultry industry in Austria by shipping twelve hundred baby chicks to that country in the spring of 1947. These chicks were very carefully distributed to selected poultry breeders. Both of these projects were apparently carried through with considerable success. Heifers for refugees were distributed beginning in 1955.

Eventually, the entire Brethren program in Austria was concentrated on meeting the needs of the displaced persons and refugees, who often had no place to go and no one to help them. The Brethren were especially interested in the *Volksdeutsche* refugees who were not eligible for assistance from UNRRA or its successor, the International Refugee Organization, because they were German in origin and hence not "allied" displaced persons. Also, the Ecumenical Refugee Commission of the World Council and the American interdenominational agency, Church World Service, were primarily interested in the "allied" displaced persons. The result was that no American agency except the Brethren Service Commission at first took any interest in the *Volksdeutsche*.

The Displaced Persons Act, enacted by the United States Government in 1948, did not apply to the *Volksdeutsche*. However, the Brethren cooperated with the government by providing the necessary papers for more than one thousand displaced persons to resettle in the United States. Then, when the Act was amended in 1950 to include the ethnic German, the Brethren were able to provide the papers for one hundred fifteen of these families to resettle in the United States before the available visas for this group were exhausted. In the years prior to 1950 the Brethren had developed a program of relief and rehabilitation for the *Volksdeutsche*, located in the Austrian city of Linz. The program included a youth vocational training project, material aid distribution, English courses, and a hospital and public health center. Perhaps the outstanding contribution was assistance given to the Austrian government in establishing a sanitarium for tubercular refugees at Thalham near St. Georgen. In these ways, the Brethren had done all that they could to help the *Volksdeutsche* to improve their condition both in Europe and in the United States. A later project which drew attention was the permanent work camp (established in cooperation with the Mennonites) which reconstructed the well-known Protestant school in Vienna *(Karlsschule)*.

A final European relief project which is worth some attention was developed by the World Council of Churches under Brethren leadership in Greece. The fighting during and after World War II had devastated much of northern Greece, and the World Council was eager to help because the Greek Orthodox Church was a member of the Council. However, it was very difficult to gain permission to send a Protestant relief team into Greece, because of the sensitivities of the Greek Church. Because of their growing reputation for nonpartisan service, the Brethren were asked to explore the possibilities of work in Greece, and M. R. Zigler was sent to Greece by the World Council in November 1949. Probably, Zigler did not expect to receive an invitation to send a team into Greece, for no other Protestant had received one previously, but to his surprise the archbishop dispatched the request for assistance on the day after Zigler left.

Now the pressure was placed on the Brethren Service Commission and the World Council to respond to this invitation. After some difficult negotiations in Geneva and in America which covered most of the next twelve months, the leader of the Brethren relief team arrived in northern Greece in the area around Ioannina in the fall of 1950. Although some emergency relief supplies were provided, the emphasis was placed on long-range agricultural rehabilitation. In addition to the distribution of chickens, livestock, tools, and other equipment, the introduction of hybrid seed corn increased the corn yield tremendously.

This World Council project in Greece which the Brethren sponsored and promoted received universally favorable acclaim. Perhaps the highest praise came from the Greek archbishop who wrote that "the work performed by these fine young people . . . is extremely valuable and effective and will render much good in the near future towards the education of the villagers through methods taught by your groups." Moreover, he was "exceedingly grateful for these great accomplishments which show a spirit of Christian solidarity of a more stable and concrete nature," and he was "highly satisfied at the cooperation and proof of brotherly love shown by the church through the setting up of such programs for the public benefit."

During the decades of the 1950s and the 1960s the Brethren continued to be alert to the needs of suffering people around the world, whether their suffering was caused by war or by natural disaster. In 1966, 25 years after the organization of the Brethren Service Commission, there were 432 persons working in 15 countries overseas and in 21 of the United States. The scope of the program has been reduced, and the work has tended to be done even more fully through ecumenical agencies. An example is the organization of the International Voluntary Services Agency (IVS) with personnel in the Near East and Asia. The emphasis seems to have been on meeting immediate needs through the distribution of material aid.

Social Action in the United States

Several projects among the many which the Brethren developed in the United States ought to be included in this discussion. The young people who became a part of the Brethren Volunteer Service program beginning in 1948 were especially eager to engage in social service projects, and the church found ways to utilize their interests. One of the projects which were opened to these young people was located at Falfurrias, Texas, where the Brethren had developed an interest in the needs of the Mexican-Americans along the border as early as 1918. John Stump, a Brethren minister who had moved from Indiana to Texas and had become prosperous in the cattle business, provided the funds to establish a farm and school for training Mexican children. The project had languished and finally was taken over by the Brethren Service Committee in the 1940s. The program at Falfurrias was admirably suited for the needs of volunteer service and a sizable percentage of the volunteers during the first twenty years was assigned to Falfurrias.

They strengthened the religious and community program with the Mexican-Americans, carried on a large-scale construction and rehabilitation program, and enabled the farm gradually to be placed in full cultivation.

Meeting the religious and social needs of the multitudes of migrant workers who roamed the Atlantic seaboard area from Florida to Delaware was also a natural field for a Brethren Volunteer Service project. Myron Miller, the peace activities director in the Southeastern Region of the church, saw the possibilities and led in the establishment of a year-round program at Pahokee, Florida. The program concentrated on maintaining day nurseries which took care of the children while the parents worked in the fields. The work in the migrant camps proved to be meeting a very definite need and was continued.

The Brethren have had a long-standing interest in the welfare of the Negro American. Prior to the Civil War, slave owners were not admitted to membership in the church and the Annual Conference minutes include numerous references to the Brethren refusal to have anything to do with human slavery. At the same time it proved to be very difficult for the Negroes to fit into the Brethren cultural pattern of separatism, and very few Negroes have become members of the church. In the nineteenth century there were occasional Negro congregations begun. During the first two decades of the twentieth century, the Brethren established two projects among the Negroes in Arkansas and in Colorado, but both of these were relatively short-lived. They seemed to have been based largely on evangelizing the Negro rather than an attempt to meet his social and physical needs. Later, in the 1940s there was a new wave of interest in integrating local congregations and in establishing special projects among Negroes in areas of the South where there were no Brethren congregations, but neither of these interests was actually implemented on any significant scale. Participants in Brethren Volunteer Service were used in a few interracial and Negro projects, but even that aspect of work with the Negroes did not develop as expected. The most successful of the projects using volunteers were located in the cities of Baltimore and Washington. Although some individual Brethren have engaged in significant interracial projects, it has generally been quite difficult for the church to develop any vital projects of this type.

In contrast to the Brethren difficulty in working with the Negro American, the Brethren developed a helpful project during World War II to assist the Japanese Americans who were evicted from their homes on the Pacific coast by the United States government. Ralph Smeltzer, a young Brethren graduate student, began working in 1942 with the American Friends Service Committee in a relocation center in California. Under his leadership the Brethren became involved in establishing hostels in Chicago and in New York City which assisted about 1,500 Japanese Americans in resettling in those areas.

Conclusion

The most obvious conclusion is the phenomenal change in the social outlook of the Brethren during the twentieth century. From a group of people with the characteristics of a sect the Brethren grew and developed in their social involvement until they accepted many of the same patterns and ways as other Protestant denominations. They have accepted the idea that they have a responsibility for people outside of their church without regard for race, nationality, or creed.

One of the outstanding prophets produced by the Church of the Brethren, Dan West, recognized in 1947 that "in the last third of a century we have moved so far and so fast that were my own father to return he would not likely recognize the same church to which he belonged." He quoted one observer outside of the Church of the Brethren who had stated that the Brethren were moving "faster than any other church in America." Most of these changes, West believed, had demonstrated the "genius of the Brethren in action." To support his contention, he cited such developments as the Brethren support of the American Friends Service Committee in Spanish Civil War relief, when the Brethren had been "the only group with workers on both sides, most of the time," the Heifer Project in which Catholic and Lutheran workers cooperated, the UNRRA program which was modified by Brethren ideas and cooperation, and Church World Service, which "might not have happened without the Brethren." Certainly, West was correct that the changes in the attitude toward social involvement that had taken place in the Church of the Brethren had made a significant impact on other Christian churches and on society as a whole.

---

1. *Minutes of the Annual Meetings, 1778-1909* (Elgin, Ill.: Brethren Publishing House, 1909), Article 5, 1900, 719.

2. *Minutes of the Annual Meeting*, Article 8, 1913, 5.

3. *Ibid.*, Resolutions, 1915, 29-30.

4. *Minutes of the Annual Conference* (Elgin, Ill.: Brethren Publishing House, 1918), Resolutions, 1917, 16; Resolutions, 1918, 10.

5. *Minutes of the Annual Meeting*, Article 3, Unfinished Business (1912), 3.

6. *Minutes of the Annual Conference* (1918), Article 13, 5.

7. Documentation for these and following MS quotations are to be found in Roger E. Sappington, "The Development of Social Polity in the Church of the Brethren: 1908-1958" (Ph.D. dissertation, Duke University, 1959), published in shortened form as *Brethren Social Policy: 1908-1958* (Elgin, Ill.: Brethren Press, 1961).

8. *Minutes of the Special General Conference, 1918* (Elgin, Ill.: Brethren Publishing House, 1918), p. 6.

9. Quoted in Rufus D. Bowman, *The Church of the Brethren and War, 1708-1941* (Elgin, Ill.: Brethren Publishing House, 1944), 183-184.

10. *Ibid.*, 184-189.

11. The Civilian Conservation Corps had been established in 1933 as a part of the "New Deal" of President Franklin D. Roosevelt to provide useful employment for American young men. The camps were located in rural and forested areas.

12. *Minutes of the Annual Conference* (1917), 14.

8

MISSIONS

B. Merle Crouse

The Brethren are a people with a sense of mission. The Great Commission (Matthew 28:19-20), along with the Sermon on the Mount, the eighteenth chapter of Matthew, the thirteenth chapter of John, and the book of James, has been one of the key texts for Brethren. At times the Great Commission text has been used more for justifying the practice of trine immersion baptism than for sending God's people into the world, but its constant missionary imperative has always been heeded to some extent.

The Brethren have a rich history of missionary endeavor. Participation in the Protestant foreign missionary movement has been serious. Mission has become an essential element of the faith and is a dominant theme in the present-day life of the Church of the Brethren. The otherworldly benefits of being a new creature in Christ have not always received primary emphasis. The new way to live as Christians in this world is not necessarily of more importance, but it is thought of as essential for the Christian and is given more emphasis in the traditional Brethren message.

The Brethren have always been convinced that they have something Christian to do out there among the nations. The struggle to define that something seems to be harder today than it has been in times past as obvious human needs become more authoritative and the New Testament less studied. The ebb and flow of history have given varying emphases to the Brethren missionary intention through the years. This chapter traces briefly the various stages of Brethren mission history.

The Missionary Attitude and Activities of the Early Brethren in Europe (1708-1733)

The early Brethren in Europe were well-known for their zealous missionary spirit and activity. They were both respected for their sincerity and denounced for their persistent and bothersome inroads among the people of the established churches. They were convinced that God had ordained them to take their message to their world.

Alexander Mack, Jr., in his preface to the first American edition (1774) of his father's writings, reflects the urgent call to witness and to grow that the first Brethren felt on the occasion of their founding baptismal service. "Thus all eight were baptized in an early morning hour. After they had all emerged from the water, and had dressed themselves again, they were all immediately clothed inwardly with great joyfulness. This significant word was then impressed on them through grace: 'Be fruitful and multiply.' "[1]

The first eight Brethren at Schwarzenau had been Christians and members of the established churches before their baptism in the River Eder. Of the men, one was Lutheran and four were Reformed. All of them had taken a spiritual pilgrimage out of the churches and had met in the Radical Pietist circle of Schwarzenau. Their new baptism now disassociated them from the Pietists and set them apart in a sectarian movement of their own.

Their rationale for forming a new church reveals their missionary intention and the source of their zeal. They felt true Christianity to have been lost with the spiritual decline evident in the established churches. They sought the restitution of the primitive church by uniting like-minded, awakened Christians into a new body free of traditional creeds and rites but committed to New Testament teachings and practices as they understood them after much searching and study together.

Alexander Mack's letter to Count Charles August in 1711 contains a clear statement of his missionary message and rationale.

> Now I will freely and publicly confess that my crime is that Jesus Christ, the King of kings and Lord of lords, desires that we do what we are doing — that the sinner shall repent and believe in the Lord Jesus and should be baptized in water upon his confession of faith. He should then seek to carry out everything Jesus has commanded and publicly bequeathed in His Testament. If we are doing wrong herein, against the revealed word of the Holy Scriptures, be it in teaching, way of life, or conduct, we would gladly receive instruction. If, however, no one can prove this on the basis of the Holy Scriptures, and yet persecutes us despite this, we would gladly suffer and bear it for the sake of the teachings of Jesus Christ.[2]

Before the baptisms at Schwarzenau in 1708 that gave birth to the Church of the Brethren, Alexander Mack spent much time in study with his close friend, the Radical Pietist Ernst Christoph Hochmann von Hochenau. Hochmann, for a time, preached earnest missionary sermons to the Jews, exhorting them to seek conversion to Christ in view of his imminent return. Mack often accompanied Hochmann on missionary journeys in Germany. They preached for revival and renewal among their countrymen of the established churches, witnessing for a holier life, a closer fellowship among believers, and for spiritual union with God.

Later, Mack led the Brethren missionary efforts. They went out to teach, evangelize, and baptize converts into their church. Their mission field was limited to the Christian world of their time. They won adherents from the Reformed, the Lutherans, the Separatists and the Mennonites. Their appeal to each group was different though their intention was the same: to be instrumental in bringing about a faithful and obedient church like the New Testament church.

The message to the Reformed and Lutherans was new life in Christ for a spiritually barren church. The Separatists had found new wine but provided no wineskins to hold it in. To them the appeal was for an outward church in agreement with the inward spiritual church of which they were already a part. The Brethren agreed essentially with the Mennonites in everything but their form of baptism. Mennonite baptism was for adults only, but the Brethren insisted that pouring was not a biblical form. A fairly large number of Mennonites were baptized again in the Brethren mode of trine immersion, convinced by biblical argument and zeal.

Brethren missionary success drew fire from the established churches, from the Radical Pietists, and from civil authorities who were not eager to have the delicate religious situation disturbed. That which for Brethren was authentic and necessary missionary work for true conversion to Christ was understood as offensive proselytism by the groups who suffered loss because of it.

The Brethren experienced sizable church growth in Europe. The Schwarzenau group, under the care of Alexander Mack, became a well-organized, active congregation. From this group preachers were sent out into the Rhine Valley and as far as Switzerland. Scattered converts were baptized in the Palatinate and in the Marienborn area as well as in Wittgenstein. The Marienborn congregation for the most part eventually moved to Krefeld. The Krefeld Brethren baptized a group of six men from Solingen whose story of steadfastness and faith as prisoners in Düsseldorf and Jülich illustrates the best of the early Brethren spirit.

Mounting suppression and economic need led to emigration of the Brethren from Germany, beginning in 1719. The Schwarzenau church moved to Surhuisterveen in West Friesland in 1720. According to Brumbaugh, twelve Hollanders joined the church during the nine years of sojourn in West Friesland.[3] Estimates of the European membership of the Brethren range from the two hundred fifty-five names compiled by Brumbaugh[4] to the figure of one thousand cited by a later leader.[5] The latter estimate is certainly an exaggeration while Brumbaugh's list was hardly complete. The total population of baptized Brethren in Europe must have included about three hundred persons.

The Missionary Efforts and Expansion of the Colonial Brethren (1719-1778)

It took time for the colonizing Brethren to regain the missionary momentum once theirs in Europe. The group of immigrants under Peter Becker arrived in Philadelphia in 1719 and scattered from Germantown into the surrounding region in search of land and work. The bitter misunderstandings of the church in Krefeld certainly made for cautiousness and some loss of zeal for a time among these former members. Their new homeland was strange and unknown and they had to learn how to live in it after the patterns of the Pennsylvania new world. After four years in the colonies, the Brethren reorganized themselves on Christmas Day, 1723, baptized six members, and held a love feast.

The Brethren had organized themselves, but more than that was happening. They received a renewed joy and fervor to seek out the scattered Brethren in the hinterland and to witness to others of the German-speaking communities. They were caught up in an awakening that gave rapid growth to the group and moved the spirit of their neighbors over a broad region.

On October 23, 1724, the fourteen male members set out from Germantown on a missionary tour to strengthen members of the Brethren diaspora and to preach for the awakening of others. Their journey took them to Skippack, Falckner's Swamp, Oley, and Coventry on the Schuylkill, where they visited the new brethren of the Christmas baptisms. At Coventry, two more were baptized, a love feast was held on November 8, and the second Brethren congregation was organized with nine members.

As originally planned, the missionary tour was to have ended at the Schuylkill. However, news reached them that there were several awakened people in the Conestoga area and that their ministry was needed. The *Ephrata Chronicle* has recorded important details of the visit to Conestoga.

> A meeting was held at Höhn's on the following day, November 12, at which the Superintendent [Conrad Beissel] was present. At this meeting extraordinary revival powers were manifested. The Brethren spoke with such power concerning baptism and the divine purpose concerning fallen man involved therein, that after the close of the meeting five persons applied for baptism, namely the before-mentioned Höhn, his wife, John Mayer and his wife, and Joseph Shäfer, who were at once baptized in apostolic fashion by Peter Becker in the Pequea stream. Soon a sixth one followed these, namely Veronica, the wife of Isaac Frederick.[6]

Conrad Beissel, who later founded the monastic community of Ephrata and led many Brethren into schism, was also baptized in the same service. In the evening a love feast took place in Höhn's house. The next Sunday Sigmund Landert and his wife were baptized and the first congregation of Lancaster County organized with Conrad Beissel chosen as preacher in charge.

The ordinances of baptism and the love feast and their meaning for the Brethren were the key to their missionary message and method. Baptism meant that an old life of compromise with the world was now buried forever. It represented cleansing and commitment to a holy life of obedience as called for by Jesus in the Sermon on the Mount. The baptismal rite itself was a first step of obedience. Baptism was an ordinance authorized and performed by the church, that is, the community of believers and not by a sacerdotal clergy. Candidates were approved by the church and the service of baptism was a highly significant and joyful worship service of the whole congregation. It was the outward symbol of an inward reality for the believer. Baptism cut the convert off from many former relationships and made him part of a new family with Christ as Lord and the other baptized members as brethren. Baptism meant a leaving of one world and the joining of another.

The love feast was the celebration of the principal elements of the believer's new world. Feetwashing was both a symbol and an experience of service and humility, a renewal of the church's readiness to love one another and to obey Christ. The common supper affirmed the fraternal bonds of the Brethren. The receiving of the broken bread and the wine renewed the baptismal vows, binding the believer to his Lord. Brethren evangelism was related very directly to these rites. The organization of new congregations was sealed with the love feast celebration.

For the most part, the colonial congregations met in the homes of the members, often on a rotating basis. Many Brethren homes and barns were

built with the church meetings in mind. The first simple meetinghouse was
built in 1770 by the Germantown church. The White Oak church held its
first love feast in 1736 and met in the homes of its members until 1859.
Church meetings in the homes encouraged a warm social dimension within
the fellowship.

Leaders in the churches were developed and called from among the
baptized men who went through a kind of apprenticeship in the church.
Those who showed gifts for understanding people and for understanding
and teaching the faith were chosen by their congregation and ordained by
other ordained leaders.

The expansion of the Brethren from Germantown through the colonies
to the west and south was dependent upon two patterns of missionary work.
The "home community missionary method" was responsible for the rapid
growth of the Brethren in the colonial period. This involved evangelism by
members and leaders of the congregations within their immediate communities
and surrounding neighborhoods. When distant members could form a group
of eight or more baptized members and when leadership could be provided,
a new congregation was formed. Like the growth and division of cells in
living tissue, so was the effectiveness of the home community missionary
method for forming new congregations and inspiring them to be fruitful
and multiply.

The Conestoga congregation illustrates the effectiveness of the home
community missionary method. The congregation was organized in 1724,
then divided in 1732, when the Beissel group removed to Ephrata. In 1908
J. G. Royer spoke of Conestoga's growth in this way:

> Conestoga was one of the first organized colonial churches. In 1730 it had
> about thirty-five communicants. In 1748 it had 200; in 1770, having by that
> time received over 400 into fellowship it had only 86 communicants. From the
> very beginning, Conestoga church was now weakened by emigration, then re-
> cruited and strengthened by the faithful, earnest application of the home-com-
> munity missionary method.
>
> What can we say for colonial Conestoga today? for we still have her with
> us. Her territory has been divided and subdivided until there are now within
> her original boundary twenty congregations with a total membership of nearly
> 5,000 souls.[7]

A more recent reporter from the Conestoga church adds: "As a result of three
divisions, in 1772, 1864, and 1897, and subsequent subdivisions, Conestoga
has become the mother church of all the congregations in Lancaster, Dauphin,
Lebanon, Berks, and Schuylkill counties, and, in fact, of most of the congregations comprising the Eastern District of Pennsylvania."[8] In 1969 the
Conestoga congregation had a membership of 494 members.[9]

The "emigration or colonization method" started with the movement of
the German congregations within Germany and then to the colonies and to
West Friesland. The westward expansion of the church after the Revolutionary War was dependent upon this pattern. Extension of the colonial church
into Maryland and farther south was by emigration of Brethren families from
established congregations to new territories.

Morgan Edwards reported statistics for the period around 1770 of the
Brethren in Maryland and farther south. According to his research there

were five congregations in Maryland with 452 members, one congregation in Virginia with thirty-six members, three congregations in North Carolina with 100 members and three congregations in South Carolina with about 100 members. Two of the latter congregations were English-speaking, and one had a Negro member who was baptized in January 1770. According to Edwards' figures, in 1770 there were 1,505 members in twenty-eight congregations in the colonies from New Jersey to South Carolina.[10] More migration into Virginia took place in 1775.

The Brethren missionary history of the colonial era includes the publication of Luther's translation of the Bible in 1743 by Christopher Sauer, Sr. His son, Christopher, Jr., the Brethren elder, reprinted the Bible in 1763 and again in 1776. This publication made the Bible available for most of the German population of the colonies. Other publications from the Sauer press continually fed the Germans practical, pious Christian orientation in matters of faith, politics, and daily living. The colonial period of the Brethren closed with the confiscation of the Sauer Press in 1778.

The Missionary Spirit and Expansion of the Brethren in Home Missions (1778-1968)

The war hurried the exodus of the Brethren from Pennsylvania to settlement on new frontier land. Dove analyzes the reasons for Brethren migration in this way:

1. Religious intolerance of the growing population in other sects toward the Germans of the Separatist type, such as the Brethren, induced their desire to seek seclusion in the underdeveloped frontier country.

2. Rapid development of the Pennsylvania Colony increased land values and the sale of land was profitable in eastern Pennsylvania.

3. Fertile land could be bought cheaper in undeveloped sections of the country, than in eastern Pennsylvania.

4. Exaggerated reports concerning the opportunity of the frontier were circulated among the German farmers of Pennsylvania, inviting settlers.

5. Missionary zeal led Brethren to plant their religion and culture in new territories.[11]

The result of this migration was rapid church development in other territories. The eastern Pennsylvania Brethren moved into middle and western Pennsylvania and down through Maryland and Virginia to North Carolina and Tennessee and westward to the Mississippi Valley. In spite of war and Indian disturbances the membership doubled by 1825. Ohio and Indiana became strongholds of the Church of the Brethren. The first church in Indiana was organized in 1809. By 1866 there were fifty-five congregations in the state, divided into three districts.[12]

By 1882 the membership had increased to about 58,000 and had followed the frontier development to the west coast. The first members to locate in the far west arrived in Oregon in 1850 from Indiana. Brethren colonization had reached its farthest extension by 1850 but migration continued to Kansas, North Dakota, the Northwest, Canada, California, and Florida.

Churches were established through the promotion of land sales, sponsored in some cases by Brethren and in other cases by railroad and real estate men who took note of the Brethren and Mennonite pattern of colonization. The Brethren churches of North Dakota, Montana, Idaho, and Washington owe their existence in large measure to enterprising land promoters of the Great Northern Railroad, the Oregon Short Line, and the Northern Pacific Railway. The Canadian Pacific Railroad was responsible for Brethren settlement in western Canada.

The missionary movement of the Brethren by land purchase and colonization was over by 1918. In later years a few Brethren moved to Florida and organized rural churches. One small colony was established in Cuba for several years but eventually moved back to the mainland. Brethren expansion in Europe was determined to a large extent by the policies for religious freedom of civil governments. In the United States, up to World War I it was determined by the availability of fertile land.

During the first fifty years of the nineteenth century, the Brethren tended to close themselves off from others. The German life and language were threatened by the English language and the developing American culture. Fraternal relations with other churches were disapproved of. Education was suspect as a door to becoming vain and worldly. The group consciousness that held the Brethren together was still undergirded by sincere Bible study but tended toward a traditional sectarian unity rather than helping persons discover profound spiritual truths. The mood of many Annual Meeting minutes suggests defensiveness and self-conscious protectionism. Yet the church grew well.

By 1850 the Church of the Brethren began to change. There were both interest and agitation for education, publications, and missionary work. The life and work of John Kline of Virginia suggests a return to the kind of attitude that made the younger Christopher Sauer a great Christian leader in the church and in his community. Kline was a farmer and a self-made physician. He traveled and corresponded with church leaders and political leaders in his opposition to slavery and in his interest to save the unity of the nation and of the church during the Civil War crisis. He was a zealous missionary who preached and developed new churches, traveling thousands of miles on horseback. He stirred the denomination to a renewed missionary consciousness, proposing the sending of two men to the Oregon country to raise up churches with the scattered Brethren settlers. M. R. Zigler describes Kline's evangelistic fervor:

> He took very seriously the Great Commission, which to him and the Brethren of those days was interpreted to mean starting small units near the mother congregation, and then following through with constant care until these units became congregations and began to extend themselves in the spirit of the Great Commission.

> This call to evangelism led him into areas far beyond his local church and the State of Virginia. The evidence is clear that he was invited back again and again to give administrative advice and inspiration to small groups that were emerging. . . . Up until the time of his death he continued to visit the sick and give spiritual counsel, to visit churches for council meetings, to preach, to officiate at love feasts, and to pray with others. He gave close and satisfactory administrative attention to members of the local congregation at Linville Creek. All these activities led to active participation in the Annual Meeting. He joined the fellowship of leaders in moving the Church of the Brethren with its twenty

thousand members to united action, and in developing a denominational plan for implementing the Great Commission.[13]

John Kline was one of the mid-nineteenth century leaders with a big vision for the church. In his time the church began to promote higher education and *The Gospel Visitor* was published. John S. Flory reports of the first stirrings for foreign mission work in the church: "In 1852 a query from Virginia asked the Annual Conference to consider a plan for foreign mission work. Brother Kline heartily endorsed and urged the matter. While the Conference took no action, a committee was later appointed, of which he was a member, to consider the matter and bring a report to the Conference. He was heartily interested in preaching the Gospel of Christ to the whole World."[14]

The Annual Conference of 1853 recommended that any members wishing to move westward locate where they were most needed by the church. In 1860 Conference appointed James Quinter and Daniel P. Sayler as secretary and treasurer of a board set up to seek personnel for strengthening the members in Oregon and California. In 1870 two ministers from Indiana, Jacob Miller and Daniel Sturgis, were appointed for the work in the West and were provided expenses for the mission. Appeals for mission workers for the state of Maine and for Alabama and Tennessee came to the church in 1872 and 1875. In 1885 city work was begun in Chicago. Foreign work was begun in Denmark in 1876. Mission activities began to be coordinated with the appointment of a mission board in 1880. Brethren missions had begun a new era in which the church's energies were directed to new fields both at home and in other lands.

By 1882, the membership of the Church of the Brethren was between 55,000 and 60,000.[15] By 1916, the membership had doubled. Thirty years later it reached 182,000, and in 1966, over 190,000 in North America.[16]

Home mission efforts from the late nineteenth century to the present have been carried on primarily through the initiative of national and district agencies of the church. This is in contrast to the early practice of founding new congregations through the extension of congregational activities. Following the trends of urbanizing America, the home mission churches of the past forty years have been established in the cities. From 1940 to 1960 the number of urban members of the Church of the Brethren increased rapidly. The report of the General Brotherhood Board to the 1968 Annual Conference entitled "An Urban Ministry for Today's People" lists 336 urban congregations in the church, almost one third of the total number of congregations. The report presents a positive attitude and strategy for the mission of the churches in the cities.[17] It is obvious that the future growth of the Church of the Brethren in the United States will depend on the work done in urban communities.

Foreign Missions in the Church of the Brethren From 1876
1. Scandinavia

The growing conscience for foreign missions began to translate into action in 1876, when Christian Hope, a Dane, was sent to the land of his birth as the first missionary of the Brethren in America to a foreign land. He had been a Lutheran until his search for a church holding to New Testament principles led him to be baptized in the Hickory Grove church, Illinois, in 1874. Hope had a friend in Denmark, Christian Hansen, who also longed to be part of a church like the Brethren. A special meeting of the Northern Illinois District on November 12, 1875, in the Cherry Grove church treated the request from Christian Hope to send missionaries to Denmark. The delegates made the following resolutions:

> This meeting [is] to call a brother to the ministry who can preach in the Danish language, and to select two brethren to accompany him to Denmark. One of those to be chosen should be able to speak in the German language. . . . This the church accepted, and proceeded to elect a minister, all present participating in the choice. The lot fell upon Brother Christian Hope.
>
> The delegates then proceeded to select two brethren as already stated. The choice fell upon Brethren Enoch Eby and Paul Wetzel.[18]

The Hope family was in Denmark by February 1876. In May of that year Christian Hansen and a girl were baptized. By the middle of 1877, six more joined the Brethren. In October 1877, Enoch Eby and Daniel Fry arrived in Denmark to organize the church, ordain Danish leadership, and encourage the new group of believers. C. C. Eskildsen was ordained and given official oversight of the Danish church.

Christian Hope was related to the work in Denmark for twenty-three years. Other missionaries carried on and eventually saw the church extended to Sweden. At one time the Church of the Brethren in Scandinavia reached a membership of 61 in the two Danish churches and 171 in five Swedish congregations. There were three Danish and ten Swedish ministers. After fifty years, the church in America recalled its missionaries and began to phase out its support. Emigration took its toll of the Scandinavian membership. The 1955 *Yearbook*, which was the last one to list Brethren members in Scandinavia, records fifteen members in Denmark and twenty-nine in Sweden.

Supervision of the Scandinavian mission was the responsibility of the pioneering Northern Illinois District from November 1875 to May 1880, when Annual Conference appointed a denominational Foreign and Domestic Mission Board which accepted the care of that work.

2. Turkey

The Foreign and Domestic Mission Board was replaced in 1884 by the General Church Erection and Missionary Committee. Elder D. L. Miller, one of the members of this committee, had traveled extensively to the lands of the New Testament churches and had published a description of the contemporary situation of Christianity in western Asia Minor. The interest aroused by this writing led the General Missionary Committee in February 1895 to decide to open mission work in that part of Turkey.

G. J. Fercken, a native of the area, was chosen as the first missionary. He came into the Church of the Brethren after ten years as an Episcopalian minister. His Dutch father and French mother had educated him in the Greek, Arabic, French, and English languages. For years he had done linguistic work in Izmir (Smyrna) and other parts of the East. The Northern

District of Illinois, in which he was a member, recommended him for the work in Turkey and at Conference in 1895 he was appointed.

The lofty dream of the Brethren for this work is suggested in an announcement that appeared in the *Gospel Messenger* in mid-1895: "Asia Minor mission is now being opened; a more promising field has never presented itself to the Brethren Church. It is simply reestablishing primitive Christianity among the seven churches spoken of in Revelation. 'Seven Churches of Asia,' by D. L. Miller, gives a full account of the mission field. The book is sold in the interests of this mission; and the first cost is now fully paid. . . . All profits go to this mission."[19]

The Fercken family arrived in Turkey on July 13, 1895. Izmir was chosen as the mission center. They received permission from the Turkish government to carry on Christian work and set about their task. Within ten months, Fercken had been ordained to the eldership by a group of Brethren representatives from America, several people had been baptized, a church organized, a minister and deacon elected, two love feasts held, and an orphanage established. Before 1900, twenty-five children were in the orphanage.

In 1897 Elder Fercken began a mission station in Aydin, a city of forty-five thousand located approximately fifty miles to the south and east of Izmir, not far from the ruins of Ephesus. The Aydin work had been a mission field of the Congregational Church, which left some members there when the area was abandoned. The Brethren station was opened in 1897, when two Armenian Congregationalists asked for baptism. In 1898 a church was organized in Aydin. Moyer says:

> Fercken's report on Easter, 1898, after two years and nine months of work, showed two organized churches and one out-station with a total membership of thirty-nine, one elder, three ministers, and one deacon. Thirteen had been baptized during the year, and a new out-station had been opened at Alasheir (Philadelphia of Revelation) with five members, one of whom was a minister. The members of the Asia Minor mission were all Armenians and Greeks who had previously been professed Christians, and the work of the mission was entirely among these peoples.[20]

The Armenian church members had welcomed the Brethren mission in its first years, especially because of the orphanage and its service to needy Armenian children. When several of the orphans were baptized in 1898, their attitude became unfriendly. Their influence with the Moslem Turkish government brought antagonism against Fercken, who had to leave the country. His departure began the decline of the flourishing Brethren work. The board received a careful report made by D. L. Miller and four other Brethren who investigated the situation. The board's decision to send other missionaries and continue the work was never effectively implemented. National leaders with some support from America carried on until soon after 1909, when marital problems of the leading minister led to his separation from the church and to the closing of the mission.

3. Switzerland and France

The General Mission Board, in its January 1899 meeting, asked G. J. Fercken to investigate Switzerland as a possible field and to initiate work there if it seemed advisable. Again, development was rapid. In June 1899 a Sunday school was started at Lancy, a small village near Geneva. By September several Swiss and one Frenchman were baptized and a Swiss church was organized. In October Fercken baptized a group in Oyonnax, France, and organized the first church in that country. A minister and a deacon were elected in the French church. At the close of 1899 there were two churches, one in each country, and nearly thirty members. A meeting-house was built in Lancy in 1900 with American funds but was so poorly located that the board authorized its sale in 1901. The church continued meeting in a rented place in Geneva.

By June 1904 there were fifty-seven members in the two countries. In 1905 the board sought another missionary to go to France but found no one ready to go. In 1906, Fercken left the Brethren and went into the Swedenborgian faith. The further history of Brethren activities in the area is provided by Moyer:

> The churches in France and Switzerland were then committed to the charge of Adrian Pellet, a Swiss who had come from the Salvation Army into the Church of the Brethren a few years before, and had been in the ministry for some time. In the summer of 1906, a new station had been opened at Nantua, France. The records for that year show Switzerland to have had a membership of forty, and France a membership of nineteen. Pellet had his headquarters at Geneva, and continued his work from there with apparent competency and success. In 1907, however, the mission in Geneva was closed, and Pellet was located at Oyonnax, France.[21]

In 1909, there were serious problems with the Swiss minister. In 1911, Paul Mohler and his wife Lucy went as missionaries from America to France. He found the work seriously injured by Pellet's errors and the mission in such disrepute that it was considered impossible to carry on. The board decided to close the field in August 1912 and called the Mohlers home.

This was the last Brethren attempt to work among nominally Christian people until the beginning of the mission in Ecuador in 1946. The work in Turkey, France, and Switzerland seems to have had good possibilities for success but floundered because of unstable leadership and possibly because the missionaries and national workers were not given solid sustaining fellowship. They had no fellow workers with whom to counsel and by whom to be strengthened for their difficult work. The people of Brethren tradition in America seemed not yet to be ready to accept the cost of leaving home to do the work to which the church had committed herself.

4. India

The mission experience gained in Turkey and Europe prepared the Brethren for entrance into the non-Christian fields of Asia. Wilbur B. Stover, his wife, Mary Emmert Stover, and Bertha Ryan founded the mission work in India in 1894. The Brethren chose a field north of Bombay, centered at Bulsar, involving Gujarati and Marathi language groups. Evangelistic work began in March 1895 by holding preaching and teaching meetings in the Bulsar railway library. In April 1897 the first eleven converts in India were baptized. The following September, five more were baptized. Other missionaries joined the team that same year. By the end of 1899 there were forty-five members in the Indian church. The congregation in Bulsar was organized in February 1899. In 1901 other churches were organized in Jalalpor and Anklesvar and related to one another as the First District of India.

The bubonic plague and severe famine struck India from 1896 into the 1900s. The Brethren set up orphanages and distributed food to thousands of destitute families. At one time six hundred orphans were under the care of the mission. Many people asked to be Christian during the famines. Motives were mixed. The danger of taking in "rice" Christians was great. The mission baptized carefully but took in hundreds of new members, many of whom returned to their old religions and reentered caste when the crisis was over. Some of them matured into good Christians. The orphans were given vocational and Bible training. Many of them became Christians and some have served in the ministry of the Indian Church of the Brethren.

By 1929 ninety-three missionaries had worked in India and the church had 3,944 members with 30 deacons and 15 ministers. The congregation at Vyara was the largest congregation the Brethren have ever had anywhere, with 1,590 members.[22] The fifteen congregations were divided into the Gujarati-speaking First District and the Marathi-speaking Second District. The high point of membership in the Indian church was reached in 1956 with 9,481 members. Since that time there has been a decline in the membership in India which numbered 8,628 in 1968.

In 1917 there were three Indian ministers. In 1966, twenty-four of the twenty-five congregations had part-time or full-time pastors. Of the 40,000 rupees used for pastoral support in the Indian church in 1967, all but 4,000 were given by Indians. Very soon the Indian Christians will be supporting their local work completely.

At an early stage in its development, the work in India combined medical, educational, and other social services with its evangelistic activity. The plague and the famines made medical work imperative in the first years. Dr. O. H. Yereman, a convert from the work in Turkey, arrived in 1903 as the first Brethren medical missionary. In 1954 there were two medical centers, in Bulsar and Dahanu, which treated 25,000 cases each during the year, most of them non-Christians.[23]

Educational work began in the orphanages and expanded to include a network of ninety elementary schools, several boarding schools and hostels, a teacher training school, a Bible school and the Rural Service Training Center. In 1951, 5,300 children were in mission-run elementary schools. A key evangelistic method was to provide education under Christian teachers. The Indian government has now taken over the support and operation of most of the elementary schools.

Agricultural improvement and economic uplift have been part of the concern of many individual missionaries in India. In 1952, the Rural Service Training Center was opened in Anklesvar with an Indian agriculturalist in charge. This all-Gujarat interdenominational center is now preparing a goodly group of rural extension men for work in improved crops and seeds and better methods of land use. The students are trained to go out to serve as *gram sevaks*, that is, as community development workers in the villages. The Rural

Service Center maintains a relationship with them and gives them a sense of fellowship and purpose for their work.

The Indian field is the first extensive illustration of the consistent Brethren mission practice from 1900 to the present, of investing a large proportion of mission resources in social services. Social work has been a complementary expression of the gospel along with aggressive evangelistic witness.

The Indian church is recently coming out of its "compound complex" and is beginning to seek involvement with the secular Indian world. The Independence movement received little or no participation from the Brethren in India whose attitude has been one of isolation from national affairs. Younger Indian Brethren are appearing who are trained and motivated to be dynamic community as well as church leaders, if the older church will challenge them to exploit their "Indian-ness" for the edification of the church and to apply their Christianity to the development of India.

The Indian Brethren have joined the Church of North India, a union of Christians from a variety of denominational traditions. Thus, the Indian members of the Church of the Brethren became part of a sister church in 1970.

5. *China*

In 1908, two hundred years after the birth of the church in Germany, and fourteen years after the founding of work in India, the Brethren opened mission work in China. Five missionaries landed in Shanghai in September of that year. The first mission station was set up in the city of Ping Ting Chow, Shansi Province, in 1910. In April of that year the first two Brethren converts were baptized. A second station was opened at Liao Chow in February 1912. On September 11, 1912, the two stations were organized into congregations, the Ping Ting church with a membership of eight and the Liao church with nine.

Evangelistic work in North China expanded to other communities so that by 1939 there were 2,670 members in five organized churches. There were three ordained Chinese pastors and forty-eight paid evangelists of whom twenty-nine were women.[24] A 1948 estimate of membership, after missionaries had not been with the churches for two years, gives 3,075 members among the Chinese Brethren in the North.

Another field opened in South China in 1918 as a result of the initiative of Moy Gwong Han, a member of the Brethren Chinese Fellowship in Chicago. From 1918 to 1948, three single women from America and three Chinese Christians related to the Chicago Fellowship worked in the village of On Fun, Kwangtung Province. By that time the church had 340 members scattered in fifty-five villages, and an elementary school of 270 pupils. In 1948 and 1949 representatives of the American church visited South China and arranged for the On Fun congregation to join the Kwangtung Synod of the Church of Christ in China.[25]

In 1911 a primary school was opened in Ping Ting. In 1912 a boys' orphanage was founded. In 1924 the mission operated twenty-seven schools serving 1,030 students. This included four Bible schools and two high schools. Adult education was part of the educational program.

Medical work began in 1914 and reached a high point in 1924 with three hospitals and extensive outpatient and public health work. Three missionary and three Chinese doctors were working at that time. In 1917 and 1918 most of the mission staff was deployed in an intensive effort to control a pneumonic plague epidemic. Famine relief was a regular part of the work for many years. In 1921-22 all the missionaries worked in famine relief, underwritten by $150,000 from the Brethren in America and large contributions from the International Red Cross and other agencies.

The years of Brethren work in China had been very stormy and unstable politically. In 1911 all the missionaries were evacuated from their areas for three months during the Chinese Revolution. In 1927 the missionaries moved out for ten months during the Chinese Civil War. In 1936 three missionaries were killed by the Japanese and all mission personnel was evacuated in 1940 for a period of six years because of Japanese occupation and World War II. In 1949-1950 missionaries had to leave again because of the Communist take-over. Since then they have been unable to return. In September 1953, the China budget and all missionary activity of the Church of the Brethren related to China ended.

Little is known of the present condition of the Chinese Brethren. The church in China is going through a time of suffering and cleansing. It has also certainly become more authentically Chinese in thought and expression than it would have under foreign domination. Some day when it is possible to have fellowship again, the Chinese Christians will have much to share with their brethren of the rest of the world.

Relief and rehabilitation work is part of the Brethren story in China. In addition to the great efforts made during the plague and the famines, relief work was carried on following World War II with refugees and in an emergency food production program. The Heifer Project located 2,400 heifers in China. The Brethren Service Commission cooperated with the United Nations Relief and Rehabilitation Administration and the Chinese government in sending volunteers from America to China to reclaim land no longer in production and to train Chinese to use farm machinery. This work won the respect of both Nationalist and Communist authorities before it was terminated by the Communist take-over.

6. Nigeria

Fourteen years after mission beginnings in China, A. D. Helser and H. Stover Kulp went to Nigeria to establish Brethren work. They broke ground in March 1922 in Garkida on the Hawal River, Bornu Province, in Northeastern Nigeria. The area was populated by animist tribes governed by Mohammedan rulers. By comity agreement, the Church of the Brethren mission eventually came to be responsible for an area located in Bornu and Adamawa Provinces, working with Bura, Margi, Higi, Whona, and Chibuk language groups. The territory is 150 miles in length and fifty miles in width with a population today of some 600,000.

Missionary activity was limited to the Garkida area for the first four or five years. In 1927 a new station was started at Lassa with the Margi tribe. In 1929 leprosy work was begun at Garkida with help from the government and the American Leprosy Mission. In 1951 the Leper Colony had

1,700 patients from forty-five tribes. There was a Leper Colony church of 170 members and also a school of 300.

New mission stations opened up in Marama, Chibuk, Wandali, and many other villages, often with a missionary family living at each place. Evangelistic work has usually been combined with medical services and elementary schooling in the centers of village work. The Brethren mission in Nigeria started a practice of giving classes of religious instruction in the villages. These classes have won many people to Christ and are important feeders for the churches. In 1951 there were 1,053 members in the eight Nigerian churches. By 1961 there were 6,649 members and twenty-four congregations. In 1968 the membership had grown to 18,412 in forty-one congregations. In recent years a mass movement has begun in the Brethren area of Nigeria with about 2,500 people coming into the churches each year. The problem of the church is to develop leadership fast enough to integrate so many people into the churches, to take care of the thousands of older members, and at the same time to reach out toward new groups ready to turn to Christianity.

In 1951 a class for pastors was started at Chibuk. In 1959 the Theological College of Northern Nigeria was begun with several denominations cooperating; Kulp Bible School was founded in more recent years. The Waka Teacher Training College and Secondary Schools help with training laymen. The Nigeria Program Report of 1966 comments on the leadership problem:

> In 1966 the greatest problem of the Church is lack of leadership. There is every indication that the Nigerian Church will continue to grow at a rapid rate. If we say, for example, that there will be 2,000 people coming into the church every year for the next few years, what should they have in the area of leadership? At the present rate, we are turning out about fifteen lay leaders from the Kulp Bible School every year and an average of one or two men a year from Theological College of Northern Nigeria. This means that we are turning out leaders at the rate of about one to every one hundred twenty-eight new converts. This does not care for the 12,000 who are already in the church. We are also turning out men and women from Teacher Training College and Secondary Schools who help in the leadership problem. However, it should be remembered that only a small proportion of the Kulp Bible School leaders will be working full time for the church. Any way that you look at it, it can hardly be said that the church is holding its own on leadership, let alone gaining. We will need to gain in our leadership training capacity. We presently have in-service training in an annual Classes of Religious Instruction course, an annual ministers' retreat, and various courses in Women's Work, Girls Life Brigade, Boys Brigade, etc. Additional programs need to be opened up in this area.[26]

In 1966, the medical program included one doctor doing public health work in the villages. There were three hospitals with heavy work loads: Lassa Hospital with sixty-four beds, handling 72,312 cases during the year, Garkida Hospital with eighty beds, serving 363,840 cases, and the Leprosarium hospital of eighty-six beds. More than 530 patients were residing in the leprosy settlement; another 1,397 patients were seen in outpatient clinics supervised by Leprosarium personnel. The mission operates six registered dispensaries and other first-aid stations which treated 26,880 new patients during the year and handled 265,000 medical attendances. The small medical staff at Chibuk was instrumental in controlling a serious meningitis epidemic in their area, treating 379 cases and holding the fatality list to 32.

The educational work of the Church of the Brethren mission in Nigeria has been a strategic part of the evangelistic effort and has become an important part of the national public education system. The Waka Schools include a Teacher Training College, which had 341 students, and the Secondary School with 205 students enrolled in 1966. Most of the faculty are Brethren personnel with the government providing almost all of the budget.

The Brethren had thirty-six elementary schools with 195 teachers and 6,658 pupils in operation in 1966. Twenty-six of these schools were turned over to the government in 1967 but continue to be centers for religious training as provided for by government regulation.

A program of rural development has been growing in areas of influence and scope of services for Nigerian farmers. They are given aid and encouragement for replacing hand work with more efficient tools, both for oxen and tractor. They are receiving new seed and are using commercial fertilizers and better agricultural practices. In 1966 sixteen Kulp Bible School trainees were doing extension work with rural families.

The work in Northeastern Nigeria is now done as a cooperative effort of the Church of the Brethren in America, the dynamic Nigerian church of Brethren heritage known as the Eastern District (Lardin Gabas) of the Church of Christ in the Sudan, the Brethren Church of Ashland, Ohio, and the Basel Mission of Europe.

Ivan Eikenberry has described the church in Nigeria as being at the boil and with a full head of steam: "In almost the entire church area, we have what has been called a people movement. It seems to be the fulness of time for the community; the pot is at the boil. Years of planting are bringing harvest. Years of love quietly demonstrated in Christian community service are shouting their witness. Membership is increasing explosively."[27] Brethren missionary witness in Nigeria has started a fire on the dry tinder of hungry hearts and in an ancient society ripe for change.

7. Ecuador

Ecuador came under Brethren concern during World War II. The first project was an inner-city youth program in Quito, opened in 1943 and operated to the end of the war by a group of Brethren Service men. This work was later turned over to government agencies. The wartime Brethren Service activities in Ecuador and Puerto Rico brought the needs of Latin America to the attention of the Church of the Brethren. They saw in Ecuador, a nominally Roman Catholic country, a ready mission field for Brethren witness.

The Benton Rhoades family went to Ecuador in 1946 and began work in the Calderón Valley, an Indian community twelve miles north of Quito. Agricultural and community development, health and medical services, education and evangelism combined into an effective program. In 1953 the first congregation was organized in Calderón with thirteen members, all Indians. An Indian minister was called and installed as pastor. The following year brought twenty more members to the church of whom eleven were mestizos of the non-Indian Ecuadorian culture.

In 1959, a second area of work was opened in Las Delicias, a village of the jungle country near the town of Santo Domingo. An international work camp gave the evangelistic impact that brought a new group of believers into being. The first baptismal service was held in 1960 and the church in Las Delicias was organized in 1962. By July 1965, the Brethren had organized two more congregations in the Santo Domingo zone and one more to the north of Calderón. At that time the Brethren congregations and their two hundred members joined with several congregations of other traditions to form the United Evangelical Church of Ecuador.

This young church is small in number and big in ideals and aspiration. It is a national body that now works in partnership with the Church of the Brethren, the United Andean Indian Mission (a joint effort of the United Presbyterian Church in the United States of America, the Presbyterian Church in the United States, the United Church of Christ, and the United Methodist Church) and the Board of Missions of the Methodist Churches of Latin America. The United Evangelical Church of Ecuador has struggled faithfully to find its style and to unite the variety of traditions that it includes. There have been conflicts. Missionaries and national leaders have had to learn to dialogue in depth and to adjust their biases and relationships drastically. The adjustment has been painful but there seems to be good progress. The church is growing in numbers and maturity. Missionaries are finding their place in the church's program and fellowship.

The United Evangelical Church of Ecuador was founded with 305 members in 1965. In early 1969 it had over 500 members in thirteen congregations. Missionaries and monetary assistance from the three cooperating mission boards subsidize the church's program. The church is now beginning to work seriously at self-support for its local church programs through stewardship education, planning, and systematic offerings in the churches. The church founded a training school for lay leaders and the ministry in 1966, the Center of Theological Studies. The Center has enrolled more than two hundred students in its various courses. These include continuing education for pastors, a course for music leaders, and the basic ministerial course which is offered at two levels and given in regional centers for nonresident, part-time students. The extension system is an effort to reach church leaders in their communities with recognized theological training. This type of program has found acceptance rapidly in the last five years in several Latin American countries. The Center of Theological Studies is becoming a joint project with the Evangelical Covenant Church in Ecuador at the present time and may come to have the sponsorship and participation of other national churches in the future.

Brethren mission efforts have had success in elementary education through an Indian school in Calderón and secondary education through scholarships. This school is now subsidized in part by the government and will eventually pass into government hands. Literacy work and vocational training are reaching older youth and adults.

Medical work began in the Rhoades' first year. Three clinics in the

Calderón area are operated primarily with Ecuadorian personnel. Dr. John Horning has done pioneer work in family planning on a national scale, promoting and training for responsible parenthood and birth control through the Evangelical churches, Ecuadorian doctors, and civic leaders.

The Brethren Foundation, the social service agency related to the Brethren mission, is responsible for the educational, medical, and economic uplift ministries. The Foundation is involved in a growing program of community and economic development both in high Andean communities and in the warm jungle areas now being colonized.

The missionary appeal of the Brethren and of most Evangelicals in Ecuador to nominal Roman Catholics is to return to true Christianity, as witnessed to by the New Testament, that is, to seek the living Christ and to commit one's life to him as Savior and Lord. Since Vatican Council II the Roman Catholics have responded with much greater openness than was possible formerly. Relationships with the Roman Catholic Church are also in a rapid state of transition in Ecuador.

The United Evangelical Church of Ecuador is also witnessing vigorously to its sister Evangelical churches with the message that the walls of the Evangelical ghettos must come down and that the faith means not only the saving of souls, but also the transformation and improvement of man's lot in this world. The United Church is speaking also to the cooperating North American churches, especially with its zeal and audacity to make great plans and push forward big programs in spite of its numerical smallness. The United Church is also protesting a tendency of the churches from the North to be satisfied with a secularized social service that does not relate well to the national churches and tends to become an ecclesiastically sponsored Point Four program. The United Church is saying that such social service harms the church and cheapens the service by immunizing nonbelievers from the gospel message and giving them less than they need and long for. All Christian service is related to God's redeeming action when it was born and should inspire hope and wistfulness in men to seek an inward new life in Christ.

8. Indonesia

The youngest Brethren field is Indonesia, which opened in the late 1950s. Christianity had been there for many decades before the Brethren arrived, and no new work has been established by Brethren missionaries. It is not likely that they will start new work in that land because the approach to Indonesia is unique in Brethren mission history. In cooperation with other non-Indonesian churches the Brethren are strengthening the existing Indonesian Evangelical churches with missionary personnel sent to do carefully defined, much needed tasks for which the Indonesians need help.

Brethren personnel in Indonesia have served in educational and medical capacities. The two fraternal workers presently there are both involved in education. One teaches in a theological school, the other acts as a minister to students in Djakarta.

Partnership Missions: The Brethren Missionary Attitude
and Strategy for Today.

Partnership missions, as in the case of the Indonesian work, that is, working as a service within the programs and structures of existing national churches, will be the prevailing pattern for Brethren missions in the coming years. The Annual Conference of the Church of the Brethren in 1955 defined this strategy in the following terms:

> An indigenous church is not only self-supporting, self-propagating, and self-governing, but also, insofar as Christian principles permit, identifies itself with the culture of the country where it is located. . . .
>
> It is our policy to encourage these new churches to assume financial and administrative responsibility for their churches as rapidly as possible. In order that they may make a more effective witness in non-Christian lands, we encourage them to affiliate with the over-all Protestant church in their respective areas. . . . Our Nigerian church . . . has been active in attempting to form the Church of the Sudan. Our church in Ecuador is part of the Evangelical Church in Ecuador.
>
> If our efforts to encourage the building of indigenous churches abroad succeed we should naturally expect that these churches will become less dependent on the American church for finance, for administration, and for personnel. It may be that the time will come when they will no longer be tied to us administratively but will affiliate with the total Protestant church in their homelands. If this happens it is to be expected that the fellowship between our church in America and their churches abroad will continue throughout the years through exchange of spiritual leadership and the sharing of resources. Churches abroad will probably continue to look to their mother churches for financial help for running their institutions. They will likely continue to welcome and even to seek the help of well-trained Christian workers from North America. . . .
>
> When we teach these young churches we cast our bread upon the waters. If our work is well done it will not return to us void. What matters is that Christ be born in them and that they go on witnessing for him.[28]

The Brethren are still pacifists, still baptize by trine immersion, and celebrate the love feast with the washing of feet. This means they are still sectarian. However, their attitude has become increasingly respectful and ecumenical in their relationships with other churches. Their missionary intention for these and the coming days may shift far afield from their heritage if they do not walk with great sensitivity to New Testament values, the precarious and paradoxical road which they are choosing, that of a sectarian theology with an ecumenical strategy. May their future history record more Christian creativity and faithfulness than compromise.

1. Alexander Mack, Jr., quoted in D. F. Durnbaugh, ed., *European Origins of the Brethren* (Elgin, Ill.: Brethren Press, 1958), 122.

2. Alexander Mack, Sr., quoted in Durnbaugh, *European Origins*, 163.

3. Martin G. Brumbaugh, *A History of the German Baptist Brethren in Europe and America* (Elgin, Ill.: Brethren Publishing House, 1899), 54-70. The publishing house will hereafter be cited as "BPH."

4. *Ibid.*, 54-70.

5. T. T. Myers, "The Birth of the Schwarzenau Church and Its Activities," in D. L. Miller, ed., *Two Centuries of the Church of the Brethren* (Elgin, Ill.: BPH, 1908), 39.

6. *Chronicon Ephratense,* quoted in D. F. Durnbaugh, ed., *The Brethren in Colonial America* (Elgin, Ill.: Brethren Press, 1967), 66.

7. J. G. Royer, "The Growth to the Mississippi," in D. L. Miller, *Two Centuries,* 78.

8. Guy R. Saylor, ed., *History of the Church of the Brethren, Eastern Pennsylvania, 1915-1965* (Lancaster, Pa.: Church of the Brethren, Eastern District of Pennsylvania, 1965), 20-21.

9. *Church of the Brethren Yearbook* (1970), 82-83.

10. Morgan Edwards, *Materials Toward a History of the American Baptists,* quoted in Durnbaugh, *Brethren in Colonial America,* 186-191.

11. Frederick D. Dove, *Cultural Changes in the Church of the Brethren* (Elgin, Ill.: BPH, 1932), 58.

12. Otho Winger, *History and Doctrines of the Church of the Brethren* (Elgin, Ill.: BPH, 1919), 77-78.

13. M. R. Zigler, "Elder John Kline — Churchman," *Brethren Life and Thought,* IX (Summer 1964), 15-16.

14. John S. Flory, *Builders of the Church of the Brethren* (Elgin, Ill.: BPH, 1925), 94.

15. Howard O. Miller, *Record of the Faithful,* quoted in Floyd E. Mallott, *Studies in Brethren History* (Elgin, Ill.: BPH, 1954), 106-107.

16. Mallott, *Studies,* 111; *Church of the Brethren Yearbook* (1947 and 1967).

17. "1968 Report of the General Brotherhood Board," *Annual Conference Minutes, Church of the Brethren* (Elgin, Ill.: 1968), 66-69.

18. Matthew M. Eshelman, *The History of the Danish Mission,* quoted in Elgin S. Moyer, *Missions in the Church of the Brethren* (Elgin, Ill.: BPH, 1931), 153.

19. General Missionary and Tract Committee, *Gospel Messenger* (July 24, 1895), as quoted by Moyer, *Missions,* 160.

20. Moyer, *Missions,* 162.

21. *Ibid.,* 167-168.

22. *Ibid.,* 178-179.

23. Wendell Flory, *Brethren Missions in India* (Elgin, Ill.: Foreign Mission Commission, 1955), 18.

24. Wendell Flory, "A History of the Brethren Involvement in China," *Brethren Life and Thought,* XI (Autumn 1966), 35.

25. *Ibid.,* 41.

26. Roger Ingold, ed., "Church Report," Annual Report, Church of the Brethren Mission, Nigeria, 1966, 1-2.

27. Ivan Eikenberry, *Which Way in Nigeria?* (Elgin, Ill.: Church of the Brethren General Offices, 1959), 9-10.

28. "Report on the Foreign Mission Program and Policy," *Conference Minutes . . . Annual Conference of the Church of the Brethren* (Elgin, Ill.: 1955), 67.

9

ECUMENICAL RELATIONSHIPS

Edward K. Ziegler

The Church of the Brethren today believes in full cooperation with other churches and participates heartily and responsibly in many cooperative Christian movements. But the present stance of the Church of the Brethren toward other churches represents an almost total reversal of its earlier positions.

When the church was founded in Germany in 1708, it was the expression of a vigorous protest against many of the practices and beliefs of the main-line churches of that day in Europe. Its approach to other churches was polemical and proselyting. The early history of the Brethren shows that the leaders were often imprisoned and punished in various ways for their bitter attacks upon the state churches and for their insistence upon rebaptizing persons from other churches who were persuaded to join them. In this attitude they were not alone. A spirit of mistrust and of divisiveness was prevalent. The established churches were intolerant of dissent or of movements toward renewal within the churches. There was little irenic spirit displayed either by the established churches or by their unwanted offspring.

When the Brethren migrated to the American colonies, the more irenic spirit of the Pennsylvania Quakers who were their hosts began to permeate the church. While the Brethren, and indeed most of the Germanic sects, tended to hold themselves aloof from English-speaking groups, there was far more tolerance and interchange of views among religious communities than had been possible in Europe.

An episode of great significance in the history of the Brethren was their participation in the synods convened by the Moravian leader, Count Nicolas Ludwig von Zinzendorf. The *Unitas Fratrum* or Moravian Church, known in Germany as the *Brüdergemeine,* was a movement with strong mystical and missionary emphases, growing out of the early Hussite association of Christians. Many of the Moravians, driven by persecution and attracted by the promise of religious freedom, came to the American colonies about the same time as the Brethren.

From the beginning of his association with the Moravians, Count Zinzendorf had a broad ecumenical outlook. He had a vision of the reunification of the various denominations into a federation, a "Congregation of God in the

Spirit." He hoped to establish not a monolithic church, but a union according to the motto, "In essentials unity, in nonessentials diversity, in all things charity." Zinzendorf believed that the Moravians were uniquely fitted to lead such a movement and that Pennsylvania with its climate of religious freedom and its multiplicity of German sectarians would be the ideal place to launch his bold experiment. In 1741, with the inspiration of Zinzendorf's presence and counsel, Henry Antes, a Reformed minister, sent out a general invitation to a synod to convene in Germantown on New Year's Day, 1742. The purpose of the synod was to confer about the common faith and interests of the churches and to seek ways of closer cooperation. Held at frequent intervals across the next several months, the synods tried earnestly to find grounds of unity and ultimately a union of the sects.

Brethren leaders were invited to these synods and attended at least three of the meetings. But alarmed by what they saw as syncretistic tendencies and repelled by the rather high-handed leadership of the Count, the Brethren withdrew. A momentous consequence of this ecumenical contact was the decision of the Brethren to hold their own Great Council in 1742. Out of this Council grew the Annual Conferences of the Brethren which to the present time constitute the highest governing body of the Church of the Brethren.[1]

For the next 150 years, there is little evidence in Brethren history or literature of any interest in ecumenical contacts. They cooperated locally with other groups, it is true, in the use of meetinghouses and cemeteries. They also made common cause with the Mennonites in appealing to the authorities for recognition of their pacifist witness. However, there was a period in the latter half of the nineteenth century when their isolation was interrupted by a series of acrimonious debates with representatives of other denominations, especially Baptists and Disciples. The published volumes containing the texts of these debates show intense polemical spirit and a desire on both sides to show that the debaters represented the sole repository of divine truth essential to salvation. These debates were typical of the spirit of most denominations just before what may be called the dawn of the ecumenical era.

Early Ecumenical Contacts

It was not until the powerful ferments of the missionary and the Sunday school movements began to influence American Protestantism that the Brethren began to take the first cautious steps toward ecumenism. When the Brethren first sent missionaries to India in 1894, their workers were encouraged to cooperate closely with other missions. From the very beginning they observed the principle of comity. Wherever the Brethren foreign missionaries have gone they have been in the forefront of ecumenical activity. Inevitably their ecumenical experience and spirit have had a profound effect upon the home church. It can be truthfully said that the foreign mission interests in the Church of the Brethren have been the pioneers of ecumenical interest and concern.

Long before the church at large became interested in working with other denominations, the leaders in Christian education began to enjoy such contacts. For many years, Brethren editors have shared with their colleagues in the planning of the International Sunday School Lessons and other areas of curriculum. In the early days of the Sunday school movement, Brethren were strongly discouraged from going to the popular Sunday school conventions. But by 1908, Brethren were attending the International Sunday School Convention at Jerusalem, and in increasing number shared in succeeding International Conventions.

In 1916, J. H. B. Williams, then assistant secretary of the General Mission Board of the Church of the Brethren (its most influential administrative unit for many years), wrote to inquire of the Federal Council of Churches what steps would be required for the Church of the Brethren to become a member of the Council. He apparently believed that the church had moved by then far enough from its earlier separatist position at least to consider such membership. About this same time, as the shadows of World War I moved over the world, Brethren, Friends, and Mennonites developed a degree of cooperation and intense dialogue in their common problems as peace churches in a time of war.

After World War I, in 1919, major Protestant churches in America prepared a campaign to capitalize on the growing interest of many Christians in social issues and international problems. They started a grandiose ecumenical venture named the Interchurch World Movement. Brethren leaders attended the planning conferences, and the boards of the church voted to commit the denomination to full participation in the movement. However, upon referring this action to Annual Conference for approval, they found strong resistance and disapproval. The boards were required to withdraw from the movement. The Church of the Brethren paid in full all its financial obligations to the movement, which soon afterward collapsed. The Brethren, like others, were caught up in the enthusiasm for a brave new world which characterized the movement, but the mood of the total church was more timid. While this costly venture into ecumenism may have set back Brethren ecumenicity twenty years, the church at least had the satisfaction of knowing that the ill-starred movement had had powerful influence for justice in the settling of the famous steel strikes and in securing more humane working conditions for steel workers.

Conciliar Connections

For the past thirty years, the principal involvement of the Church of the Brethren in ecumenical affairs has been through the conciliar movement. In 1936 the Council of Boards of the church appointed M. R. Zigler to represent the Church of the Brethren at the Oxford Conference on Life and Work and the Edinburgh Conference on Faith and Order, both held in the summer of 1937. Zigler brought back enthusiastic reports to the boards, which then appointed a strong committee to relate the Brethren to these movements. Zigler was continued as the Brethren representative to the consultations of world Christian leaders exploring the formation of a World Council of Churches.

During this same period serious study was being given to the question of Brethren participation in the Federal Council of Churches. In 1938, the

Council of Boards voted: (1) that various departments responsible for church program be authorized to cooperate with the corresponding departments of the Federal Council, especially in such areas as peace, temperance, relief, missions, and evangelism; (2) that the Council of Boards authorize an appropriation to the Federal Council from the budgets of the concerned Boards; and (3) that the Council of Boards authorize fraternal representation only, at the forthcoming biennial meeting of the Federal Council. Again, M. R. Zigler was appointed as the Brethren representative.

By 1941, sufficient progress had been made in cooperation and sufficient knowledge of the working of the Federal Council of Churches gained that the Council of Boards could make the following statement recommending full participation of the Church of the Brethren in the Federal Council and in the World Council of Churches (in process of formation):

Since the Church of the Brethren has for a number of years shared partially in the program of the Federal Council of Churches in America by unofficial representation in certain sections of the Council; and since the Conference was officially represented at the World Ecumenical Conferences of Oxford and Edinburgh in 1937; and since much progress has been made toward a World Council of Churches in order to give Protestantism a strong voice in the many strategic situations which now exist throughout the world; and since the World Council as well as the Federal Council is now actively engaged in peace movements of major proportions and is concerned especially with the problem of the conscientious objector, which has been an important concern of the Church of the Brethren for more than two hundred years;

Therefore, the Council of Boards recommends that Annual Conference of 1941 authorize constituent membership both in the World Council of Churches and in the Federal Council of Churches of Christ in America and take steps to appoint official representatives to the Councils of these bodies when our membership has been officially approved by the proper authorities.

It is understood that the Church of the Brethren shall not be bound by any action of these Councils and in no way compromises its doctrinal position by this action. This authorization is made out of a desire to share in the larger fellowship of the Protestant world and to be a more effective comrade of other Christian groups in those great movements for peace and world reconciliation to which we all in Christ owe a common loyalty.[2]

The 1941 Annual Conference adopted this recommendation by a very large majority vote, and appointed as its official representatives to the Federal Council M. R. Zigler, D. W. Kurtz, Rufus D. Bowman, Paul H. Bowman, Sr., and Edward K. Ziegler. Representatives to the World Council were appointed at a later time. There were repercussions in the church to this historic action and repeated queries to Annual Conference asking that the church withdraw from the councils. Thorough debates on the question of membership in the councils were held in 1945 and in 1968. Each time, the position of the church of full and responsible membership in the councils was reaffirmed, with increasingly large majority votes.

When the time came for the first Assembly of the World Council of Churches (1948), the Brethren sent their full complement of delegates to the historic meeting in Amsterdam. In the meantime, a full representation was sent to each meeting of the Federal Council. Brethren became actively involved in the activities of major departments of the Council. The Brethren were also participating in other interdenominational agencies such as the

Foreign Missions Conference, the Home Missions Council, the Stewardship Council, the Student Volunteer Movement for Foreign Missions, and the International Council of Christian Education. When these and other agencies joined with the Federal Council of Churches in 1950 in the formation of the National Council of Churches of Christ in the U.S.A., the Church of the Brethren from the beginning voted approval and fully participated.

Ecumenical Action

Until very recent times, the Brethren have not made significant contribution to theological thought in the wider church. The area of greatest competence has seemed to be in the fields of peace, social concern and action, relief, and certain specialized aspects of overseas missionary work. During the 1930s and 1940s, the ecumenical contribution was largely shaped by the interests and ability of the persons selected to represent the church. M. R. Zigler, who during this time was the chief Brethren exponent of ecumenical cooperation and the first Brethren representative to the councils, was not a theologian but a churchman of profound humanitarian concerns. He was always prodding and pleading with the councils to be involved in the quest for world peace and in those humanitarian activities which would not only bind up the wounds of past wars but prevent future ones. These emphases were not only Zigler's personal bias, but were inherent in the Brethren apprehension of the gospel and its relevance in our modern world. He was strongly supported in his insistence upon these practical issues by the church which sent him and by the colleagues who also represented the Church of the Brethren in the conciliar movement.

In his earlier years, Zigler helped to initiate a strong rural emphasis in the Council of Churches, and a series of national convocations on Town and Country Church which brought together leaders of the rural church movement for many years. After World War II, Zigler spent eleven fruitful years in Europe as the head of the Brethren's vast program of relief and rehabilitation and as the liaison with the World Council of Churches offices in Geneva. He not only administered a far-reaching program for the Brethren, but also saw the development of the Heifers for Relief program and assisted in setting up the World Council's effective worldwide ministry to refugees and the victims of disaster. Zigler's own competence and the role of the Church of the Brethren were recognized in his being given a seat on the powerful Central Committee of the World Council, on which he served until 1961.

Norman J. Baugher, who was executive secretary of the General Board of the Church of the Brethren from 1953 until his untimely death in 1968 also served a term on the Central Committee from 1961 until his death. While the Church of the Brethren is certainly one of the smaller member churches in the World Council, she takes her membership very seriously, sends her full complement of delegates to all its meetings, and has given important leadership to those phases of the Council program which are consistent with the genius of the Church of the Brethren.

Brethren participation in the work of the National Council of Churches has likewise been hearty and responsible. Considering the size of the church, it has given a very large number of leaders to the Council. Norman J.

Baugher served two terms as a vice-president of the Council, giving powerful leadership in peace and long-range planning. Andrew W. Cordier, long prominent on the United Nations staff and former president of Columbia University, has also been a vice-president of the Council. Brethren have given considerable influential leadership in such departments of the Council's activities as peace, worship, evangelism, race relations, and stewardship. Church World Service, which is the department of the National Council channeling the gifts and compassionate concerns of the churches to the hungry and homeless around the world, not only owed much to Brethren initiative and leadership, but entrusted the administration of all its centers for collecting and processing relief materials to the Brethren Service Commission of the Church of the Brethren.

Another area where the Brethren have been responsibly engaged in the conciliar movement is in state and local councils of churches. A startling number of lay and professional leaders of these councils has been provided by the Church of the Brethren. State Council executives in Connecticut, Massachusetts, Pennsylvania, Virginia, Illinois, Kansas, Arizona, and Washington have been Brethren. A large number of local area and city council executives have also been recruited from the Brethren. In most areas where the Brethren are, they participate fully in council activities.

Mention was made earlier of the significant involvement of Brethren in ecumenical work in the countries where they have missions. A brief survey of this direction is here appropriate. In India Brethren missionaries and national leaders have long been active in national and provincial Christian councils, in literary and translation activities, and more recently in the formation of the Church of North India. This church, which came into being in late 1970 is a merger of Anglican, Baptist, Brethren, Disciple, Methodist, and Presbyterian traditions. The Church of the Brethren in India has voted to enter fully into this emerging church.

In Nigeria, the Brethren early pressed for the formation of a United Church of the Sudan, and continue to be the strongest group moving in this direction, while fully cooperating with such movements for unity which the Church in Nigeria is ready to sustain. In China, during the years when missionary activity was still permitted there, Brethren missionaries and Chinese pastors were powerful leaders in movements toward a united, indigenous, Chinese Christian Church. The churches established and nurtured by the Brethren in Ecuador led in the formation of the United Evangelical Church of Ecuador. In Indonesia, instead of seeking to establish a Church of the Brethren, Brethren missionaries have been seconded to the Church of Indonesia, and have worked happily under the direction of Indonesian church leaders.

Perhaps one of the most important contributions of the Church of the Brethren to the ecumenical movement in overseas missions has been in the area of agricultural missions. Many Brethren missionaries were themselves products of a strong rural Christian culture, were well trained for working among rural people, and deeply concerned about the rural billions in the lands where they served. They helped to establish programs of rural mission work which were outstandingly relevant to the needs of the people and were deeply appreciated by national leaders. Thus it is not strange that the Rural Missions Cooperating Committee and Agricultural Missions, Inc., which is the major ecumenical clearing house and training agency for rural missions, has had strong Brethren leadership. Ira W. Moomaw, a world leader in the fields of rural education and the problems of hunger, was for a number of years the executive director of this world organization, after a distinguished career as a missionary in India. He was followed in this post by another Brethren rural expert, J. Benton Rhoades. Moomaw has written a number of provocative books about world problems of hunger and rural education. Another Brethren missionary and pastor, Edward K. Ziegler, has written in the fields of rural church worship and the training of rural ministers, books which are being widely used in seminaries and rural churches around the world.

The outbreak of World War II found the Brethren open and eager for cooperation with others sharing their deep concern for the Christian position regarding war and peace, and the problems of the conscientious objector to war. While this concern was shared most deeply by the Friends, the Mennonites and other Brethren bodies, there was a large sector in other churches as well which was ready for cooperative effort and planning. Raymond Wilson of the Friends, Orie Miller of the Mennonites, and M. R. Zigler, along with other leaders in peace activities, were able to forge a program for conscientious objectors to serve under church auspices in "work of national importance," which was acceptable to the United States government's Selective Service organization. A National Service Board for Religious Objectors was organized. While there have been some criticism and some disillusionment concerning this program for conscientious objectors, it was the best plan which could then be devised for giving these young persons opportunity for significant service activities instead of going to prison or compromising their convictions by entering so-called noncombatant military service.

Brethren have continued to lead out in this area of guidance and counsel for conscientious objectors and the administration of activities in which they are allowed to serve. For many years, W. Harold Row, formerly executive secretary of the Brethren Service Commission, has given strong leadership in this field, as well as in the whole area of relief and service and peace activities in the ecumenical movement. An imaginative approach to the problems of hunger was sparked by Brethren relief worker Dan West while he was administering relief to Spanish refugees during the unhappy civil war in that land. He thought of the practicality of sending live bred heifers to countries where there was a shortage of milk and cattle. This program, initiated by the Brethren, soon became widely ecumenical, and has continued throughout the years sending hundreds of thousands of cattle, goats, sheep, and other animals to impoverished peoples. Brethren have also given able leadership to CROP (Christian overseas relief program), by which the churches channel their contributions of food for world hunger.

Much of what has been described thus far deals with the involvement of the Church of the Brethren in the life and work areas of ecumenical

Christian concern, where, indeed, the Brethren have deep interest and some degree of experience and competence. More recently, there has been Brethren participation in the faith and order division in the person of Warren F. Groff, dean of Bethany Theological Seminary.

Ecumenical Conversations

Another area of ecumenical relationships has to do with the conversations carried on to foster closer fellowship with other Christian bodies, which may or may not lead to merger of churches. It is important now to examine what progress the Brethren have made in this aspect of ecumenical life. Here the stance of the Brethren is inevitably conditioned by their history and by their understanding of the nature of the church. From the beginning of the Brethren involvement in Germany, there have been strong separatist tendencies in the church. Since the Church of the Brethren has been moving more into the mainstream of Protestant church life in the past fifty years, there has been a great deal of thoughtful scrutiny of our ecumenical posture.

A matter in which Brethren have a particularly tender conscience is the relationship with the other Brethren bodies which have broken from the main body of the church. In 1881 a very conservative group (Old German Baptist Brethren) left the church, and has remained as an island of social and ecclesiastical conservatism ever since. The following year another and larger group, more aggressive and progressive than the main body, also separated. Across the years, this latter group, known simply as the Brethren Church, has become more conservative theologically than the Church of the Brethren. Some thirty years ago, this group was split by the modernist-fundamentalist controversy, giving birth to a fundamentalist group called the National Fellowship of Brethren Churches. The Church of the Brethren has hoped and prayed that the unhappy division within the Brethren family itself might somehow be healed. So far as the Old German Baptist Brethren on the one side and the fundamentalist Fellowship of Brethren Churches on the other is concerned, these seems to be little hope of ultimate reconciliation with the Church of the Brethren.

With the Brethren Church, however, there is growing rapport and cooperation. For some years there has been a successful combined missionary program in Nigeria. To maintain and foster this relationship, the Church of the Brethren has for many years had a Fraternal Relations Committee. Intermittently, friendly talks are carried on with this group, clarifying differences, sharing insights, and exploring avenues of further cooperation. There appears to be little likelihood of organic reunion of these two groups in the near future, however.

As ecumenical contacts have increased in the area of program, there is a growing interest in the church in conversations which might lead to possible organic union with other church bodies. The Fraternal Relations Committee, which in 1934 became a permanent committee of the Annual Conference of the church, initiated such conversations or was authorized by Annual Conference to respond to overtures from other denominations for such talks. As a means of acquainting the total church with the nature and scope of these talks, the Fraternal Relations Committee has presented to Annual Conference on many occasions fraternal delegates or visitors from the various communions with whom they have been conversing. The committee has also sought to provide materials and settings for ecumenical education. Wherever the committee has found that its ecumenical contacts called for joint action and program, its concerns were referred to the appropriate board or commission of the church for implementation.

Among the most fruitful and rewarding contacts with other denominations which the Fraternal Relations Committee has had have been the sustained conversations with others in the Free Church tradition. The many areas of common concern with the Mennonites and Quakers have led to a series of formal consultations with them. In 1964 and again in 1968 conferences were held in which several branches each of Brethren, Friends, and Mennonites have shared their insights and concerns. The most recent of these consultations, held in November 1968, at New Windsor, Maryland, brought together sixty representatives of nine groups in this tradition to discuss for three days the role of the peace churches in today's world. Such consultations are not designed to lead to merger, but they do provide opportunity for sharing concerns, insights, common faith, and differences with great sincerity and depth.

Further cementing of the relationships between these groups who share so much of a common heritage and outlook has occurred in two recent conferences on the "Believers' Church." In these conferences Baptists, Disciples, and others in the Free Church tradition have also been involved. The concepts of the Believers' Church and radical discipleship have proved to be a strong bond of interest and material for serious ecumenical conversation. An influential group of Brethren churchmen and theologians believes that the ecumenical future of the Brethren lies in increasingly strong relationships within the group of churches which hold these concepts to be of prime importance. Still conscious of its heritage in the left wing of the Reformation and of its roots in the Pietist and Anabaptist traditions, the Church of the Brethren is uncomfortable in movements toward union with churches which do not hold these concepts.

Among the Mennonite groups, the Brethren have found most intimate and practical relationships with the General Conference Mennonite Church. For thirteen years, 1945-1958, Mennonite Biblical Seminary and Bethany Biblical Seminary shared campus, faculty, and all classroom activities. This creative relationship was terminated when the Mennonites decided to move toward a united Mennonite ministerial training program centered at Elkhart and Goshen, Indiana, and the Brethren deemed it necessary to move to a new campus in the western suburbs of Chicago.

The Brethren have carried on ecumenical conversations also with several smaller bodies. Among them was the General Eldership of the Churches of God in North America. This group, comprising some 38,000 members, shares a common habitat with the strongest areas of Brethren population and has had many common interests and practices with the Church of the Brethren. After several years of conversations and a series of grass-roots conferences of laymen and pastors of both churches, it was agreed that merger between the two would not be a viable ecumenical direction for either. Brief conversations have also been held with the Church of God, (Anderson, Indiana). The Brethren share some publishing interests with this group. Fruitful conversations are still being held with the Evangelical Free Church of North America.

The most intense and serious conversations concerning possible merger have been carried on over the past eight years with the American Baptist Convention (formerly Northern Baptist Convention). With this denomination, talks have proceeded to the point of working out principles for a possible plan of church union which are being studied with great care by local churches both singly and in community or state groupings of the churches. Thorough study has gone into all the ecclesiological and theological issues which might draw the churches together or tend to drive them apart. Areas of greatest divergence are in church polity and in the emphasis upon peace. Baptists are congregational in church polity while the Brethren enjoy a form of representative polity. Baptists support the military chaplaincy, while Brethren are adamantly opposed to this form of ministry to persons in the armed forces. Theologically, the two churches are very similar. In early 1969 it was mutually decided not to press for union in the near future, but rather to focus on joint efforts of Christian mission.

A unique ecumenical privilege has been the cordial exchange of visits between the Brethren and the Holy Orthodox Church of Russia. This relationship, growing out of the Russian Church's desire to be in dialogue with an American church which is concerned for peace, dates back to a meeting of Russian and Brethren delegates at the Third Assembly of the World Council of Churches at New Delhi, India, in 1961. In the years since then exchanges of visits by delegations of the churches were made in 1963 and in 1967. In the latter exchange the Russian delegation was led by Metropolitan Nikodim of Leningrad and Ladoga, chairman of the department for external church affairs of the Moscow patriarchate. The Brethren leader has been W. Harold Row. This exchange of Christian dialogue across the "Iron Curtain" is rooted in the hope that peace may come to the war-broken world in the twentieth century and in the firm conviction that the churches may point the way to a just and lasting peace.

Brethren have been involved in two movements in Europe of great ecumenical import. One is a series of conferences sponsored by the peace churches and the International Fellowship of Reconciliation, in which their representatives engage in dialogue with theologians from other European churches. These conferences have been called the Puidoux Conferences, from the location in Switzerland of the first such gathering. These meetings, under the stimulus provided originally by M. R. Zigler, have been characterized by high-level scholarly debate and discussion.

W. Harold Row and other Brethren have also participated actively in the Christian Peace Conferences of Prague, which are international meetings of significant groups of theologians and churchmen, including those from the churches behind the communist frontier, those from the West, and those from the Third World. The fact of its location gives special importance to this conference. While American participation is welcomed in the conference, it is not dominant. The Brethren participants have reported an especially warm welcome.

The most vigorous debate on ecumenicity within the Church of the Brethren in recent years has come about through the challenge of the Consultation on Church Union (COCU). In December 1961, Dr. Eugene Carson Blake, stated clerk of the United Presbyterian Church in the U.S.A., at the invitation of the then Episcopal Bishop James A. Pike, preached a sermon in Grace Cathedral, San Francisco, on the eve of the triennial meeting of the National Council of Churches, in which he pleaded for the formation of a new united church which should be "truly evangelical, truly catholic, and truly reformed." Originally addressed to the Protestant Episcopal Church, the United Presbyterian Church, the Methodist Church, and the United Church of Christ, Blake's powerful appeal soon attracted other denominations, and the annual meetings of the Consultation since that time have included ten denominations as full participant members (now nine since the formation of the United Methodist Church). From the beginning, other churches which are not ready for full participation in COCU have been invited and welcomed as observer-consultant churches. While at first the relationship was more observer than consultant, the churches which have accepted this role have been playing an increasingly important part in the discussions. The Church of the Brethren has had observer-consultants present from the first meeting.

In 1965, the Brethren and others were asked whether they would welcome an invitation at that point to become full participants in the Consultation. After a year of study and the publication of considerable material on the subject, the Annual Conference of the Church of the Brethren voted in June 1966 by an overwhelming majority to continue the observer-consultant relationship, but not to accept full membership at that time. Perhaps no issue before the Church of the Brethren in many years has so deeply stirred the church or so intensely divided it. The action of the Conference declining full membership in COCU was interpreted by some as a retreat into narrow sectarianism or as a surrender to resurgent fundamentalism. On the other hand, the debate clearly showed that the most vocal and persuasive opponents of affiliation with COCU were those who saw the Church of the Brethren hearkening to a different drummer; they saw the Brethren as champions of the Free Church tradition and of radical discipleship. They saw the role of the church not in isolationism, but as a strong minority voice in the body of the church universal, sustained by a strong church entity, speaking out prophetically in the councils of churches, and cooperating fully and trustfully with other Christian groups. To be sure, a minority within the church led by a group called the Brethren Revival Fellowship was opposed to any form of cooperation, except with equally conservative groups. This group helped to swell the tide of opposition to COCU.

Sober reflection would show that the Brethren refusal to enter fully into membership in COCU indicates the desire of the church to maintain a strong peace witness and a quality of radical discipleship which they do not see as viable within the shape of the church emerging from the Consultation. The option to join COCU, however, was kept open, and is still open. Two years after the historic debate on the issue, Annual Conference again studied the question of affiliation. After another spirited debate, Conference voted not to reopen the decision, but by a smaller majority than in 1966. However, the number of observer-consultants was increased from two to four, the maximum allowed by the Consultation authorities. The Church of the Brethren may in time be drawn irresistibly toward a united and uniting church which under God may emerge.

The same Annual Conference which rejected so decisively the option to become a full participant in COCU voted to pursue a somewhat different ecumenical direction:

> Annual Conference voted to (a) Reaffirm our resolute and profound commitment to cooperation with our brethren in Christ through local, state, national and world councils of churches, and urge Brethren through their local churches to responsible participation in the councils.
>
> (b) Move as rapidly as possible to explore possible mergers of our church with such churches or groups of churches as are sufficiently similar to us in doctrine, polity, and mission that merger may be feasible and productive. We see the Church of the Brethren as serving under God as a bridge church, actively seeking to promote cooperation and possible merger with a constellation of churches which are close to us in doctrine and polity and with whom we can share in the concepts of mission which we now see to be the will of God for our time.[3]

Because of the increasing magnitude of the tasks entrusted to the Fraternal Relations Committee and of the change in direction seen in the 1966 Annual Conference action, the General Board of the church was asked to explore some new structuring for ecumenical concerns. After two years of study, the Fraternal Relations Committee was replaced by an Interchurch Relations Committee, responsible equally to Annual Conference and the General Board of the Church, with somewhat wider powers than those held by the earlier committee. This new committee is engaged in continued study of new ecumenical directions for the Church of the Brethren, is holding conversations in depth with the Commission on Christian Unity of the American Baptist Convention, and is working with the General Board for fuller cooperation with other churches through the Councils of Churches.

The committee sees its task as basically that of guiding the Church of the Brethren through this time when all ecclesiastical structures must be under the gaze of God to see whether they truly share in God's mission in and to the world. That God wills the visibility of his church in the world, there can be no doubt. That the Church of the Brethren has something unique to share with the whole Church of Jesus Christ is firmly and humbly believed. How that contribution of the insights God has given her can best be made to the whole church is not clearly seen. If, like a grain of wheat falling into the earth to die that it may bring forth more fruit, the Church of the Brethren must truly lose its life in order to save it, then the Church of the Brethren will be ready to take that road.

The Church of the Brethren, like most of her sister churches, is passing through a time of crisis of identity. But there are many thoughtful persons in the church who firmly believe that its destiny is inextricably tied up with that of the whole church of Christ. Isolationism is past and done with. It is impossible to be separatist in this day and continue to be the church. The Church of the Brethren, therefore, seeks divine guidance that it may be faithful to God's calling and may be a vital and responsible part of the total church.

There will certainly be vast realignments throughout the whole church of Jesus Christ. One important and necessary grouping will be that of the churches which share the Anabaptist, Free Church, radical discipleship kind of church vision. Very likely the Church of the Brethren will find its destiny under God in such a group. Whether such a group of churches with such vision can be a part of the great church which may emerge from the Consultation on Church Union is an open question. It may well be that a certain amount of pluralism in holy obedience may be necessary for the health and effectiveness in mission of the church. What the Church of the Brethren has been given is important for God's mission in the world. The concern is that it be used where it can be shared most helpfully and conspicuously. The prayer of the Brethren, with that of the Lord, is that all his folk may be one, one under God, one as God the Father and Christ are one, so that the world may believe in God's mission and turn to him and be saved.

---

1. Donald F. Durnbaugh, ed., *The Brethren in Colonial America* (Elgin, Ill.: Brethren Press, 1967), chap. 3.

2. *Minutes of the Annual Conferences of the Church of the Brethren, 1923-1944* (Elgin, Ill.: 1946), 162.

3. *Minutes of the 180th Recorded Annual Conference of the Church of the Brethren, June 21-26, 1966*, 50.

10

STATISTICS AND ADDRESSES

Donald F. Durnbaugh

I. *Historical Statistics (North America)*[1]

Year	Congregations	Ministers	Members	Source
1770	28	43	1,505	Morgan Edwards
1850	145*	300*	10,000*	David Benedict
1882	497	1,701	57,749	Howard Miller
1890	720	1,622	61,101	U. S. Census
1900	800*	2,397	75,000*	Brethren *Almanac*
1910	896	3,012	82,215	*Missionary Visitor*
1920	1,004	3,400	96,076	Brethren *Yearbook*
1930	1,029	2,735	138,173	Brethren *Yearbook*
1940	1,017	2,754	176,908	Brethren *Yearbook*
1950	1,029	2,900	186,201	Brethren *Yearbook*
1960	1,077	2,686	200,217	Brethren *Yearbook*

(* — estimate)

II. *Current Statistics (September 30, 1969)*[2]

District	Congregations	Pastors	Members	Total Giving
Florida, Georgia and Puerto Rico	14	11	1,590	$ 187,278
Idaho and Western Montana	8	5	954	70,343
Illinois and Wisconsin	49	34	7,290	750,126
Indiana, Middle	37	25	6,202	576,331
Indiana, Northern	50	41	9,774	1,166,574
Indiana, Southern	22	16	2,786	318,684
Iowa and Minnesota	43	33	4,961	456,739
Michigan	22	17	2,588	286,889
Mid-Atlantic	60	46	13,663	1,181,908
Missouri	13	6	1,030	75,571
Missouri, Southern, and Arkansas	11	2	559	33,123
North Atlantic	18	18	3,203	381,825
Ohio, Northern	58	51	9,378	1,021,390
Ohio, Southern	59	53	12,577	1,258,834
Oregon-Washington	20	18	3,028	299,175

Pacific Southwest	38	33	7,931	898,009
Pennsylvania, Eastern	45	30	15,688	1,658,687
Pennsylvania, Middle	52	36	12,104	939,405
Pennsylvania, Southern	39	22	9,490	929,931
Pennsylvania, Western	68	46	13,183	1,036,239
Shenandoah (North Virginia)	77	47	15,482	1,147,332
Southeastern	46	12	3,078	176,837
Southern Plains	13	9	1,115	100,663
Virginia, First	41	27	8,306	580,474
Virginia, Southern	40	20	6,787	331,155
Western Plains	51	37	6,047	561,877
West Marva (Maryland, West Va.)	51	21	6,584	295,085
(Subtotal)	(1045)	(716)	(185,198)	(16,720,484)
India, First	21	20	7,745	7,052
India, Second	4	4	1,054	1,272
Nigeria	41	33	17,711	18,478*
(Subtotal)	(66)	(57)	(26,510)	(26,812)
Total	*1,111*	773	*211,708*	*$16,747,296*

(* 1968 figure)

III. *Annual Conferences (1880-1970)*[a]

Year Place	Moderator	Moderator's Profession
1880 Lanark, Ill.	Enoch Eby	Schoolteacher
1881 Ashland, Ohio	Enoch Eby	Schoolteacher
1882 Milford Junction, Ind.	Enoch Eby	Schoolteacher
1883 Bismarck Grove, Kans.	Enoch Eby	Schoolteacher
1884 Dayton, Ohio	Enoch Eby	Schoolteacher
1885 Mexico, Pa.	John Wise	Schoolteacher/farmer
1886 Pitsburg, Ohio	D. E. Price	Farmer
1887 Ottawa, Kans.	Enoch Eby	Schoolteacher
1888 N. Manchester, Ind.	Enoch Eby	Schoolteacher
1889 Harrisonburg, Va.	S. S. Mohler	Farmer
1890 Pertle Springs, Mo.	Enoch Eby	Schoolteacher
1891 Hagerstown, Md.	Daniel Vaniman	Schoolteacher
1892 Cedar Rapids, Iowa	Daniel Vaniman	Schoolteacher
1893 Muncie, Ind.	D. E. Price	Farmer
1894 Meyersdale, Pa.	Enoch Eby	Schoolteacher
1895 Decatur, Ill.	Enoch Eby	Schoolteacher
1896 Ottawa, Kans.	D. E. Price	Farmer
1897 Frederick, Md.	L. W. Teeter	Teacher/writer
1898 Naperville, Ill.	W. R. Deeter	Farmer
1899 Roanoke, Va.	L. T. Holsinger	Farmer/businessman
1900 N. Manchester, Ind.	D. L. Miller	Businessman/publisher
1901 Lincoln, Neb.	Daniel Vaniman	Schoolteacher
1902 Harrisburg, Pa.	D. L. Miller	Businessman/publisher
1903 Bellefontaine, Ohio	S. F. Sanger	Businessman

Year	Place	Moderator	Moderator's Profession
1904	Carthage, Mo.	H. C. Early	Farmer/businessman
1905	Bristol, Tenn.	John Zuck	undetermined
1906	Springfield, Ill.	S. F. Sanger	Businessman
1907	Los Angeles, Calif.	L. T. Holsinger	Farmer/businessman
1908	Des Moines, Iowa	H. C. Early	Farmer/businessman
1909	Harrisonburg, Va.	D. M. Garver	Farmer/businessman
1910	Winona Lake, Ind.	H. C. Early	Farmer/businessman
1911	St. Joseph, Mo.	D. M. Garver	Farmer/businessman
1912	York, Pa.	H. C. Early	Farmer/businessman
1913	Winona Lake, Ind.	D. M. Garver	Farmer/businessman
1914	Seattle, Wash.	Frank Fisher	Superintendent of institution
1915	Hershey, Pa.	H. C. Early	Farmer/businessman
1916	Winona Lake, Ind.	I. W. Taylor	Cabinetmaker
1917	Wichita, Kans.	H. C. Early	Farmer/businessman
1918	Hershey, Pa.	I. W. Taylor	Cabinetmaker
1919	Winona Lake, Ind.	H. C. Early	Farmer/businessman
1920	Sedalia, Mo.	I. W. Taylor	Cabinetmaker
1921	Hershey, Pa.	Otho Winger	College president
1922	Winona Lake, Ind.	I. W. Taylor	Cabinetmaker
1923	Calgary, Alberta, Canada	Otho Winger	College president
1924	Hershey, Pa.	J. J. Yoder	College professor
1925	Winona Lake, Ind.	Otho Winger	College president
1926	Lincoln, Neb.	D. W. Kurtz	College president
1927	Hershey, Pa.	J. W. Lear	Seminary professor
1928	La Verne, Calif.	Otho Winger	College president
1929	N. Manchester, Ind.	H. K. Ober	Pastor
1930	Hershey, Pa.	James M. Moore	Pastor
1931	Colorado Springs, Colo.	Otho Winger	College president
1932	Anderson, Ind.	D. W. Kurtz	Seminary president
1933	Hershey, Pa.	Charles D. Bonsack	Denominational executive
1934	Ames, Iowa	Otho Winger	College president
1935	Winona Lake, Ind.	Charles C. Ellis	College president
1936	Hershey, Pa.	D. W. Kurtz	Seminary president
1937	Nampa, Idaho	Paul H. Bowman	College president
1938	Lawrence, Kans.	Vernon F. Schwalm	College president
1939	Anderson, Ind.	D. W. Kurtz	Pastor
1940	Ocean Grove, N. J.	Rufus D. Bowman	Seminary president
1941	La Verne, Calif.	C. Ernest Davis	College president
1942	Asheville, N. C.	Paul H. Bowman	College president
1943	McPherson, Kans.	W. W. Peters	College president
1944	Huntingdon, Pa.	Charles C. Ellis	College president (retired)
1945	N. Manchester, Ind.	Warren D. Bowman	Pastor
1946	Wenatchee, Wash.	Rufus Bucher	Pastor

Year Place	Moderator	Moderator's Profession
1947 Orlando, Fla.	Rufus D. Bowman	Seminary president
1948 Colorado Springs, Colo.	Calvert N. Ellis	College president
1949 Ocean Grove, N. J.	Paul H. Bowman	College president
1950 Grand Rapids, Mich.	Charles C. Ellis	College president (retired)
1951 San Jose, Calif.	Desmond W. Bittinger	College president
1952 Richmond, Va.	R. W. Schlosser	College professor
1953 Colorado Springs, Colo.	Vernon F. Schwalm	College president
1954 Ocean Grove, N. J.	William M. Beahm	Seminary dean
1955 Grand Rapids, Mich.	A. Stauffer Curry	Denominational executive
1956 Eugene, Oregon	Paul M. Robinson	Seminary president
1957 Richmond, Va.	A. C. Baugher	College president
1958 Des Moines, Iowa	Desmond W. Bittinger	College president
1959 Ocean Grove, N. J.	William M. Beahm	Seminary dean
1960 Champaign-Urbana, Ill.	Edward K. Ziegler	Pastor
1961 Long Beach, Calif.	Charles E. Zunkel	Pastor
1962 Ocean Grove, N. J.	Nevin H. Zuck	Pastor
1963 Champaign-Urbana, Ill.	Harry K. Zeller, Jr.	Pastor
1964 Lincoln, Neb.	DeWitt L. Miller	Pastor
1965 Ocean Grove, N. J.	A. Stauffer Curry	Denominational executive
1966 Louisville, Ky.	*Dan West	Denominational executive (retired)
1967 Eugene, Oregon	Raymond R. Peters	Pastor
1968 Ocean Grove, N. J.	M. Guy West	Pastor
1969 Louisville, Ky.	Morley J. Mays	College president
1970 Lincoln, Neb.	A. G. Breidenstine	College dean (retired)

(* first layman elected as moderator)

IV. *Offices*

   North America

General Offices, 1451 Dundee Avenue, Elgin, Illinois 60120

   General Secretary, S. Loren Bowman

   Associate General Secretaries: World Ministries Commission, Joel K. Thompson; Parish Ministries Commission, Earle W. Fike, Jr.; General Services Commission, Galen B. Ogden.

   Treasurer, Robert Greiner

Washington Office, 110 Maryland Avenue, N.W., Washington, D. C. 20002

   Representative, W. Harold Row

   Abroad

Ecuador — Casilla 455, Quito

   Field Secretary, George M. Kreps

India — Dharampur Road, Bulsar, Bulsar District, Gujarat State

   Executive Secretary, Ishwarlal L. Christachari

Indonesia — Institut Theologia, Geredja Protestan Maluku, Djl. Tanah Lapan
      Ketjil, Amboina
    Fraternal Worker, Fumitaka Matsuoka
Indonesia — Dewan Geredja di Indonesia, Djl. Salemba Raya 10, Djakarta
    Fraternal Worker, Donald Fancher
Nigeria — C.B.M., Box 626, Jos, Benue-Plateau State
    Field Secretary, Roger L. Ingold
Switzerland — 150 Route de Ferney, 1211 Geneva 20
    Director in Europe, Dale Ott

V. *Institutions*
    Colleges and Theological Schools
        North America
California
    La Verne College, La Verne, Calif. 91750
Illinois
    Bethany Theological Seminary, Oak Brook, Ill. 60521
Indiana
    Grace College and Seminary, Winona Lake, Ind. 46590 (Grace Brethren)
    Manchester College, No. Manchester, Ind. 46962
Kansas
    McPherson College, McPherson, Kans. 67460
Ohio
    Ashland College and Seminary, Ashland, Ohio 44805 (Brethren Church)
Pennsylvania
    Elizabethtown College, Elizabethtown, Pa. 17022
    Juniata College, Huntingdon, Pa. 16652
Virginia
  Bridgewater College, Bridgewater, Va. 22812
        Abroad
Ecuador
    Center of Theological Studies, Casilla 455, Quito (in cooperation with
      other denominations)
India
    Gujarat United School of Theology, I. P. Mission, Ellis Bridge,
      Ahmedabad, Gujarat State (in cooperation with other denomina-
      tions)
    Vocational Training College, Anklesvar, Broach District, Gujarat State
Nigeria
    Kulp Bible School, Kwarhi, P.O. Box, Mubi, North East State
    Theological College of Northern Nigeria, Bukuru, via Jos, North East
      State (in cooperation with other denominations)
    Waka Teacher Training College, P.O. Box, via Yola, North East State
    Medical and Homes for Aging
        North America
California
    Hillcrest Homes, La Verne, Calif. 91750
    Long Beach Brethren Manor, Long Beach, Calif. 90806

Florida
Florida Brethren Home, Sebring, Fla. 33870
Illinois
Bethany Brethren Hospital, Chicago, Ill. 60624
East Garfield Park Hospital, Chicago, Ill. 60624
The Home, Girard, Ill. 62640
Pinecrest Manor, Mt. Morris, Ill. 61054
Indiana
Timbercrest Home, No. Manchester, Ind. 46962
Iowa
Spurgeon Manor, Dallas Center, Iowa 50063
Kansas
The Cedars, McPherson, Kans. 67460
Maryland
Fahrney-Keedy Memorial Home, Boonsboro, Md. 21713
Ohio
Agape Acres, Ashland, Ohio, 44805
Brethren Home, Greenville, Ohio 45331
Good Shepherd Home, Fostoria, Ohio 44830
West View Manor, Wooster, Ohio 44691
Pennsylvania
Peter Becker Memorial Home, Harleysville, Pa. 19438
The Brethren Home, Neffsville, Pa. 17556
The Brethren Home, New Oxford, Pa. 17450
Brethren Home, Windber, Pa. 15963
Morrison Cove Home, Martinsburg, Pa. 16662
Tennessee
John M. Reed Home, Limestone, Tenn. 37681
Virginia
Brethren Home for Aging, Bridgewater, Va. 22812
Friendship Manor, Roanoke, Va. 24012

Abroad

India
Brethren Mission Hospital, Dahanu Road, Thana District, Maharastra State
Nigeria
Adamawa Provincial Leprosarium, Garkida, via Yola, North East State
Garkida Hospital, Garkida, via Yola, North East State
Mission Hospital, Lassa, P.O. Mubi, via Yola, North East State
Puerto Rico
Castañer Hospital, Castañer, Puerto Rico 00631

Service Centers
North America

California
Church World Service Center, Modesto, Calif. 65352

Indiana
    Church World Service Center, Nappanee, Ind. 46550
Maryland
    New Windsor Service Center, New Windsor, Md. 21776
Texas
    Church World Service Center, Houston, Texas 77021
        Abroad
India
    Rural Service Center, Anklesvar, Broach District, Gujarat State (for community development)

VI. *Historical Libraries and Archives*

Brethren Historical Library, General Offices, Church of the Brethren, Elgin, Ill. 60120
Bethany Theological Seminary Library, Oak Brook, Ill. 60521
See also the colleges listed above.

---

1. The sources used for the table of historical statistics in North America are: Morgan Edwards, *Materials Toward a History of the American Baptists* (Philadelphia: Crukshank and Collins, 1770ff.), reprinted in D. F. Durnbaugh, ed., *The Brethren in Colonial America* (Elgin, Ill.: Brethren Press, 1967), 173-191; David Benedict, *A General History of the Baptist Denomination in America* (New York: Colby and Co., 1848), 913, 959; Howard Miller, *Record of the Faithful* (Lewisburg, Pa.: J. R. Cornelius, 1882), 67; *Special Reports, Religious Bodies: 1906* (Washington, D. C.: Bureau of the Census, 1910), 22; *The Brethren Family Almanac* (1901), 27-38; *The Missionary Visitor*, XII (June 1910, 185; Church of the Brethren *Yearbook* (Elgin, Ill.: 1921ff.). John Price assisted in compiling the statistics.

2. Church of the Brethren *1970 Yearbook* (Elgin, Ill.: 1970), 140-141.

3. Church of the Brethren *1957 Yearbook* (Elgin, Ill.: 1957), 3-4; Church of the Brethren *1966 Yearbook* (Elgin, Ill.: 1966), 3. Information on moderators' professions was obtained from scattered sources.

11

DOCUMENTS

Donald F. Durnbaugh

I. *An Open Letter to the Palatine Pietists (1708)*

Before the first Brethren baptism in 1708 the eight participants sent out an open letter to like-minded Pietists in the Palatinate. The unknown writer told how the desire for baptism became known to them during the visit of two "foreign brethren," possibly Dutch Collegiants. It provides insight into the motivations leading to the formation of the Brethren movement.

To All Those Beloved Called in Christ Jesus. Greetings!

Under the providence of God, in Christ Jesus the beloved, I announce and make known to the brethren beloved in God the wonderful divine ordinance which has revealed itself among brethren through their manifest confession about the true baptism. According to the Holy Scriptures, Jesus Christ, our Savior, received this true baptism from John the Baptist. When John, however, refused, our dear Savior said, ". . . for thus it is fitting for us to fulfil all righteousness" [Matthew 3:15]. After he had been baptized, a voice from heaven called, "This is my beloved son, with whom I am well pleased [Matthew 3:17]. Listen to him" [Matthew 17:5]. John bore record saying, "I saw the Spirit descend as a dove from heaven, and it remained on him" [John 1:32].

I must first describe the beginning, when all of us, in varying numbers of years ago (indeed, one experienced a strong agitation of the heart already five years ago) expressed to several brethren: "You men, dear brethren. We must be baptized according to the teachings of Jesus Christ and the apostles." However, when this was opposed, it was passed over, but was not completely erased from our hearts. At various times I had an occasion to admit or realize before God and my conscience that it would still occur, and I was assured of it in my heart. In the past two years the other brethren were moved in their consciences that they must be baptized, but none of us knew of the others' concern. Quite by accident, when two foreign brethren visited us, that which was in our hearts was revealed. Our inner joy increased and we were strengthened in the Lord not to be negligent, and to come together in the fear of the Lord. Each one revealed and opened the depths of his heart. As we found that we all agreed with one spirit in this high calling, we have decided to announce this to our beloved brethren through an open letter. This is to see whether they also find themselves convinced in their hearts to help confirm this high calling to the pride and glory of our Savior Jesus Christ, and to follow the Creator and Fulfiller of our faith. We drew lots, and the lot has fallen on the most unworthy.

Dear brethren, please have patience with this simple letter, as the dear Savior and Redeemer has patience with all of us, and hears and sustains us in His long-suffering.

I also want to remind the dear brethren that we must publicly profess that which Christ Jesus taught and did without hesitation or fear of man. We need not be ashamed and must above all suffer and endure all things with rejoicing.

"Joy! Joy! More joy! Christ prevents all suffering. Bliss! Bliss! More bliss! Christ is the sum of grace!"

Concerning baptism, Christ, the first-born is our forerunner, of whom the apostles and many thousands testified with their blood that Jesus Christ was the Son of the living God. Now Jesus did not only teach, but also acted and commanded, saying to His disciples: "Go therefore and make disciples of all nations (and make known to them Jesus, the Son of God, that they may believe on Him, that He is the same), baptizing them in the name of the Father and of the Son and of the Holy Spirit, teaching them to observe all that I have commanded you" (Matthew 28 [19, 20]). Dear brethren! What is then better than being obedient and not despising the commandment of the Lord Jesus Christ, the King of all Glory? This, especially as we have left all sects because of the misuses concerning infant baptism, communion, and church system, and unanimously profess that these are not according to the teaching of Jesus Christ. We profess that they are rather man's statutes and commandments, and therefore do not baptize our children, and testify that we were not really baptized.

We should, however, remind ourselves of our baptismal covenant, and profess at the same time that it is man's commandment and teaching established after the statutes of the world, and does not follow simply the teaching of Jesus Christ. Oh, beloved brethren in the Lord, we will not be able to meet the test at that time when the Lord [Hausherr] will come and require from us the obedience which He has commanded of us. We have been unfaithful servants, as we knew, recognized, and professed the will of the dear Lord. Oh, there is still time today, dear brethren, before the sun of justice sets and the time breaks upon us of which Jesus says that one can work no more! Is it not highly necessary that we go to meet the Son of God on the holy path, and kiss Him, before His wrath is kindled?

Dear brethren, we cannot err, as He — the Way, the Truth, and the Eternal Life — goes before us, and His teaching, namely Jesus Christ's, is sealed by His blood. His disciples have loyally followed Him and sealed it with their blood. Saint John faithfully explains to us in his second epistle that many deceivers have come into the world, and gives us the sign that whosoever does not remain in the teaching of Christ has no God. However, whosoever does remain in the teaching of Jesus Christ has both the Father and the Son. When we consider the eternal providence of God, which stands so clearly in the written teaching of Jesus Christ despite all controversy, does not this also seem a great miracle, that the almighty God so cares for us that we have a sure guide, and that a light always appears for us in the darkness? May God be eternally praised and glorified for His goodness, grace, and mercy, which He still evidences even to this hour.

In the second chapter of the Acts of the Apostles, it says that the multitude was so convinced by the sermon of Peter that they spoke, " 'Brethren, what shall we do?' And Peter said to them, 'Repent, and be baptized every one of you in the name of Jesus Christ . . . ,' " and it is added, "For the promise is to you and to your children and to all that are far off, every one whom the Lord our God calls to Him" [Acts 2:37-39]. Now the apostles remained single-mindedly obedient and did not lay any emphasis on whether the Holy Spirit came to the persons before or after the baptism; rather, they remained firmly by the commandment of their Father and baptized those who had shown themselves repentant. This needs little proof, dear brethren, as the entire New Testament is full of it. It can, however, easily be seen that this is no slight or poor matter which can be taken lightly. It cannot possibly be that all obviously disorderly persons are accepted for baptism, when it is known that they are without true remorse and repentance.

There is also an exact relationship and brotherly discipline, according to the teaching of Jesus Christ and His apostles. When a person does not better himself, after faithful warning, he must be expelled and cannot be treated any more as a brother. We are truly assured that our Lord Jesus Christ, who at that time was given power and might in heaven and on the earth, is the initiator of our action, and will know how to carry it through wisely, and also provide here the one and the other to whom He will entrust wisdom and understanding. The ways of the Lord will then be orderly prepared, without giving offense and annoyance to the God-loving brethren and sisters. For the world, however, Christ and His disciples are a stumbling block and an annoyance, and it takes offense at the Word on which they are founded.

Dear brethren, it will certainly not require much more proof, as each one who is from God will be taught everything by the anointing, and will well understand the importance of baptism. Paul writes (Romans 6), "Do you not know that all of us who have been baptized into Christ Jesus were baptized into his death? We were buried therefore with him by baptism into death, so that as Christ was raised from the dead by the glory of the Father, we too might walk in newness of life" [3 and 4]. This is then the covenant of a good conscience with God, as Peter writes in First Peter 3:21 and explains very clearly that as the great flood cleansed the first world, so they have explained baptism, that from now on, all of the old sins and uncleanliness shall be washed away through baptism. For as a person is cleansed outwardly through water, so is the inner person cleansed through the blood of Jesus Christ in faith. The Holy Spirit gives His testimony thereto. These are the three witnesses on earth, of which St. John speaks (1 John [5]:8).

I am quite convinced that you, dear brethren, are more familiar with the Holy Scriptures about this than I am, concerning Jesus Christ's teaching, action, life, and conduct. Your hearts will be, with ours, so mightily convinced that if an angel came from heaven and proclaimed something different we would not accept it. I do not doubt that some one could ignore this ordinance, and consider it unnecessary without the loss of his salvation if grounded in God. I also do not doubt that some out of folly for their own opinions may fail to do as our Lord Jesus Christ has done. But as Christ our head and keeper lowered himself into the water, so must we of necessity, as His members, be immersed with Him. Moreover, we do not write one point which is not from the teachings of Christ and His apostles out of the freedom of conscience which each one has. It may be that God has revealed to us, where possibly presumption is practiced. We live in the appearance of good and simple work and wish to eat our own bread in quiet conduct according to the teaching of St. Paul, the apostle. Where, however, God places different work on a brother, which may well be harder than physical work, then each one should attend to his own work to which God has called him, in the fear of the Lord. That I would like to have someone to be as I am, is very deceptive, for each should live according to his calling.

So then, if some more brethren wish to begin this high act of baptism with us out of brotherly unity according to the teachings of Christ and the apostles, we announce in humbleness that we are interceding together in prayer and fasting with God. We will choose him whom the Lord gives as the baptizer as God will reveal to us. If we then begin in the footsteps of the Lord Jesus to live according to His commandment, then we can also hold communion together according to the commandment of Christ and His apostles in the fear of the Lord. We now wish from the bottom of our hearts, grace, peace, and love for all brethren, from God our Father in Jesus Christ, His beloved Son, through the Holy Spirit. May the triune God seal, strengthen, found, and confirm His eternal truth in our hearts, that we may highly respect all that which is commanded through God. Let nothing depart from our hearts, but rather let us think upon it, talk about it, and also tell our children, that they also learn to observe the commandments and witness of God. Yes, the Lord God of our fathers, the God of Abraham, be praised, the God of Isaac, and of Jacob, be highly exalted, and His name be glorified to the end of the world.

[Summer, 1708]   [One of the first eight][1]

II. *Petition to the Pennsylvania Assembly (1775)*

The peace churches in Pennsylvania were under strong pressure in 1775 to join the military uprising against the British. On October 27, 1775, the Society of Friends (Quakers) submitted a memorial to the legislature reaffirming their peace position. The following month the Brethren and the Mennonites presented a joint petition in the same vein.

A Short and Sincere Declaration.

To our Honorable Assembly, and all others in high or low station of administration, and to all friends and inhabitants of this country, to whose sight this may come, be they English or German.

In the first place we acknowledge us indebted to the most high God, who created heaven and earth, the only good being, to thank Him for all His great goodness and manifold mercies and love through our Saviour Jesus Christ, who is come to save the souls of men, having all power in heaven and on earth.

Further we find ourselves indebted to be thankful to our late worthy Assembly, for their giving so good an advice in these troublesome times to all ranks of people in *Pennsylvania,* particularly in allowing those, who, by the doctrine of our Saviour Jesus Christ are persuaded in their conscience to love their enemies and not to resist evil, to enjoy the liberty of the conscience, for which, as also for all the good things we enjoyed under their care, we heartily thank that worthy body of assembly, and all high and low in office who have advised to such a peaceful measure, hoping and confiding that they, and all others entrusted with power in this hitherto blessed province, may be moved by the same spirit of grace which animated the first founder of this province, our late worthy proprietor *William Penn,* to grant liberty of conscience to all its inhabitants, that they may in the great and memorable day of judgment be put on the right hand of the just judge, who judges without respect of person, and hear of Him these blessed words: *Come, O blessed of my Father, inherit the kingdom prepared for you, . . . what you did to one of the least of these my brethren, you did it to me,* among which number (i.e. *the least of Christ's brethren*) we by His grace hope to be ranked; and every lenity and favour shown to such tender conscienced, although weak followers of this our blessed Saviour, will not be forgotten by Him in that great day.

The advice to those who do not find freedom of conscience to take up arms, that they ought to be helpful to those who are in need and distressed circumstances, we receive with cheerfulness toward all men of what station they may be — it being our principle to feed the hungry and give the thisty drink. We have dedicated ourselves to serve all men in every thing that can be helpful to the preservation of men's lives, but we find no freedom in giving, or doing, or assisting in any thing by which men's lives are destroyed or hurt. We beg the patience of all those who believe we err in this point.

We are always ready, according to *Christ's* command to *Peter,* to pay the tribute, that we may offend no man, and so we are willing to pay taxes, *and to render unto Caesar those things that are Caesar's and to God those things that are God's,* although we think ourselves very weak to give God His due honor, He being a spirit and life, and we only dust and ashes.

We are also willing to be subject to the higher powers, and to give in the manner *Paul* directs us: *For he does not bear the sword in vain; he is the servant of God, to execute his wrath on the wrongdoer.*

This testimony we lay down before our worthy Assembly, and all other persons in government, letting them know that we are thankful as above mentioned, and that we are not at liberty in conscience to take up arms to conquer our enemies, but rather to pray to God, who has power in heaven and on earth, for *us* and *them.*

We also crave the patience of all the inhabitants of this country; what they think to see clearer in the doctrine of the blessed Jesus Christ, we will leave to them and God, finding ourselves very poor. For faith is to proceed out of the word of God, which is life and spirit, and a power of God, and our conscience is to be instructed by the same; therefore we beg for patience.

Our small gift, which we have given, we give to those who have power over us, that we may not offend them, as Christ taught us by the tribute penny.

We heartily pray that God would govern all hearts of our rulers, be they high or low, to mediate those good things which will pertain to our and their happiness.

The above declaration, signed by a number of elders and teachers of the Society of Mennonists, and some of the German Baptists, presented to the Honorable House of Assembly on the 7th day of November, 1775, was most graciously received.[2]

III. *The Goshen Statement on War (1918)*

In January 1918 an especially called conference of the Church of the Brethren met in Goshen, Indiana, to prepare a statement on the proper reaction of members of the church to World War I. The first section contained a letter to leading officials of the United States government. The second, here republished, contained a biblical and theological discussion on the subject of war. The third section provided for organization to care for the denomination's peace concerns.

Statement of Special Conference of the Church of the Brethren to the Churches and the Drafted Brethren.

Amidst all the confusion that is upon the earth at this time, and with the force and argument resident in the circumstances of the present war, the appeals to reason and human judgment, in regard to the claims of justice and freedom, we appreciate the difficult dilemma into which men are brought in deciding their position and course. In it all, however, we must know that the final authority and determining arbiter for us must be found, not in our feeling or popular acclaim, or persuasions of men, or in our own reasoning, but in the New Testament, which we claim as our creed, — a revelation of God's Will, a standard of human conduct both as to morals and religion.

Therefore this Conference of the Church of the Brethren hereby declares her continued adherence to the principles of nonresistance, held by the Church since its organization in 1708.

I. We believe that war or any participation in war is wrong and entirely incompatible with the spirit, example, and teachings of Jesus Christ.

II. That we can not conscientiously engage in any activity or perform any function, contributing to the destruction of human life.

THE FOUNDATIONS OF OUR BELIEF

I. THE OLD TESTAMENT WAS FULFILLED IN CHRIST, HENCE NOT THE CHRISTIAN'S GUIDE.

"Think not that I came to destroy the law or the prophets: I came not to destroy but to fulfill" (Matt. 5:17). "For Christ is the end of the law unto righteousness to every one that believeth" (Rom. 10:4). "So that the law is become our (Jews) tutor to bring us unto Christ, that we might be justified by faith. But now that faith is come, we are no longer under a tutor" (Gal. 3:24, 25). "For he (Christ) is our peace, who made both one, and brake down the middle wall of partition, having abolished in his flesh the enmity, even the law of commandments contained in ordinances; that he might create in himself of the two one new man, so making peace" (Eph. 2:14, 15). "God, having of old time spoken unto the fathers in the prophets by divers portions and in divers manners, hath at the end of these days spoken unto us in his Son, whom he appointed heir of all things, through whom also he made the worlds" (Heb. 1:1, 2).

II. SOME TEACHINGS OF THE NEW TESTAMENT, THE CHRISTIAN'S RULE OF ACTION.

1. Christians are servants of Christ. "But if any man hath not the Spirit of Christ, he is none of his" (Rom. 8:9). "Have this mind in you, which was also in Christ Jesus" (Philip. 2:5).

2. Love motivates the Christian's conduct. "Hereby know we love, because he laid down his life for us: and we ought to lay down our lives for the brethren" (1 John 3:16). "Ye have heard that it was said, Thou shalt love thy neighbor, and hate thine enemy: but I say unto you, Love your enemies, and pray for them that persecute you; that ye may be sons of your Father who is in heaven" (Matt. 5:43-45). "But I say unto you that hear, Love your enemies, do good to them that hate you, bless them that curse you, pray for them that despitefully use you. To him that smiteth thee on the one cheek offer also the other; . . . And as ye would that men should do to you, do ye also to them likewise. And if ye love them that love you, what thank have ye? for even sinners love those that love them. And if ye do good to them that do good to you, what thank have ye? for even sinners love those that love them. . . . But love your enemies, and do them good. . . . and your reward shall be great, and ye shall be sons of the Most High" (Luke 6:27-35).

3. Human life sacred. "Ye have heard that it was said to them of old time, Thou shalt not kill; and whosoever shall kill shall be in danger of the judgment: but I say unto you, that every one who is angry with his brother shall be in danger of the judgment; and whosoever shall say to his brother, Raca, shall be in danger of the council" (Matt. 5:21, 22).

4. Physical resistance and revenge incompatible with Christian conduct. "Ye have heard that it was said, An eye for an eye, and a tooth for a tooth: but I say unto you, Resist not him that is evil: but whosoever smiteth thee on thy right cheek, turn to him the other also" (Matt. 5:38, 39). "Render to no man evil for evil. Take thought for things honorable in the sight of all men. If it be possible, as much as in you lieth, be at peace with all men. Avenge not yourselves, beloved, but give place unto the wrath of God: for it is written, Vengeance belongeth unto me; I will recompense, saith the Lord. But if thine enemy hunger, feed him; if he thirst, give him to drink: for in so doing thou shalt heap coals of fire upon his head. Be not overcome of evil, but overcome evil with good" (Rom. 12:17-21). "Then saith Jesus unto him, Put up again thy sword into its place: for all they that take the sword shall perish with the sword" (Matt. 26:52). "Jesus answered (Pilate), My

kingdom is not of this world: if my kingdom were of this world, then would my servants fight, that I should not be delivered to the Jews: but now is my kingdom not from hence" (John 18:36). "For though we walk in the flesh, we do not war according to the flesh (for the weapons of our warfare are not of the flesh, but mighty before God to the casting down of strongholds)" (2 Cor. 10:3, 4).

5. Suffering for righteousness' sake a Christian's duty and privilege. "Blessed are ye when men shall reproach you, and persecute you, and say all manner of evil against you falsely, for my sake. Rejoice, and be exceeding glad: for great is your reward in heaven: for so persecuted they the prophets that were before you" (Matt. 5:11, 12). "Behold, I send you forth as sheep in the midst of wolves: be ye therefore wise as serpents, and harmless as doves. But beware of men: for they will deliver you up to councils, and in their synagogues they will scourge you; yea and before governors and kings shall ye be brought for my sake, for a testimony to them and to the Gentiles. But when they deliver you up, be not anxious how or what ye shall speak; . . . For it is not ye that speak, but the Spirit of your Father that speaketh in you" (Matt. 10:16-20). "If ye were of the world, the world would love its own: but because ye are not of the world, but I chose you out of the world, therefore, the world hateth you" (John 15:19). "But call to remembrance the former days, in which, after ye were enlightened, ye endured a great conflict of sufferings; partly, being made a gazing stock both by reproaches and afflictions; and partly, becoming partakers with them that were so used. For ye both had compassion on them that were in bonds, and took joyfully the spoiling of your possessions, knowing that ye have for yourselves a better possession and an abiding one. Cast not away therefore your boldness, which hath greater recompense of reward. For ye have need of patience, that, having done the will of God, ye may receive the promise" (Heb. 10:32-36).

6. The instructions of John the Baptist to the soldiers (Luke 3:14), and the Lord's suggestion that they sell their cloaks and buy swords, and his final saying that two swords are sufficient (Luke 22:35-38), when studied in the text and context, are against military warfare, rather than in its favor.

III. THE LORD'S EXAMPLE

"Because Christ also suffered for you, leaving you an example, that ye should follow his steps; who did no sin, neither was guile found in his mouth: who, when he was reviled, reviled not again; when he suffered, threatened not; but committed himself to him that judgeth righteously: who his own self bare our sins in his body upon the tree, that we, having died unto sins, might live unto righteousness; by whose stripes ye were healed" (1 Peter 2:21-24).

"And the soldiers led him away within the court, . . . and they call together the whole band. And they clothe him with purple, and platting a crown of thorns, they put it on him; and they began to salute him, Hail, King of the Jews! And they smote his head with a reed, and spat upon him, and bowing their knees worshipped him. And when they had mocked him, they took off from him the purple, and put on him his garments. And they led him out to crucify him" (Mark 15:16-20, and to the end of the chapter).

"And when they had come unto the place which is called The Skull, there they crucified him, and the malefactors, one on the right hand and the other on the left. And Jesus said, Father, forgive them; for they know not what they do" (Luke 23:33-34, and to the end of the chapter).

IV. THE TEACHINGS AND EXAMPLE OF THE APOSTOLIC CHURCH

The Apostolic church and early church fathers endured, without physical resistance, the persecutions of the Jewish and heathen peoples, and ever taught and consistently followed the principles of peace.

The Church's Attitude Toward the Government

I. We are loyal citizens of this great nation, which has been and is now a safeguard of our religious liberties and the protector of our homes and loved ones.

II. Our attitude towards Civil Governments and rulers should be carefully taken into account. We are taught that Governments are ordained of God, and that the administrators of Government are ministers of God. As such we are to be in subjection to them (Rom. 13:1-7). We are admonished to pray for the rulers and magistrates and for those in authority (1 Tim. 2:1-2).

The word and authority of God, however, must be final and supreme over all. And when the demands of men and of Governments conflict with the Word of God, we are then bound by the latter, regardless of consequences. "Whether it is right in the sight of God to hearken unto you (magistrates) rather than unto God, judge ye" (Acts 4:19). "But Peter and the apostles answered and said, We must obey God rather than men" (Acts 5:29). Therefore we urge, —

First. That our various congregations pray without ceasing for the rulers of our nation that the nation may again enjoy peace, and that blood-shedding and destruction may cease.

Second. That they contribute liberally to the relief of human suffering, both in men and money.

Third. That they express their gratitude to God for our favored position and freedom from the devastation of war, by giving freely of our substance for constructive relief work, such as Red Cross, Y.M.C.A., Friends' Relief Work, or through our own Service Committee.

Fourth. We urge our people to put forth their utmost effort in this world crisis, laboring with their hands, cultivating our fields and gardens and vacant lands, planting only such crops as will contribute to the real necessities of life; also that they practice the greatest economy in clothing, food, and all supplies which may, mechanically or otherwise, aid in the production and transportation of food, clothing and fuel, so that a suffering and hungering world may be clothed, warmed and fed.

Appeal for Greater Efforts in Church and Mission Work

The present crisis has aroused the self-sacrifice of all classes of people in the interests of suffering humanity. The spirit of sacrifice is with us. Our young people are restless to do something commensurate with the sacrifices of others, but they must have a cause.

We urge that the supreme cause of the Kingdom of God be held up before them so repeatedly and continuously that they will enlist in its service. Our young people should be made to see that there can be no permanent peace without Christianity, and Christianity can not become real in the world without heroic, self-sacrificing work of missions. The world will not be safe for democracy until it is safe for truth. The greatest service we can render humanity is the promotion of the Kingdom of God. And all the pent-up energy of the church can here find an outlet in the work of religious education, which includes all Christian work.

We need more pastors, and churches should elect and encourage suitable brethren for this work. The Sunday-schools have a great task to inculcate the true Gospel into the hearts of man, in this age of materialism, skepticism, and carnage. We urge that special efforts be made to secure volunteers for our mission work. As others give their sons for the trenches, we should give ours for the salvation of the world. When the spirit of self-sacrifice is manifest on every hand, it is opportune to enlist the young people in the holy cause of missions, where they can give their lives in a living sacrifice for the things that endure.

We urge upon the whole church to increase greatly her offerings for the cause of missions. The excess profits, due to the war, should all be given for the promotion of the Kingdom of God, of which the mission work is a most vital part. We believe, with Dr. [John R.] Mott and Sherwood Eddy, that, during this world crisis, no one should "lay up treasure on earth," but give all that he can for the salvation of the world.

The gospel of Jesus Christ is the source and foundation of all our blessings, and the only hope of enduring peace. Therefore let us give our lives and our means to promote his Gospel, at home and abroad.

Other Provisions

We are petitioning the Government to give our drafted brethren such industrial noncombatant service as will contribute constructively to the necessity, health and comfort of hungering, suffering humanity, either here or elsewhere.

We further urge our brethren not to enlist in any service which would, in any way, compromise our time-honored position in relation to war; also that they refrain from wearing the military uniform. The tenets of the church forbid military drilling, or learning the art or arts of war, or doing anything which contributes to the destruction of human life or property.

We commend the loyalty of the brethren in the Camps for their firm stand in not participating in the arts of war. We do not wish to oppose the consciences of those brethren who, in some Camps, found work which they felt they could conscientiously do, but we urge them to do only such work as will not involve them in the arts of destruction.[3]

IV. The Revised "Brethren's Card" (1923)

A brief compilation of Brethren beliefs was prepared and distributed in the early twentieth century by the Tract Committee. In 1922-1923 this statement was revised by request of Annual Conference delegates, and approved for circulation with the understanding that it should not be considered a creed.

The Church of the Brethren
Formerly Called Dunkers

1. This body of Christians originated early in the eighteenth century, the church being a natural outgrowth of the Pietistic movement following the Reformation.

2. Firmly accepts and teaches the fundamental evangelical doctrines of the inspiration of the Bible, the personality of the Holy Spirit, the virgin birth, the deity of Christ, the sin-pardoning value of his atonement, his resurrection from the tomb, ascension and personal and visible return, and the resurrection, both of the just and unjust (John 5:28, 29; 1 Thess. 4:13-18).

3. Observes the following New Testament rites: Baptism of penitent believers by trine immersion for the remission of sins (Matt. 28:19; Acts 2:38); feet-washing (John 13:1-20; 1 Tim. 5:10); love feast (Luke 22:20; John 13:4; 1 Cor. 11:17-34; Jude 12); communion (Matt. 26:26-30); the Christian salutation (Rom. 16:16; Acts 20:37); proper appearance in worship (1 Cor. 11:2-16); the anointing for healing in the name of the Lord (James 5:13-18; Mark 6:13); laying on of hands (Acts 8:17; 19:6; 1 Tim. 4:14). These rites are representative of spiritual facts which obtain in the lives of true believers, and as such are essential factors in the development of the Christian life.

4. Emphasizes daily devotion for the individual, and family worship for the home (Eph. 6:18-20; Philipp. 4:8, 9); stewardship of time, talents and money (Matt. 25:14-30); taking care of the fatherless, widows, poor, sick and aged (Acts 6:1-7).

5. Opposes on Scriptural grounds: War and the taking of human life (Matt. 5:21-26, 43, 44; Rom. 12:19-21; Isa. 53:7-12); violence in personal and industrial controversy (Matt. 7:12; Rom. 13:8-10); intemperance in all things (Titus 2:2; Gal. 5:19-26; Eph. 5:18); going to law, especially against our Christian brethren (1 Cor. 6:1-9); divorce and remarriage except for the one Scriptural reason (Matt. 19:9); every form of oath (Matt. 5:33-37; James 5:12); membership in secret, oath-bound societies (2 Cor. 6:14-18); games of chance and sinful amusements (1 Thess. 5:22; 1 Peter 2:11; Rom. 12:17); extravagant and immodest dress (1 Tim. 2:8-10; 1 Peter 3:1-6).

6. Labors earnestly, in harmony with the Great Commission, for the evangelization of the world, for the conversion of men to Jesus Christ; and for the realization of the life of Jesus Christ in every believer (Matt. 28:18-20; Mark 16:15, 16; 2 Cor. 3:18).

7. Maintains the New Testament as its only creed, in harmony with which the above brief doctrinal statement is made.[*]

V. *Declaration of Principles and Purposes for Conference Delegates (1946)*

In the reorganization of the church polity worked out in 1946-1947, there is a statement of "declaration of principles and purposes." Members of the Standing Committee of Annual Conference and Conference delegates are asked to accept these. This is therefore as close to a creed as is found in the Church of the Brethren.

(1) I again declare my faith in, and grateful acceptance of, Jesus Christ, "the only begotten Son of God," as my personal Savior; and the Bible as God's infallible Word of Truth, and the New Testament as the ultimate rule of faith and practice for men (John 1:14; 3:16, 36; 12:47-48; Luke 21:33; Acts 10:43; 2 Timothy 3:16).

(2) It is my sincere endeavor, in submission to God's Holy Spirit, to make my life, at all times, in purpose and in act, a true expression of the teaching of Jesus and his apostles (1 Corinthians 10:31-33; Romans 12:1-2).

(3) I pledge my loyalty, my life and influence, to the Church of the Brethren and to her doctrines and practices as taught by the Scriptures and defined by her General Conference (1 Peter 1:13-16; 3:3-4; James 5:12; Luke 3:14; 1 Corinthians 6:1-8; John 18:20; 1 Peter 5:13-14; John 13; 1 Corinthians 11:1-21).

(4) As a delegate to the above-named Conference, I promise prayerfully to consider with open mind and a teachable spirit all matters presented, and to act, by voice and vote, in good faith, for the best interests of the church, that she may continue to be "the pillar and ground of the truth" (1 Thessalonians 5:17; Romans 14:22-23).[5]

VI. A Message to Fellow Christians in All Lands (1958)

As part of the observance of the two-hundred-fiftieth anniversary of the founding of the Church of the Brethren, a statement was presented to the Central Committee of the World Council of Churches, Nyborg, Denmark, August 22, 1958. It was directed to all Christians.

The Church of the Brethren, prior to 1908 known as the German Baptist Brethren, is celebrating in the year 1958 the 250th anniversary of its founding. In this our anniversary year, we desire to extend greetings to our fellow Christians throughout the world, particularly to those communions in the membership of the World Council of Churches.

[There follows a historical sketch of the early Brethren, here omitted.]
They contended for freedom of worship and the free exercise of conscience. They conceded to no earthly power authority over the human spirit. They believed in reconciliation between man and man and in the peaceful arbitration of disputes between nation and nation. They renounced war and the taking of human life. On the basis of religious conviction they refused military training and service. They rejected the civil oath as contrary to New Testament teaching and as an affront to their integrity. They were Biblical Christians and sought to demonstrate in daily life the teachings of the gospel.

The Brethren accepted the Lordship of Christ as a cardinal tenet of their faith. They looked to him as their Leader and Savior. Rejecting as they did creeds and dogma, they became theologically nontechnical and exercised broader latitude in matters of doctrine than they did in what they considered the practical and more urgent issues of daily living. The Lordship of Christ implied for them absolute obedience to him who was to them the Master of every life and of all life. On this premise they considered man's life here as temporary and transient and all life precious in the sight of God. They could, therefore, do violence to no human being. Man, in their view, was of infinite worth and possessed rights as a child of God which could not be denied him.

The Brethren were not ascetic. They did, however, develop a doctrine of nonworldliness and accepted disciplines austere and removed from the immediate ends of life. The Brethren were less involved in the physical comforts and the accumulation of wealth than in the deeper meanings and the final fulfillment of life.

The Lordship of Christ also undergirded their doctrine of peace and nonretaliation. They strove for harmony among themselves and with their neighbors. They deplored conflict in the social order and sought to alleviate passion and violent conflict between races and nations. They regarded all war as sin. Every war for them was civil war inasmuch as it involved hate, bitterness, and destruction within the family of God and among his children.

The Church of the Brethren, now a body of 210,000 members, has sponsored the church of Christ in India, Africa, and China. We have lately established the church in Ecuador, South America, as a ministry to the Calderón Indians of that country. Our ministry of relief, material aid, refugee resettlement, and rehabilitation has been extended to five continents of the world.

We are committed in America and other countries both in theory and in practice when possible to the policy of comity and visible unity. We have no intention or desire to establish congregational units in areas where we carry on relief work except when clear need for such a ministry is demonstrated by indigenous groups and when it can be done in a prevailing pattern of Christian co-operation. We desire to serve in the spirit of ecumenicity and in the name of our Lord Jesus Christ, to the end that human distress may be relieved, communities and individuals rehabilitated, and the gospel proclaimed in areas of spiritual retardation.

The Church of the Brethren, a co-operating communion of the World Council, is also a member of the National Council of Churches of Christ in the United States of America. We are affiliated with Church World Service and with numerous other intercommunion movements such as the National Service Board for Religious Ojectors in the United States of America, the American Bible Society, and the Heifer Project which owes its origin to the Brethren.

On this 250th anniversary of our beginning, we humbly acknowledge our indebtedness to the past. We have been the recipient of contributions from the total church and from the centuries of Christian thought and worship which had already preceded our beginning. Except for the continuing witness of the apostles and martyrs, and generations of devout men and women, we could never have known Christ. We recognize in gratitude "the clouds of witnesses" through whom the word of life has been made available to us.

We acknowledge ourselves debtors to those pioneers of Protestant Christianity who contended for the purity of the church and for the rediscovery of the mind of Christ, and who in their quest for truth demonstrated the adventurous spirit of the disciples and the early apostles. They have contributed to our belief in the centrality of the Scriptures, to our concern for practical piety, and to our reliance upon internal rather than external authority. We confess our excesses in emphasizing the danger of creeds, and our failure to contribute more positively to the undergirding of the Christian faith in its doctrinal and theological structure. This we do, however, without surrendering our conviction that there is an inner witness of the Holy Spirit which now and always has relevance to religious thought and experience.

We desire the fellowship of the universal church in searching out the bases of unity in Christ and sharing the variableness of the Christian faith with which God has endowed the members of his body. We, too, stand under the Lordship of Christ, our common Leader and Savior, confessing our fealty to him in all areas of life, admitting our proneness to unfaithfulness, and penitent for our tendency toward religious exclusiveness.

We seek openness of mind and heart that we may perceive what God, who has spoken to us in our history, is saying to us in our own day. It is our prayer that in so doing we may be drawn closer to the God who loves us, to the Christ who is our Lord, and to fellow members of the community of faith who are our brothers.

We could not be true to the light which we believe has been shed abroad in our hearts without at least sharing with our fellow Christians the following concerns:

First: We urge the Universal Church of Christ, in this time of supreme need in the life of the world and of dramatic possibilities for the kingdom of God, to recognize the relevancy of goodwill and resolute love in the affairs of men and of nations. Let us as Christians demonstrate throughout the world our concern and compassion for distressed and disadvantaged peoples of all races that a climate of trust and brotherhood may emerge in which peace among nations, races, and peoples may have positive promise of success.

Second: Realizing how desperately urgent it is that nations turn from the suicidal madness of war and preparation for war, to the settlement of disagreements in the spirit of reconciliation and also recognizing that the convictions concerning the establishment of peace and justice and liberty which have been elaborated in the ecumenical movement have not yet penetrated the wider membership of the churches, we urge the consideration of a world assembly of churches in a special and concerted effort to undergird every sincere approach to peace among the nations to the end that they may be persuaded to seek security, not on the basis of fear and preponderance of arms, but on the basis of reason, understanding, and goodwill.

Third: We beseech our fellow Christian bodies through the common voice of the World Council of Churches to seek on the part of the governments of the world, recognition of the right of conscience and religious conviction in regard to participation in war and military service. We seek for men everywhere freedom to follow unrestricted and unafraid the inner light of love and the divine will. We implore for all such persons the privilege to serve mankind as positive, constructive, and creative citizens of their respective governments.

That there may come to pass among the Christians of the world genuine unity grounded in Christ our Lord; that the Church of Christ may be the instrument of unity for the total life of the children of men; and that races and peoples and classes may be drawn more closely together by the One whom we worship and serve, we pledge our ceaseless prayers and our continuing effort, and beseech for our fellowship the prayers of the Church Universal.°

VII. *Statement of the Church of the Brethren on War (1970)*

From time to time the Church of the Brethren has put its antiwar position on record, particularly for the use of its members in dealing with military conscription. The most recent statement was adopted in June 1970. It is based on an Annual Conference resolution of 1948, revised in 1957, 1968, and 1970.

The Church of the Brethren regards with sorrow and deep concern our nation's increasing movement toward a permanently militaristic outlook. Two devastating world wars, the conflict in Korea, the Vietnam War, and the many international crises of recent decades have produced an alarming change in American attitudes toward war and peace. The American public may come to accept as normal and inevitable the prospect that the nation must be prepared to go to war at any moment, that every young man must spend time in military service, that an overwhelming share of our *heavy* federal taxes must be devoted to military needs, and that this country must always be willing to assume the military burdens of weaker allies, actual or potential.

Because of our complete dissent from these assumptions, the Church of the Brethren desires again, as at other times in its history, to declare its convictions about war and peace, military service and conscription, the use of tax money for military purposes, the right of Christian conscience, and the responsibility of Christian citizenship.

1. THE CHURCH AND SPIRITUAL NURTURE

The Church of the Brethren seeks by processes of education and spiritual nurture to help its members to allow a spirit of peace and an attitude of nonviolence to develop within themselves as an outgrowth of deep religious conviction. They are encouraged to demonstrate this spirit in their daily relationships in the home, the school, business, and the community.

For this purpose we provide our services of worship, our preaching ministry, our Sunday and weekday educational efforts, our summer camps, our colleges and seminary, our personal counseling, our volunteer service program, our continuing ministry in relief and rehabilitation, and our entire church-extension program. We seek thereby to lead individuals into such intimate contact with Jesus Christ, our Lord, that they will commit themselves to him and to the manner of life which he taught and exemplified.

We believe that such commitment leads to the way of love and of nonviolence as a central principle of Christian conduct, knowing full well that, in so doing, violence may fall upon us as it did upon Jesus. We recognize that there are varying degrees of achievement of this sought-for result in individuals and churches. But we seek to maintain a deep and growing fellowship among ourselves and between ourselves and our Master in order that we might increasingly know his purpose and do his will.

2. THE CHURCH AND CONSCIENCE

The church has stood likewise for the principle of freedom of worship and freedom of conscience. The church itself respects the right of the individual conscience within its membership and has never set up an authoritative creed. Instead, it accepts the entire New Testament as its rule of faith and practice and seeks to lead its members to comprehend and accept for themselves the mind of Christ as the guide for their convictions and conduct.

We believe that no government has the authority to abrogate the right of individual conscience. "We must obey God rather than men" (Acts 5:29).

The official position of the Church of the Brethren is that all war is sin and that we seek the right of conscientious objection to all war. We seek no special privileges from our government. What we seek for ourselves, we seek for all — the right of individual conscience. We affirm that this conscientious objection may include all wars, declared or undeclared; particular wars; and particular forms of warfare. We also affirm that conscientious objection may be based on grounds more inclusive than institutional religion.

3. THE CHURCH AND WAR

The Church of the Brethren, since its beginning in 1708, has repeatedly declared its position against war. Our understanding of the life and the teaching of Christ as revealed in the New Testament led our Annual Conference to state in 1785 that we should not "submit to the higher powers so as to make ourselves their instruments to shed human blood." In 1918 at our Annual Conference we stated that "we believe that war or any participation in war is wrong and incompatible with the spirit, example, and teachings of Jesus Christ." Again in 1934 Annual Conference resolved that "all war is sin. We, therefore, cannot encourage, engage in, or willingly profit from armed conflict at home, or abroad. We cannot, in the event of war, accept military service or support the military machine in any capacity." This conviction, which we reaffirmed in 1948 and now reaffirm again, grew out of such teachings of Christ as the following:

"Love your enemies, do good to those who hate you, bless those who curse you, pray for those who abuse you. To him who strikes you on the cheek, offer the other also . . . " (Luke 6:27, 28).

"So whatever you wish that men would do to you, do so to them; for this is the law and the prophets" (Matthew 7:12).

"Put your sword back into its place; for all who take the sword will perish by the sword" (Matthew 26:52).

4. THE CHURCH AND CONSCRIPTION

The Church of the Brethren feels constrained by Christ's teachings to lead its people to develop convictions against war. The church cannot concede to the state the authority to conscript citizens for military training or military service against their conscience.

The church will seek to fulfill its prophetic role in this matter in two ways: by seeking to change political structures and by influencing individual members.

The church will seek to use its influence to abolish or radically restructure the system which conscripts persons for military purposes.

The church pledges its support and continuing fellowship to all of our draft-age members who face conscription. We recognize that some feel obligated to render full or noncombative military service and we respect all who make such a decision.

We commend to all of draft age, their parents, counselors and fellow members, the alternative positions of (1) Alternative Service as conscientious objectors engaging in constructive civilian work, or (2) Open, nonviolent noncooperation with the system of conscription. The church pledges itself to renew and redouble its effort to interpret to the membership of the church at all levels of the church's life these positions which we believe are in harmony with the style of life set forth in the gospel and as expressed in the historic faith and witness of our church.

The church extends its prayers, spiritual nurture, and material aid to all who struggle and suffer in order to understand more fully and obey more perfectly the will of God.

5. THE CHURCH AND ALTERNATIVE SERVICE

The church pledges its support to the draft-age member facing conscription who chooses to engage in constructive alternative service civilian work as a conscientious objector. Such service might include participation in relief and rehabilitation in war or disaster areas anywhere in the world; technical, agricultural, medical, or educational assistance in developing countries; service in general or mental hospitals, schools for the handicapped, homes for the aged, and kindred institutions; and medical or scientific research promising constructive benefits to mankind.

The church will seek to establish, administer, and finance to the extent of its resources, projects for such service under church direction or in cooperation with other private civilian agencies.

6. THE CHURCH AND NONCOOPERATION

The church pledges its support to the draft-age member facing conscription who chooses open noncooperation with the system of conscription as a conscientious objector. Individuals who follow the lead of their conscience to this position will need the support of the church in many ways. The church will seek to meet these needs, to the extent of its resources, by providing such ministries as legal counsel, financial support, and prison visitation. To demonstrate a sense of community and fellowship with the noncooperator, congregations are encouraged to offer sanctuary and spiritual support. All members of the church who take the position of noncooperation should seek to exhibit a spirit of humility, good-will, and sincerity in making this type of courageous witness most effective, nonviolent, and Christian.

7. THE CHURCH AND MINISTERIAL EXEMPTION

The Church of the Brethren accepts the concept of the minister as one who seeks no special privilege but shares the life of his people. Therefore, the church urges those who have the possibility of ministerial exemption from the draft law to consider refusing such exemption and to confront the draft on an equal basis with the laity.

8. THE CHURCH AND SUPPORT OF NATIONAL DEFENSE

We declare again that our members should not participate in war, learn the art of war, or support war.

Although recognizing that almost all aspects of the economy are directly or indirectly connected with national defense, we encourage our members to divorce themselves as far as possible from direct association with defense industries in both employment and investment.

While recognizing the necessity of preserving academic freedom, we find recruitment by the armed forces on Brethren college campuses inconsistent with the church's position.

9. THE CHURCH AND TAXES FOR WAR PURPOSES

While the Church of the Brethren recognizes the responsibility of all citizens to pay taxes for the constructive purposes of government, we oppose the use of taxes by the government for war purposes and military expenditures. For those who are conscientiously opposed to paying taxes for these purposes, the church seeks government provision for an alternative use of such tax money for peaceful, nonmilitary purposes.

The church recognizes that its members will believe and act differently in regard to their payment of taxes when a significant percentage goes for war purposes and military expenditures. Some will pay the taxes willingly; some will pay the taxes but express a protest to the government; some will refuse to pay all or part of the taxes as a witness and a protest; and some will voluntarily limit their incomes or use of taxable services to a low enough level that they are not subject to taxation.

We call upon all of our members, congregations, institutions, and boards, to study seriously the problem of paying taxes for war purposes and investing in those government bonds which support war. We further call upon them to act in response to their study, to the leading of conscience, and to their understanding of the Christian faith. To all we pledge to maintain our continuing ministry of fellowship and spiritual concern.

10. THE CHURCH AND CITIZENSHIP

The church holds that our supreme citizenship is in the kingdom of God, but we undertake to render constructive, creative service in the existing state. We encourage our members to exercise the right of suffrage and to regard public office as an opportunity to work for good government in keeping with our Christian values. We believe that in a democracy Christians must assume responsibility for helping to create intelligent public opinion which will result in legislation in harmony with the eternal laws of God.

As Christian citizens we consider it our duty to obey all civil laws which do not violate these higher laws. We seek, however, to go beyond the demands of law, giving time, effort, life, and property in a ministry to human needs without regard to race, creed, or nationality. We attempt to reconcile conflicting persons and groups, leading them toward fuller human brotherhood under a common divine allegiance.

We believe that good citizenship extends beyond our own national boundaries and will there serve to remove the occasion for war. Convinced that good citizens in a good society must work out a better way than war to resolve international conflict, we have in recent years undertaken a diligent search for practical, effective means to that end.

The church encourages its members to study international relations and foreign policy and to confer with legislators, government executives, and other policy makers concerning these matters in the light of the Christian faith. We favor the strengthening of agencies of international cooperation; intelligent sympathy with the desire of the people in underdeveloped areas for self-determination and a higher standard of living; and intensified study and application of the peaceful, constructive uses of atomic power for the benefit of all mankind.

11. THE CHURCH AND ITS CONTINUING WITNESS

The Church of the Brethren has always believed that peace is the will of God. In the two and one-half centuries of its history it has come to understand more clearly the tremendous evil which war brings upon human beings and their society. The church, therefore, feels an increasing responsibility for the careful instruction and guidance of its members on all the problems of war and peace. It is also aware that there is room for further growth in the understanding of these questions and in ways of expressing the church's convictions in practical action.

This statement embodies the stage of thought and action which the Church of the Brethren has thus far reached in its desire to learn the will of God for our times. We undertake a continuing and growing witness and pledge ourselves to be receptive to new truth and better modes of expression as these come to our attention.[7]

---

1. A copy of the original letter is found in the Thüringisches Landeshauptarchiv, Weimar; it is published in English translation in D. F. Durnbaugh, ed., *European Origins of the Brethren* (Elgin, Ill.: Brethren Press, 1958), 115-120.

2. *A Short and Sincere Declaration* . . . ([Philadelphia: Henry Miller], 1775). It has been republished in D. F. Durnbaugh, ed., *The Brethren in Colonial America* (Elgin, Ill.: Brethren Press, 1967), 363-365.

3. *Minutes of the Special General Conference, 1918* (Elgin, Ill.: Brethren Publishing House, 1918), 3-6. The special conference is discussed in Roger E. Sappington, *Brethren Social Policy, 1908-1958* (Elgin, Ill.: Brethren Press, 1961), 42-45.

4. H. L. Hartsough *et al.*, eds., *Minutes of the Annual Conferences of the Church of the Brethren, 1923-1944* (Elgin, Ill.: Brethren Publishing House, 1946), 7-8.

5. Ora Garber, ed., *Minutes of the Annual Conferences of the Church of the Brethren, 1945-1954* (Elgin, Ill.: Brethren Publishing House, 1965), 55.

6. Church of the Brethren *Gospel Messenger* (October 4, 1958), 12-14.

7. *Statement of the Church of the Brethren on War* (Elgin, Ill.: General Offices, 1970).

BIBLIOGRAPHY

The following is a selective annotated listing of the more important publications dealing with the Church of the Brethren. Unless otherwise indicated, the publisher is the Brethren Press, Elgin, Illinois (formerly known as the Brethren Publishing House). The scholarly journal *Brethren Life and Thought* (Oak Brook, Illinois) is here abbreviated as *BLT*.

Bibliographies

Doll, Eugene E., and Funke, Anneliese M., eds. *The Ephrata Cloisters: An Annotated Bibliography.* Philadelphia: Carl Schurz Memorial Foundation, 1944. In two parts: "Sources for the History of the Ephrata Cloisters," 3-81; "Ephrata: The Printing Press of the Brotherhood, 1745-1794," 83-128; with index.

Durnbaugh, Donald F., and Shultz, L. W., eds. "A Brethren Bibliography, 1713-1963." *BLT*, IX (Winter and Spring 1964), 3-177. A list of nearly 1,300 publications by Brethren authors, in chronological order, with a checklist of Brethren periodicals and an index of authors, editors, and compilers.

Durnbaugh, Donald F., "Supplement and Index to the Brethren Bibliography." *BLT*, XI (Spring 1966), 37-64. Additions to the above, with a topical index of the entire bibliography. Also published separately.

Durnbaugh, Donald F., "A Second Supplement to the Brethren Bibliography," *BLT*, XV (Autumn 1970), 187-204.

Harley, Chester I., "A Study of the Yearbook of the Church of the Brethren." *Schwarzenau*, I (October 1939), 16-31. With an index covering the period 1871-1939.

Heckman, Marlin L., "Articles of Brethren Historical Interest in Non-Brethren Journals: A Preliminary List, 1960-1970," *BLT*, XV (Autumn 1970), 211-213.

Meynen, Emil, ed. *Bibliography on German Settlements in Colonial North America.* Leipzig: Otto Harrassowitz, 1937. A comprehensive listing, with a section on the several Brethren groups.

Sappington, Roger E., ed. "A Bibliography of Theses on the Church of the Brethren." *BLT*, III (Winter 1958), 60-70. Includes B.D., M.A., and Ph.D. theses.

Sappington, Roger E., "A Bibliography of Theses on the Church of the Brethren: Supplement to the 1958 Bibliography," *BLT*, XV (Autumn 1970), 205-210.

Seidensticker, Oswald, ed. *The First Century of German Printing in America, 1728-1830.* Philadelphia: Schaefer and Koradi, 1893. Many references to Ephrata and the Brethren.

Stapleton, A. "Researches into the First Century of German Printing in America, 1728-1831." *The Pennsylvania-German*, V (1904), 81-89, 183; VI (1905), 262-263. Additions to Seidensticker.

General History: Europe

Barthold, Friedrich W. "Die Erweckten im protestantischen Deutschland während des Ausgangs des 17. und der ersten Hälfte des 18. Jahrhunderts, besonders die frommen Grafenhöfe." *Historisches Taschenbuch*, ed. F. von Raumer, series 3, III (1852), 128-320; IV (1853), 169-390. Good general description, although unsympathetic in tone.

Blaupot ten Cate, Steven, *Geschiedenis der Doopsgezinden in Friesland.* Leeuwarden: W. Eekhoff, 1839. Has material on the Brethren in Surhuisterveen.

Brunn, Hermann. *1200 Jahre Schriesheim.* Mannheim: Südwestdeutsche Verlagsanstalt, 1964. Refers to the Mack family.

Durnbaugh, Donald F., ed. *European Origins of the Brethren.* 1958 (reprinted 1967). A source book with English translations of the important early documents.

Durnbaugh, Donald F. *The Believers' Church: The History and Character of Radical Protestantism.* New York: Macmillan, 1968.

Durnbaugh, Donald F. "Brethren Beginnings." Ph.D. dissertation, University of Pennsylvania, 1960. A narrative history, using all of the available archival materials.

Ensign, C. David. "Radical German Pietism: 1675-1760." Ph.D. dissertation, Boston University, 1955. The most comprehensive study of this movement.

Goebel, Max. *Geschichte des christlichen Lebens in der rheinisch-westphälischen evangelischen Kirche.* Coblenz: Bädeker, 1849-1860. Three volumes. A standard work based on original sources, many of which are no longer available. See especially Section 3, Volume II (pp. 681-855) and Books 2 and 3, Volume III (pp. 235-447).

Hadorn, W. *Geschichte des Pietismus in den Schweizerischen Reformierten Kirchen.* Konstanz and Emmishofen: Hirsch, 1901. See Book II: "Der unkirchliche Pietismus und die Separation" (pp. 125-253).

Hartnack, Karl. "Schwarzenau." *Wittgenstein: Blätter des Wittgensteiner Heimatvereins,* XLIV (1956), 20:83-93. Survey of major groups and individuals in Schwarzenau history, with most attention given to the Brethren.

Hartnack, Karl. "Schwarzenau an der Eder als Zufluchtsort Religionsverfolgter." *Archiv für Sippenforschung und Wappenkunde,* XVII (1940), 3:47-48; 4:70-75. Important for the list of the names.

Müller, Ernst. *Geschichte der Bernischen Täufer.* Frauenfeld: J. Hüber, 1895. Contains a detailed documentary account of the imprisonment of Christian Liebe as a galley slave.

Nieper, Fredrich. *Die ersten deutschen Auswanderer von Krefeld nach Pennsylvanien.* Neukirchen (Moers): Erziehungsverein, 1940. Along with Renkewitz, the most important European publication on the Brethren in Europe.

Renkewitz, Heinz. *Hochmann von Hochenau (1670-1721): Quellenstudien zur Geschichte des Pietismus.* Breslau: Maruschke and Berendt, 1935. The most complete and best documented European history of the Brethren origins, based on careful archival study.

Risler, Walther. "Zur Geschichte des bergischen Pietismus im frühen XVIII. Jahrhundert." *Zeitschrift des Bergischen Geschichtsvereins,* LXXVII (1960), 135-144. Detailed examination of the "Solingen Brethren. "

Ritschl, Albrecht. *Geschichte des Pietismus.* Bonn/Rhine: Adolph Marcus, 1880-1886. Three volumes. Although considered the standard history of Pietism it is extremely opinionated. Mentions the Brethren (Vol. II, 366, 374).

Schmitt, Jakob. *Die Gnade bricht durch,* second edition. Giessen: Brunnen, 1954. On the revivals in Wittgenstein, written from an evangelical perspective.

Shultz, L. W. *Schwarzenau Yesterday and Today.* Winona Lake, Ind.: Light and Life Press, 1954. With a biography of Mack by Hermann Brunn and an essay on Hochmann by Heinz Renkewitz.

Thurneysen, Eduard. "Die Basler Separatisten im ersten Viertel des achtzehnten Jahrhunderts." (Basler) *Jahrbuch* (1895), 30-78; (1896), 54-106. On the Boni brothers and other separatists.

Van Slee, J. C. *De Rijnsburger Collegianten.* Haarlem: der Erven F. Bohn, 1895. On the Dutch group in contact with the Brethren.

Vuilleumier, Henri. *Histoire de L'Eglise Réformée du Pays de Vaud.* Lausanne: Editions La Concorde, 1930. Three volumes. Mentions the Brethren activities in Bern.

Wernle, Paul. *Der schweizerische Protestantismus im XVIII. Jahrhundert.* Tübingen: J. C. B. Mohr, 1923. Three volumes. The standard work on Swiss Pietism, with mention of Liebe and Boni.

General Histories: North America

Ankrum, Freeman. *Sidelights on Brethren History.* 1962. Human interest stories.

Bittinger, Lucy. *The Germans in Colonial Times.* Philadelphia: Lippincott, 1901. Contains a well-informed outsider's description of the Brethren.

Boyle, Philip. "Baptists or German Brethren," in *He Pasa Ekklesia,* ed. I. D. Rupp. Harrisburg: author, 1844. A good depiction of the Brethren by a Maryland elder. Often reprinted.

Brumbaugh, Martin G. *A History of the German Baptist Brethren in Europe and America.* 1899 (reprinted 1961). A pioneer Brethren history, with special attention to the colonial period. Published many documents from the Abraham H. Cassel Collection.

Church of the Brethren. *Two Centuries of the Church of the Brethren.* 1908. A collection of bicentennial addresses.

Cooper, H. Austin. *Two Centuries of Brothers Valley, Church of the Brethren.* Westminster, Md.: author, 1962. Traces influences of a Western Pennsylvania congregation.

Doll, Eugene E., and Reichmann, Felix, eds. *Ephrata as Seen by Contemporaries* (1734-1752). Norristown, Pa.; Pennsylvania German Folklore Society, 1952. An excellent collection of early descriptions of the Ephrata Community, with much also on the Brethren.

Durnbaugh, Donald F., ed. *The Brethren in Colonial America.* 1967. A source book containing most of the important records and writings of the eighteenth century Brethren.

Ernst, James E. *Ephrata: A History,* ed. J. J. Stoudt. Allentown, Pa.: Pennsylvania German Folklore Society, 1963. The most recent history of the Ephrata Community.

Falkenstein, George N. *The German Baptist Brethren or Dunkers.* Lancaster, Pa.; Pennsylvania German Society, 1900. An early history, predominantly about Germantown.

Fisher, Virginia. *The Story of the Brethren.* 1957. Brethren history told in anecdotal form, for young readers.

Flory, John. *Flashlights from History.* 1932. Popularly written accounts of selected chapters of Brethren history.

Gibbons, Phoebe. *Pennsylvania Dutch and Other Essays.* Philadelphia: Lippincott, 1874. With a firsthand account of the Brethren.

Hark, J. Max, trans. *Chronicon Ephratense: A History of the Community of Seventh Day Baptists at Ephrata.* Lancaster, Pa.: S. H. Zahm, 1889. The only English translation of the Ephrata Chronicle, written by two of the Ephrata members. A basic source for the history of the colonial period.

Heckler, James Y. *Ecclesianthem, or Song of the Brethren.* Lansdale, Pa.: A. K. Thomas, 1883. An attempt to portray the history and character of the Brethren in poetry.

Holsinger, Henry R. *History of the Tunkers and the Brethren Church.* Lathrop, Calif.: author, 1901 (reprinted 1962). A basic history, written by the founder of the Brethren Church (Progressive Brethren). Has many rare illustrations and biographies.

Kent, Homer A., Sr., *250 Years . . . Conquering Frontiers.* Winona Lake, Ind.: Brethren Missionary Herald, 1958. A general history of the Brethren written from the Grace Brethren perspective.

Kimmel, J. M., ed. *Chronicles of the Brethren.* Covington, Ohio: Little Printing Co., 1951. By an Old German Baptist Brethren chronicler.

Mallott, Floyd E. *Studies in Brethren History.* 1954. A survey treatment of Brethren history, stressing the impact of industrialization in changing church behavior.

Miller, J. E. *The Story of Our Church.* 1957. A revision and enlargement of a popular history designed for young people.

Muir, Gladdys E. *Settlement of the Brethren on the Pacific Slope.* 1939. A well-documented history of Brethren expansion to the West Coast of America.

Pochmann, Henry A. *German Culture in America: Philosophical and Literary Influences.* Madison, Wis.: University of Wisconsin, 1957. A comprehensive study.

Ronk, Albert T. *History of the Brethren Church.* Ashland, Ohio: Brethren Publishing Co., 1968. A thorough study of Brethren history.

Sachse, Julius F. *The German Sectarians of Pennsylvania, 1708-1800.* Philadelphia: author, 1899-1900. Two volumes. Although these books contain much rare information they must be used with caution.

Sappington, Roger E. *Brethren Social Policy, 1908-1958.* 1961. Best study of the social program of the Brethren in the twentieth century.

Shultz, L. W. *A Mural History of the Church of the Brethren.* Milford, Ind.: Camp Alexander Mack, 1953. An outline history based upon murals painted by Medford D. Neher.

Smith, Samuel. *History of the Province of Pennsylvania,* ed. W. M. Mervine. Philadelphia: Colonial Society of Pennsylvania, 1913. Originally written in the late eighteenth century, this has an excellent chapter on the Brethren.

Winger, Otho. *History and Doctrine of the Church of the Brethren.* 1919. In textbook format, with biographies and list of publications.

Special Topics
Biographies
Cable, W. A., and Sanger, H. F., eds. *Educational Bluebook and Directory of the Church of the Brethren, 1708-1923.* 1923. Many biographical sketches of leading Brethren, with special emphasis upon those with higher education.

Church of the Brethren. *Brethren Builders in Our Century.* 1952. Thirty biographical sketches.

Flory, John S. *Builders of the Church of the Brethren.* 1925. With eleven biographical essays.

Garber, Mary. *Brethren Story Caravan.* 1950. Thirty-two biographies for children.

Garber, Mary, and others. *Brethren Trail Blazers.* 1960. Thirty-nine biographies for children.

Long, Inez. *Faces Among the Faithful.* 1962. Twenty-eight biographies of women leaders.

Miller, D. L., and Royer, Galen B., eds. *Some Who Led.* 1912. Sixty-four biographies of eighteenth and nineteenth-century leaders.

Moore, J. E. *Some Brethren Pathfinders.* Stories of twenty-seven mid-western pioneers.

Education
Bowman, Paul H., Sr. *Brethren Education in the Southeast.* Bridgewater, Va.: Bridgewater College, 1956. Describes several Brethren colleges.

Henry, Tobias F. "The Development of Religious Education in the Church of the Brethren in the United States." Ph.D. dissertation, University of Pittsburgh, 1938.

Noffsinger, J. S. *A Program for Higher Education in the Church of the Brethren.* New York: Columbia University Press, 1925. A study commissioned by the denomination.

Sharp, S. Z. *The Educational History of the Church of the Brethren.* 1923. The first comprehensive history of educational activity, by a leading Brethren educator.

Literature
Flory, John S. *Literary Activity of the German Baptist Brethren in the Eighteenth Century.* 1908. Based on a Ph.D. dissertation at the University of Virginia.

Flory, John S. "Literary Activity of the Brethren in the Nineteenth Century." *Yearbook of the Church of the Brethren* (1919), 39-45.

Grisso, Lillian, comp. *Heritage of Devotion.* 1944. An anthology of devotional literature.

Heckman, Samuel B. *The Religious Poetry of Alexander Mack, Jr.* 1912. With both the original German and English translations.

Hocker, Edward. *The Sower Printing House of Colonial Times.* Norristown, Pa.: Pennsylvania German Society, 1948. Contains a check list of the publications of all of the Sauer printers, and brief histories of the family.

McFadden, Glen. "Dunkers as Publishers." *Schwarzenau,* III (October 1941), 5-22.

Liturgy
Brumbaugh, H. B. *Church Manual,* revised edition. 1914. Long a standard manual.

Church of the Brethren. *The Brethren Hymnal.* 1951. The current hymnal.

Church of the Brethren. *Book of Worship.* 1964.

Fisher, Nevin. *The History of Brethren Hymnbooks.* Bridgewater, Va.: Beacon Publishers, 1950. A careful study of Brethren hymnody, especially the English language hymns.

Shultz, Joseph R. *The Soul of the Symbols.* Grand Rapids, Mich.: W. Eerdmans, 1966. A thorough study of the Brethren ordinances.

Ministry
Carper, Eugene C. "The Recruitment and Conservation of the Ministry in the Church of the Brethren." Ph.D. dissertation, Boston University, 1962. Two volumes.

Evans, T. Quentin. "The Brethren Pastor. Differential Conceptions of an Emerging Role." Ph.D. dissertation, Ohio State University, 1960.

Church of the Brethren. *Brethren Preaching Today.* 1947. A collection of thirty-two sermons.

Minutes

Kurtz, Henry, ed. *The Brethren's Encyclopedia.* Columbiana, Ohio: author, 1867. The first attempt to codify the pronouncements of the Annual Meetings.

Church of the Brethren. *Minutes of the Annual Meetings of the Church of the Brethren . . . 1778-1909.* 1909.

Church of the Brethren. *Revised Minutes of the Annual Meetings . . . 1778-1922.* 1922. A reduced and combined edition.

Church of the Brethren. *Minutes of the Annual Conferences . . . 1923-1944.* 1946.

Garber, Ora W., comp. *Minutes of the Annual Conferences of the Church of the Brethren, 1945-1954.* 1956.

Garber, Ora W., comp. *Minutes of the Annual Conferences of the Church of the Brethren, 1955-1964.* 1965.

Eberly, William R., comp., *Minutes of the Annual Conference of the Church of the Brethren, 1965-1969.* 1970.

Missions

Bittinger, Desmond W. *An Educational Experiment in Northern Nigeria in Its Cultural Setting.* 1941. A Ph.D. dissertation, University of Pennsylvania, 1940.

Church of the Brethren. *Our Churches in Other Lands.* 1952-1953.

Crouse, Merle, and Strietzel, Arlen. *Which Way in Ecuador?* 1961.

Eikenberry, Ivan. *Which Way in Nigeria?* 1959.

Grimley, John, and Robinson, Gordon E. *Church Growth in Central and Southern Nigeria.* Grand Rapids, Mich.: W. Eerdmans, 1966. A careful study of the mass movement into the Nigerian churches.

Moomaw, Ira W. *The Challenge of Hunger.* New York: F. Praeger, 1966. By a veteran Brethren missionary and missions executive.

Moomaw, Ira W. *Crusade Against Hunger.* New York: Harper and Row, 1966.

Moyer, Elgin. *Missions in the Church of the Brethren.* 1931. A careful study.

Royer, Galen B. *Thirty-Three Years of Missions in the Church of the Brethren.* 1913. By a long-time executive of Brethren missions.

Peace

Bowman, Rufus D. *The Church of the Brethren and War.* 1944. The basic treatment of the subject.

Brock, Peter. *Pacifism in the United States.* Princeton, N.J.: Princeton University, 1968. The definitive monograph, covering the period until 1900.

Eisan, Leslie. *Pathways of Peace.* 1948. A thorough study of Brethren Civilian Public Service projects.

Royer, Don. "The Acculturation Process and the Peace Doctrine of the Church of the Brethren in the Central Region of the United States." Ph.D. dissertation, University of Chicago, 1955.

Sanger, S. F., and Hays, Daniel, eds. *The Olive Branch of Peace.* 1907. The Brethren during the Civil War.

Weiss, Lorell. "Socio-Psychological Factors in the Pacifism of the Church of the Brethren During the Second World War." Ph.D. dissertation, University of California, 1957.

Polity

Church of the Brethren. *Organization and Polity,* revised edition. 1965.

Service

Fey, Harold E. *Cooperation in Compassion.* New York: Friendship Press, 1966. With many details on the Brethren involvement in Church World Service.

Sappington, Roger E. *Brethren Social Policy.* 1961.

Weiss, Lorell. *Ten Years of Brethren Service.* 1951. A booklet.

Sociological Studies

Dove, F. D. *Cultural Changes in the Church of the Brethren.* 1932.

Eshelman, Robert F. "A Study of Changes in the Value Patterns of the Church of the Brethren." Ph.D. dissertation, Cornell University, 1948.

Faust, Alvin G. "Cultural Patterns and Social Adjustment in the Church of the Brethren." Ph.D. dissertation, University of Pittsburgh, 1942.

Gillin, John L. *The Dunkers. A Sociological Interpretation.* New York: author, 1906. The pioneer study using sociological analysis, by a leading American sociologist.

Ziegler, Jesse. *The Broken Cup: Three Generations of Dunkers.* 1942.

Statistical Studies

Church of the Brethren. *Yearbook.* 1871ff. From 1871 to 1919 it was called the *Brethren's Almanac* and was published in different places by different publishers. From the beginning there were lists of ministers. After 1920 there were more complete statistics.

Edwards, Morgan. *Materials Toward a History of the American Baptists.* Philadelphia: Crukshank and Collins, 1770ff. The Baptist historian compiled statistics for all of the colonies, but only those for Pennsylvania and New Jersey were published. See Durnbaugh, *Brethren in Colonial America* (pp. 171-191) for Edwards' materials on the Brethren.

Miller, Howard. *Record of the Faithful.* Lewisburgh, Pa.: J. R. Cornelius, 1882. The first careful census of Brethren congregations.

Study Conferences

Bollinger, Richard. *The Church in a Changing World.* 1965. Report of a conference on "The Meaning of Membership in the Body of Christ" (1964).

Weiss, Lorell. *Therefore Brethren . . . .* 1962. A study guide based on a conference on "The Nature and Function of the Church" (1960).

--------- *Variations on a Theme.* 1969. Study materials for a conference on the topic "Faithfulness in Change" (1969).

Theology and Beliefs

Beahm, William M. *Studies in Christian Belief.* 1958. A basic statement.

Bowman, Paul H., Sr., ed. *The Adventurous Future.* 1959. Compilation of addresses for the 250th Anniversary.

Eby, Kermit. *For Brethren Only.* 1958. A personal affirmation of the Mennonite-Brethren heritage.

Eller, Vernard. *Kierkegaard and Radical Discipleship.* Princeton, N.J.: Princeton University, 1968. A comparison of the views of Kierkegaard with the early Brethren.

Frantz, Edward. *Basic Belief.* 1943. A doctrinal study by a Brethren editor.

Hogan, Herbert. "The Intellectual Impact of the 20th Century on the Church of the Brethren." Ph.D. dissertation, Claremont Graduate School, 1958.

Kurtz, D. W., and others. *Studies in Doctrine and Devotion.* 1919.

Miller, J. Allen. *Christian Doctrine.* Ashland, Ohio: Brethren Publishing Co., 1946. Studies by a former leading figure in the Brethren Church.

Nead, Peter. *Theological Writings on Various Subjects.* Dayton, Ohio: author, 1850. The most influential statement of the nineteenth century. Often reprinted.

Willoughby, William G. "The Beliefs of the Early Brethren." Ph.D. dissertation, Boston University, 1951.

Periodicals

Brethren Life and Thought. Established in 1955 by the Brethren Journal Association, as a journal of opinion and scholarship. Although independently owned, it is published in the interests of the denomination. Edward K. Ziegler, editor.

Church of the Brethren Leader. Published from 1958-1970 as an aid for church officials in the local congregations.

Messenger. This is in the direct line with the first Brethren periodical *The Monthly Gospel Visitor* (1851), although published in different towns by different publishers. From 1883 to 1964 it was called the *Gospel Messenger.* Kenneth I. Morse, present editor.

Schwarzenau. Published between 1939 and 1942 under the editorship of Floyd E. Mallott. Historical in nature.

INDEX OF PERSONS, PLACES, AND SUBJECTS